Small Business Marketing

FOR DUMMIES®

A Wiley Brand

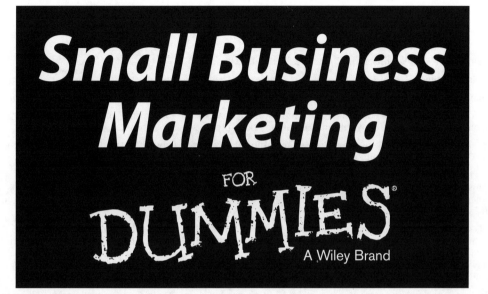

Small Business Marketing

FOR DUMMIES®
A Wiley Brand

by Paul Lancaster and Barbara Findlay Schenck

FOR DUMMIES®
A Wiley Brand

Small Business Marketing For Dummies®

Published by: **John Wiley & Sons, Ltd.,** The Atrium, Southern Gate, Chichester, www.wiley.com

This edition first published 2014

© 2014 John Wiley & Sons, Ltd, Chichester, West Sussex.

Registered office

John Wiley & Sons Ltd, The Atrium, Southern Gate, Chichester, West Sussex, PO19 8SQ, United Kingdom

For details of our global editorial offices, for customer services and for information about how to apply for permission to reuse the copyright material in this book please see our website at www.wiley.com.

The right of the author to be identified as the author of this work has been asserted in accordance with the Copyright, Designs and Patents Act 1988.

Wiley publishes in a variety of print and electronic formats and by print-on-demand. Some material included with standard print versions of this book may not be included in e-books or in print-on-demand. If this book refers to media such as a CD or DVD that is not included in the version you purchased, you may download this material at http://booksupport.wiley.com. For more information about Wiley products, visit www.wiley.com.

Designations used by companies to distinguish their products are often claimed as trademarks. All brand names and product names used in this book are trade names, service marks, trademarks or registered trademarks of their respective owners. The publisher is not associated with any product or vendor mentioned in this book.

For general information on our other products and services, please contact our Customer Care Department within the U.S. at 877-762-2974, outside the U.S. at (001) 317-572-3993, or fax 317-572-4002. For technical support, please visit www.wiley.com/techsupport.

For technical support, please visit www.wiley.com/techsupport.

A catalogue record for this book is available from the British Library.

ISBN 978-1-118-73077-5 (hardback/paperback); ISBN 978-1-118-73075-1 (ebk); ISBN 978-1-118-73080-5 (ebk)

Printed in Great Britain by TJ International, Padstow, Cornwall.

10 9 8 7 6 5 4 3 2 1

Contents at a Glance

Table of Contents

Part II: Laying the Foundation for Marketing Success ... 75

Introduction

*M*arketing is the process through which you win and keep customers. But while the definition of marketing is cast in concrete, everything about *how* businesses market has changed.

A growing number of customers now meet businesses online long before they venture through their doors. Increasingly, they form opinions based not on marketer-produced messages but on what others – or what Google – tell them about a product or business. They read online reviews more carefully than they read business brochures. And they're not hesitant to share their love or lack thereof for the companies and products they encounter, passing on their opinions not just to those within earshot but to any of the 2 billion-plus Internet users worldwide who come across their posts.

Welcome to marketing in today's screen-connected, customer-empowered world.

And welcome to *Small Business Marketing For Dummies*, written to prepare your small business to succeed in the exciting, fast-changing marketing world around you. From updated techniques for using traditional advertising and communication approaches to all-new advice for shifting marketing emphasis toward digital communications, count on the upcoming 350-plus pages to prepare you for better marketing in the following ways:

- New coverage of how to use the Internet and social media networks as your most-essential guerrilla-marketing tools.

- Revamped instructions for generating publicity in today's wired, linked and blogged world.

- Step-by-step advice for shifting from one-way to two-way marketing communications that inspire customer interactions and loyalty in today's connected and competitive marketplace.

- Updated advice and examples throughout, including the newest tips for generating product innovations, marketing communications, consumer trials, sales and loyalty.

- Expanded advice on business branding and personal branding, and how to balance the two for the health and value of your business.

Whether you're marketing on the high street or online, whether your company is a growing enterprise or a one-person shop, whether your business is starting up, making a U-turn or growing beyond your wildest expectations, this book aims to serve as your marketing partner as you plan and implement a marketing programme to reach out to the customers who will help you write your success story.

About This Book

Small Business Marketing For Dummies is especially for businesses that operate without the benefit – or the expense – of a high-powered Chief Marketing Officer (CMO), an award-winning ad agency or even a member of staff dedicated full-time to the task of managing your marketing activities.

Every example in this book is directed at the businessperson who wears all the hats and markets in whatever time remains. If that person sounds a lot like you, keep reading!

You have a business to run, customers to serve, product issues to address and a lineup of deadlines and decisions looming. You also have questions about how and how much you should be marketing, whether you need to be active online and how to best invest your time and money to draw customers to your cash register. If you fit the small business mould, you're strapped for time and need quick answers, rapid-fire advice and street-smart solutions that you can put to work immediately. This book gives you all that and more.

Foolish Assumptions

We never introduce a *For Dummies* book without reminding readers that anyone smart enough to turn to one of these yellow-and-black books is no fool. Here are a few other assumptions we make about you:

- ✔ You market a small business or organisation, probably with a tight budget and with a marketing staff made up of just you, or you and only a few others.
- ✔ You're baffled by the new marketing options you hear about every day and aren't sure how to proceed and which approaches – from traditional advertising to online and social media communications – to use.
- ✔ You're aiming for greater business success and aren't sure what marketing path to follow.

Icons Used in This Book

Marketing is full of logos, seals of approval and official stamps. In keeping with tradition, throughout the margins of this book you'll find symbols that spotlight important points, shortcuts and warnings. Watch for these icons:

This icon highlights the golden rules for small business marketing. Write them down, memorise them and use them to guide your marketing decisions and actions.

Remember the line, 'Don't tell me, show me'? This icon pops up alongside examples that show you how an idea applies in real-life marketing practices.

Not every idea is a good idea. This icon alerts you to situations that deserve your cautious evaluation. Consider it a flashing yellow light.

The bullseye marks text that helps you stretch budgets, shortcut processes, make confusing steps easy and seize low-cost, low-effort marketing opportunities.

It's not all Greek, but marketing certainly has its own jargon. When things get a little technical, this icon appears to help you through the translation.

This icon lets you know that there's a form, checklist, worksheet or resource you can find through www.dummies.com/extras/smallbusmarketing that will help you complete a step in the marketing process.

Beyond the Book

In addition to the material in the print or e-book you're reading right now, this product also comes with some access-anywhere goodies on the Web. Check out the free Cheat Sheet at www.dummies.com/cheatsheet/small busmarketinguk for some key tips and tricks for getting your business noticed.

You can also find loads of other useful resources at www.dummies.com/ extras/smallbusinessmarketing, including a link to a sheaf of forms to help you in your marketing activities. This table gives you the full run-down on what's available.

Form Number	Form Title	Description
Chapter 2: All about Customers		
Form 2-1	Customer Profile Template	A template for creating a description of customers of your business
Form 2-2	Market Segmentation Analysis	A worksheet for listing and studying revenues by geographic market area
Form 2-3	Channel Distribution Analysis	A worksheet for listing and studying revenues by distribution channel
Chapter 3: Seeing Your Product through Your Customers' Eyes		
Form 3-1	Product Line Analysis	A worksheet for listing and studying revenues by product line
Chapter 4: Sizing Up Competitors and Staking Out Market Share		
Form 4-1	Competitive Intelligence Worksheet	A form for compiling competitive information, analyses and opportunities
Chapter 5: Setting Your Goals, Objectives, Strategies, and Budgets		
Form 5-1	Statement of Purpose Worksheet	A form that lists questions to address and a template to follow when you produce the statement of purpose for your business
Form 5-2	Goals and Objectives Worksheet	A form that lists questions to address and templates to follow when you set goals and objectives for your marketing efforts
Form 5-3	Strategy-Setting Worksheet	A form that lists questions to address when you set pricing, product, promotion and place or distribution strategies
Chapter 6: Taking Stock of Your Business Image		
Form 6-1	Impression Inventory and Audit	A form for listing and rating the quality of every impression your business makes in its marketplace
Chapter 7: Forging Your Brand		
Form 7-1	Do You Have the Makings for a Powerful Brand?	A worksheet for plotting a strategy to add horsepower to your brand, from Liz Goodgold
Form 7-2	Six Brand-Management Steps	A worksheet to guide the steps necessary for building a brand for yourself or your business
Form 7-3	Test Your Tagline I.Q.	Grade your tagline by taking the Tagline Test from Eric Swartz, The Tagline Guru
Chapter 8: Creating Marketing Communications That Work		
Form 8-1	Creative Brief	Seven questions to answer before developing marketing communications

Form Number	Form Title	Description
Chapter 9: Hiring Help When You Need It		
Form 9-1	Agency Selection Checklist	Questions to answer as you evaluate each agency under consideration
Form 9-2	Website Designer Selection Checklist	Questions to answer as you evaluate each website designer under consideration
Form 9-3	Planning Your Website Worksheet	A checklist provided by Janine Warner, author of *Websites DIY For Dummies*
Chapter 10: Establishing an Online Presence		
Form 10-1	Support Site Considerations	A questionnaire to complete before investing in a support site and moving some or all customer support functions online
Form 10-2	Planning Your Mobile Website	Information and a checklist of considerations to weigh when deciding on a mobile website
Form 10-3	Is E-Commerce Right for Your Business?	Questions to weigh when deciding whether to invest in an e-commerce site
Chapter 11: Getting Interactive with Social Media		
Form 11-1	20 Tips for Becoming Successful on LinkedIn	A checklist of advice from Viveka von Rosen, CEO of Linked Into Business
Form 11-2	Checklist of Content-Generating Approaches	A list of content categories you can turn to when developing shareable content for social media interaction
Form 11-3	Social Media Tracker	A form you can use to track social media participation and effectiveness levels
Form 11-4	Social Media Programme Planning Checklist	A form listing the steps to take and issues to consider as you plan, implement and monitor your social media programme
Chapter 12: Packaging Your Message for Blogs and Other Online Channels		
Form 12-1	Blog Editorial Calendar and Post Planner	A chart for planning a month of blog posts
Chapter 14: Broadcasting Your Message on Radio, TV, and Online		
Form 14-1	Talent Release Form	A sample form for requesting talent permission agreements from those featured in your ads

Form Number	*Form Title*	*Description*
Form 14-2	Radio Advertising Checklist	A checklist to help you evaluate your radio ads
Form 14-3	TV Advertising Checklist	A checklist to help you evaluate your TV ads
Form 14-4	Planning a Webinar Checklist	A checklist detailing the steps involved in planning, announcing and hosting webinars
Chapter 15: Snail-Mailing and E-Mailing Your Customers Directly		
Form 15-1	Writing Direct Mail Letters	A checklist to use when composing the letter that accompanies traditional direct mailers
Form 15-2	Writing and Sending Effective Marketing Email	A checklist of actions to take and advice to follow when creating and sending email to your opt-in list
Form 15-3	Creating an Effective Landing Page	A list of attributes good landing pages have in common
Chapter 16: Brochures, Promotions, Trade Shows, and More		
Form 16-1	Brochure Production and Distribution Guidelines	Advice to consider when writing, designing and circulating sales literature
Form 16-2	Newsletter Production Guidelines	Advice to consider when writing, designing and circulating printed and e-newsletters
Form 16-3	Promotion Planning Guidelines	A list of promotion planning steps and considerations
Chapter 17: Public Relations and Publicity		
Form 17-1	Printed News Release Checklist	Advice to follow when writing and producing hard-copy news releases
Form 17-2	Media Interview Preparation Checklist	Help for planning for and participating in media interviews
Form 17-3	News Conference and Event Checklist	A list to follow when you're considering or planning a news event
Chapter 18: Making Impressions through Networking and Presentations		
Form 18-1	Writing Your Elevator Pitch	A formula to follow when preparing an introduction for your business
Form 18-2	Introducing Your Business by Phone	A checklist for making introductory phone calls
Form 18-3	Writing Letters or Emails to Introduce Your Business	A checklist for writing letters or email messages that introduce your business

Form Number	Form Title	Description
Chapter 20: Enhancing Customer Service and Developing Loyalty		
Form 20-1	Evaluating Your Customer Service	Questions to ask and answer as you assess the quality of customer service in your business
Form 20-2	Improving Your Customer Service	A form for benchmarking and improving customer service levels
Form 20-3	Customer Satisfaction Analysis	A checklist of approaches for winning increased business and turning customers into customers for life

Where to Go from Here

The role of marketing is to win and keep enough highly satisfied customers to keep your business not just in business but on an upward curve – and that's what this book is all about.

Hit the table of contents or index and you can dart straight to the pages that hold the advice you need right now.

Or become the marketing genius for your business by reading this book from cover to cover. It walks you through the full marketing process and helps you tailor your marketing programme, create your marketing messages and produce marketing communications that work.

For the price of this book, you can get what big businesses pay big money for: a bespoke marketing 'consultation.' Every chapter includes the latest facts and advice, and most also include how-to information from a lineup of amazing and successful experts who were generous enough to share their best tips in the pages of this book. We all wish you marketing success!

Part I

Getting Started with Small Business Marketing

In this part . . .

- ✔ Get the big marketing picture for the small business.
- ✔ Rev up your business and jump-start your marketing programme.
- ✔ Analyse and define your customers, your product and your competitors.
- ✔ Set your marketing goals, objectives, strategies and budgets.
- ✔ Shape your business's future.

Chapter 1

Framing the Marketing Process

*Y*ou're not alone if you opened this book looking for an answer to the question, 'What is marketing, anyway?' Everyone seems to know that marketing is an essential ingredient for business success, but when it comes to saying exactly what it is, they're not so sure.

People aren't sure if marketing, advertising and sales are the same or different things. And they're even less sure about what marketing involves and how to do it well.

To settle the matter right upfront, here's a plain-language description of what marketing – and this book – is all about.

Marketing is the process through which you win and keep customers.

- ✔ Marketing is the matchmaker between what your business is selling and what your customers are buying.

- ✔ Marketing covers all the steps involved in tailoring your products, messages, online and offline communications, distribution, customer service and all other business actions to meet the desires of your most important business asset: your customer.

- ✔ Marketing is a win-win partnership between your business and your market.

Marketing isn't about talking *to* your customers; on the contrary, marketing is about talking *with* them. Marketing relies on two-way communication between your business and your buyers.

Seeing the Big Picture

Marketing is a non-stop cycle. It begins with customer knowledge and goes around to customer service before it begins all over again. Along the way, it involves product development, pricing, packaging, distribution, advertising and promotion and all the steps involved in making the sale and serving the customer well.

Following the marketing wheel of fortune

Every successful marketing programme – whether for a billion-pound business or a solo entrepreneur – follows the marketing cycle illustrated in Figure 1-1. The process is exactly the same whether yours is a start-up or an existing business, whether your budget is large or small, whether your market is local or global and whether you sell through the Internet, via direct mail or through a bricks-and-mortar location.

Just start at the top of the wheel and circle around clockwise in a never-ending process to win and keep customers and to build a strong business in the process.

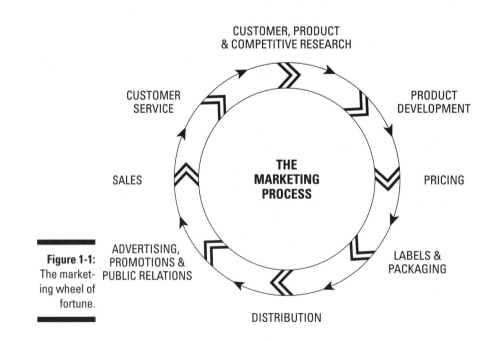

Figure 1-1: The marketing wheel of fortune.

As you loop around the marketing wheel, here are the marketing actions you take:

1. **Conduct research to gain knowledge about your customers, product, market area and competitors.**

2. **Tailor your product, pricing, packaging and distribution strategies to address your customers' needs, your market environment and your competitive realities.**

3. **Create and project marketing messages to reach your prospective customers, inspire their interest and move them toward buying decisions.**

4. **Go for and close the sale – but don't stop there.**

5. **After you make the sale, begin the customer service phase.**

   Work to develop relationships and ensure high levels of customer satisfaction so that you convert the initial sale into repeat business, loyalty and word-of-mouth advertising for your business.

6. **Interact with customers to gain insight about their wants and needs plus their use of and opinions about your products and services.**

   Combine customer knowledge with ongoing research about your market area and competitive environment. Then use your findings to fine-tune your product, pricing, packaging, distribution, promotional messages, sales and service.

And so the marketing process goes around and around.

Successful marketing has no shortcuts – you can't just jump to the sale. To build a successful business, you need to follow every step in the marketing cycle, and that's what the rest of this book is all about.

Understanding the relationship between marketing and sales

People make the mistake of thinking *marketing* is a high-powered or dressed-up way to say *sales*. Or they treat marketing and sales as two independent functions that they mesh together under the label *marketing and sales*.

In fact, sales is an essential part of marketing, but isn't and never can be a replacement for the full marketing process. Selling is one of the ways you communicate your marketing message. Selling is the point at which you offer the product, you make the case, the customer makes a purchasing decision and the business-to-customer exchange takes place.

WARNING!

Without all the marketing steps that precede the sale – fitting the product to the market in terms of features, price, packaging and distribution (or availability) and developing awareness and interest through advertising, publicity and promotions – even the best sales effort stands only a fraction of a chance for success.

Marketing: The whole is greater than the parts

Advertising. Marketing. Sales. Promotions. What are the differences? The following story has circulated the marketing world for decades and offers some good answers for what's what in the field of marketing communications:

✔ If the circus is coming to town and you paint a sign that says, 'Circus Coming to Winlaton Windy Fields on Saturday,' that's *advertising*.

✔ If you put the sign on the back of an elephant and walk it into town, that's *promotion*.

✔ If the elephant walks through the mayor's flower bed, that's *publicity*.

✔ And if you get the mayor to laugh and talk about it on the local news, that's *public relations*.

✔ If the town's residents go to the circus and you show them the many entertainment booths, explain how much fun they'll have spending money there, and answer their questions – and they ultimately spend a lot of money at the circus – that's *sales*.

Because marketing involves far more than marketing communications, I've added a second part to the circus analogy to show how the story may continue if it goes on to demonstrate where research, product development and other components of the marketing process fit in:

✔ If, before painting the sign that says, 'Circus Coming to Winlaton Windy Fields

on Saturday', you check community calendars to see whether conflicting events are scheduled, study who typically attends the circus and figure out what kinds of services and activities they prefer and how much they're willing to pay for them, that's *market research*.

✔ If you invent elephant ear pastries for people to eat while they're waiting for elephant rides, that's *product development*.

✔ If you create an offer that combines a circus ticket, an elephant ear, an elephant ride and an elephant photo, that's *packaging*.

✔ If you get a restaurant named Elephants to sell your elephant package, that's *distribution*.

✔ If you ask everyone who took an elephant ride to participate in a survey, that's *customer research*.

✔ If you follow up by sending each survey participant a thank you note, along with a two-for-one voucher to next year's circus, that's *customer service*.

✔ And if you use the survey responses to develop new products, revise pricing and enhance distribution, you've started the *marketing process* all over again.

Jump-Starting Your Marketing Programme

Small business leaders are most likely to clear their calendars and make marketing a priority at three predictable moments:

- ✔ At the time of business start-up
- ✔ When the time is right to accelerate business growth
- ✔ When they experience a bump on the road to success, perhaps due to a loss of business because of economic or competitive threats

You may have opened this book because your business is in the midst of one of those three situations right now. As you prepare to kick your marketing efforts into high gear, flip back a page or two and remind yourself that marketing isn't just about selling. Marketing is about attracting customers with great products and strong marketing communications, winning them over and then retaining their business by exceeding their expectations. As part of the reward, you achieve repeat business, loyalty, new customer referrals and a better shot at long-term business success.

Marketing a start-up business

If your business is just starting up, your marketing plan needs to address a set of decisions that existing businesses have already made. Existing companies have images to build upon, whereas your start-up business has a clean slate upon which to write exactly the right story. (If you haven't already settled on your business name, see Chapter 21.)

Before sending messages into the marketplace, answer these questions:

- ✔ What kind of customer do you want to serve? (See Chapter 2.)
- ✔ How will your product compete with existing options available to your prospective customer? (See Chapter 3.)
- ✔ What kind of business image will you need to project to gain your prospect's attention, interest and trust? (See Chapters 6 and 7.)

A business setting out to serve corporate clients would hardly want to announce itself by placing flyers on community bulletin boards. On the other end of the spectrum, a start-up aiming to win business from cost-conscious customers would probably be better off announcing a range of special offers and introductory promotions than placing large ads full of praise from affluent business leaders.

If you're marketing a start-up business, pay special attention to the chapters in Part I. They can help you identify your customers, make pricing decisions, present your product, size up your competition, set your goals and objectives, establish your market position and brand and create marketing messages that talk to the right prospects.

Growing your business

Most established businesses grow their revenues by following one of the following routes:

- Grow market share by pulling business away from competitors. (See Chapter 4.)
- Grow customer share by prompting larger transactions during each visit or by generating more frequent repeat business.
- Grow interest in new offerings that generate additional sales volume for your business. (See Chapter 3.)

Almost always, the most cost-efficient route to higher sales volume is to look inside your business first, shore up your product and service offerings and strengthen your existing customer satisfaction and spending levels *before* trying to win new prospects, which requires significantly more effort and expense. Part V offers a complete game plan to follow.

Scaling your marketing to meet your goal

Small business owners often feel overwhelmed by the marketing task. They aren't sure how much money they should dedicate to the effort, whether they need to hire marketing professionals, how to weight efforts between traditional media and online communications, and whether they need to create new ads, brochures and websites to get the job done.

Do those uncertainties sound familiar? If so, detour around the questions and get into forward motion by first putting your marketing task in perspective. Ask yourself:

- How much business are we trying to gain?
- How many clients do we want to add?

Whether you're launching a new business or accelerating the growth of an existing enterprise, defining what you're trying to achieve makes everything easier.

A social-service agency may set a goal to raise £100,000 in donor funds. An accounting firm may want to attract six corporate clients. A retailer may want to build an additional £50,000 in sales. A doctor may want to attract 100 patients for a particular new service. An e-publisher may want to achieve 500 downloads.

By setting your goal first (more on this important step in Chapter 5), the process of creating your marketing plan becomes a focused, goal-oriented and vastly easier activity. (See Chapter 23 for advice on writing a plan in ten easy steps.)

How Small Business Marketing Is Different

All marketing programmes follow the same set of steps in the marketing process (refer to Figure 1-1), but the similarities between big business marketing and small business marketing stop there. Budgets, staffing, creative approaches and communication techniques vary hugely between an international mega-marketer like, say, Coca-Cola, and a comparatively micro-budget marketer like, well, you.

This book is for *you*. Here's why.

Budget differences

As a small business marketer, you already know one difference between your marketing programme and those of the corporate behemoths that loom over you in all directions: The big guys have the big budgets. They talk about £200,000 as a discretionary line-item issue. You talk about £200,000 as an amount worthy of serious consideration or out of your league. The advice in this book is scaled to your budget, not to the million-pound jackpots you see referenced in most other marketing books.

Staffing differences

Look at the organisation chart of any major corporation. Nearly always, you find a Chief Marketing Officer (CMO). Under that position you see a bunch of other professionals, including advertising directors, sales managers, online and social-media marketing managers, research directors, customer service specialists and so on. In contrast, strong small businesses blend marketing with the leadership function. The small business organisation chart often puts responsibility for marketing in the very top box, the one with the owner's name, which likely puts *you* in the essential role of overseeing marketing as a hands-on task.

Creative differences

The top-name marketers routinely spend six figure sums to create ads with the sole purpose of building name recognition and market preference for their brands, often without a single word about a specific product or price.

Small businesses take a dramatically different approach. They want to develop name recognition just like the biggest advertisers, but their ads have to do double duty. You know firsthand that each and every small business marketing investment has to deliver immediate and measurable market action. Each effort has to stir enough purchasing activity to offset the marketing cost involved. The balancing act, and the focus of the chapters in Part IV, is to create marketing communications that build a clear brand identity while also inspiring the necessary consumer action to deliver enquiries, generate leads and prompt sales – *now!*

Strategic differences

In big businesses, bound copies of business plans are considered part of the furnishings, whereas in many small businesses, the very term *marketing plan* provokes a pang of guilt. If you just felt this typical reaction, turn to Chapter 23 for the antidote. It provides an outline for putting your plan in writing – without any mysterious jargon and with advice and examples scaled specifically to small businesses like yours.

 Truth is, creating a marketing plan is pretty straightforward and reasonably manageable. A marketing plan is one of those pay-a-little-now-or-pay-a-lot-more-later propositions. If you invest a bit of time upfront to plan your annual marketing programme, implementation of the plan becomes the easy part. But without a plan, you may spend the year racing around in response to competitive actions, market conditions and media opportunities that may or may not fit your business needs.

The small business marketing advantage

As a small business owner, you may envy the budgets, people and organisations of your big business counterparts, but you have certain advantages that they envy as well.

The heads of Fortune 500 firms allocate budgets equal to the gross national products of small countries to fund the research required to get to know and understand their customers. Meanwhile, you can talk with your customers face to face, day after day, at virtually no additional cost.

Because the whole point of marketing is to build and maintain customer relationships, no business is better configured to excel at the marketing task than the very small business.

What's more, today's customers don't just crave interactive communication with the businesses they buy from – they demand it. In the biggest of big businesses, shifting from one-way communication to two-way, interactive communication involves monumental shifts in how the business markets. Meanwhile, for your small business, shifting toward interactive marketing is simply a matter of making the choice to get online, get social, get talking and get involved in two-way communications that give your business a marketing edge. Part III includes three chapters full of advice to follow.

Making Marketing Your Key to Success

It's the simple truth that without customers, a business is out of business.

Marketing is the key to achieving customer interest, winning customer purchases, earning customer satisfaction and loyalty and keeping your small business *in* business.

Put in terms like that, marketing is the single most important activity in any business – including yours. The fact that you're holding this book means you've made a commitment, and that gives you an edge over many of your competitors. Go for it!

Chapter 2

All about Customers

In This Chapter
▶ Using various tools to analyse your business's customer base
▶ Targeting and reaching prospective customers

*E*very marketer mulls over the same questions: Who are my customers? How did they hear about me? Why do they buy from me? How can I reach more people like them?

Successful businesses use the answers to these questions to influence every product-design, pricing, distribution and communication decision they make. This chapter focuses on the only boss that really matters in business: the person with an interest in your product or service and an open wallet. Whether your business is starting up, running at full pace, or in need of a turnaround, you can use the information in this chapter to get in tune with the customers who can make or break your bottom line.

- ✔ If your business is doing well, use this chapter to create a profile of your best customers so that you can attract more just like them.

- ✔ If your business feels busy but your sales and profits are weak, this chapter can help you differentiate between the customers who are costing you time and money and the ones who are making you money – so you can direct your marketing efforts at the moneymakers.

- ✔ If your sales have hit a frustrating plateau – or worse, if they're sliding downhill – you need to get and keep more customers, full stop. That means knowing everything you can about who is buying products or services like the ones you're selling and what it takes to make those people buy from you.

Business leaders don't work for themselves; they work for their customers.

Anatomy of a Customer

Understanding who's who among your clientele is called *market segmentation* – the process of breaking down your customers into segments that share distinct similarities.

Here are some common market segmentation terms and what they mean:

- ✔ **Geographics:** Segmenting customers by their physical locations to determine the regions, counties, countries, postcodes and census districts where current and, therefore, likely prospective customers live.

- ✔ **Demographics:** Segmenting customers into groups based on factors such as age, sex, race, religion, education, marital status, income and household size.

- ✔ **Psychographics:** Segmenting customers by lifestyle characteristics, behavioural and purchasing patterns, beliefs, values and attitudes about themselves, their families and society.

- ✔ **Geodemographics:** A combination of geographics, demographics *and* psychographics. Geodemographics, also called *cluster marketing* or *lifestyle marketing,* is based on the age-old idea that birds of a feather flock together – that people who live in the same area tend to have similar backgrounds and consuming patterns. Geodemographics helps you target your marketing efforts by pinpointing neighbourhoods or geographic areas where residents share the age, income, lifestyle characteristics and buying patterns of your prospective customers.

Collecting customer information

People with the profile of your current customers are apt to become customers as well. That's why target marketing starts with customer knowledge. Small businesses fall into two groups: those with customer databases and those that serve customers whose names and addresses they never capture. A medical clinic or auto repair shop falls into the first group. A sandwich shop or convenience store likely falls into the second group, although even those who don't automatically collect customer names and information can use loyalty schemes or competitions to collect valuable customer data.

The more you know about current customers, the better prepared you are to target and reach more people just like them. Start by doing some research.

Do-it-yourself fact-finding

You can get a good start on conducting customer research without ever walking out the front door of your business. Start by focusing on information that you can collect through customer communications and contacts:

✔ **Collect addresses from shipping labels and invoices in order to group customers by location and purchase type.**

✔ **Monitor the origin of incoming phone calls.** When prospects call your business, find out where they're from and how they found you.

Keep questions conversational and brief. Remember that customers are calling to *receive* information, not to become research subjects.

- Use the caller identification feature on your phone to collect the incoming phone number prefix and area code, which enables you to track the geographic origin of customer calls.

- Your phone service provider may be able to furnish lists of incoming call area codes or dialling prefixes for your reference.

✔ **Track responses to ads and direct mailers.** Include a call to action that inspires a reaction. When prospects respond, collect their addresses and other information to build not just a database but also an enquiry profile.

✔ **Study web reports to discover more about visitors to your website.** Work with the firm that hosts and manages your site to discuss available reports and how to mine the information you collect. Also, enter your web address into Google Analytics (`www.google.com/analytics`) to access data about site visitors, including their geographic origin, language and other facts.

Be aware, though, that some internet providers hide the geographic origin of users under the label 'undefined,' and others bundle all traffic, which means you may see a good many site visitors from a distant location not relevant to your business.

Beyond studying tell-tale signs for the geographic origins of your business, put your small-business advantage to use and actually talk with your customers, using these approaches:

✔ **Survey your customers.** Use online survey services available through sites such as `www.surveymonkey.com`, which allows you to choose from a range of templates and collect responses from up to ten questions from 100 people for free. Or you can create and email a survey to customers on your own or use contest forms to collect information.

If your business attracts foot traffic, consider surveying customers in person. Whether you survey all customers or limit your effort to every *n*th customer (every tenth one, for example), keep the question period short, keep track of responses and time interviews so that your findings reflect responses from customers during various days and weeks.

When surveying customers and collecting data, keep these cautions in mind:

- Establish and share your company's privacy policy to assure customers that you respect and protect the information you collect.

- If you collect information online, visit the website of the Information Commissioner's Office (ICO) at `http://ico.org.uk` and for guidance on Data Protection.

- If you question customers in person, don't risk treating long-standing customers like strangers to your business. Instead of asking, 'Is this your first visit?' try to get at the answer indirectly, asking questions such as, 'Have you been here since we moved the reception area?' or, 'Have you stayed with us since we started our wine reception?' Savvy restaurateurs don't have to ask at all. They know that if a customer asks for directions to the bathroom, that person is likely a first-time patron. On the other hand, a waiter who overhears a customer recommending a certain menu item to a tablemate can make a safe guess that the patron is a repeat guest.

- Realise that informal studies aren't statistically valid, but provide interesting insights that help you better understand at least an informally assembled cross section of your clientele.

✓ **Observe your customers.** Without asking a single question, you can find out a lot from observing customer behaviour. What kinds of cars do your customers drive? How long do they spend during each visit to your business? Do they arrive by themselves or with others? Do those who arrive alone account for more sales or fewer sales than those who arrive accompanied by others? Where do they pause or stop in your business? Your observations help you define your customer profile while also leading to product decisions, as shown in these examples:

- A small theme park may find that most visitors stay for two hours and 15 minutes, which is long enough to want something to eat or drink. This can lead to the decision to open a café or restaurant.

- A retailer may realise that women who shop with other women spend more time and money, which may lead to a promotion that offers lunch for two after shopping on certain days of the week.

- A hotel may decide to post a restaurant display at a hallway entry where guests frequently pause.

Calling in the pros

Doing it yourself doesn't mean doing it all on your own. As you're conducting customer research, here are places where an investment in professional advice pays off:

✔ **Questionnaires:** Work out what you want to find out and create a list of questions. Then consider asking a trained market researcher to review your question wording, sequence and format. After your questions are set, you can distribute the survey on your own or with professional help. Whatever you decide, get someone with design expertise to prepare a questionnaire that makes a good visual impression on your business's behalf. Include a letter or introductory paragraph explaining why you're conducting research and how you're going to protect the privacy of answers.

✔ **Phone or in-person surveys:** Professional researchers pose questions that don't skew the results. When you ask the questions yourself, if you're not careful you may let your biases, preconceptions and business pressures leak through and sway responses. Plus, customers are more apt to be candid with third parties. (If you need proof, think of all the things people are willing to say behind someone's back that they'd never say to the person's face. The same principle applies in customer research.)

✔ **Online surveys:** Professional online survey tools are free unless you want to reach particularly large survey groups, in which case reasonably priced packages are available. If only a portion of your clientele is active online, be sure to accompany online surveys with off-line surveys in order to capture the opinions of those who don't use the Internet.

✔ **Focus groups:** If you're assembling a group of favourite clients to talk casually about a new product idea, you're fine to go it alone. But to get opinions from outsiders or insight into sensitive topics such as customer service or pricing, use a professional facilitator who is experienced in managing group dynamics so that a single dominant participant doesn't steer the group outcome.

To obtain outside assistance, contact research firms, advertising agencies, marketing firms and public-relations companies. Explain what you want to accomplish and ask whether the company can do the research for you or direct you toward the right resources.

Another good starting point is the British Library Business and IP Centre (BIPC) in London or one of its satellite centres in Birmingham, Leeds, Liverpool, Manchester, Newcastle or Sheffield, who can undertake market research for you.

Geographics: Locating your market areas

Not all businesses are geographically constrained. Most Internet businesses aren't; most restaurants are. If geography matters to your business, though, it can be an essential ingredient in arriving at your customer profile.

To target your market geographically, you need to ask, 'Where am I most likely to find potential customers, and where am I most able to inspire enough sales to offset my marketing investment?' To help you answer these questions, here's some advice:

✔ **Start with the addresses of your existing customers.** Wherever you have a concentration of customers, you likely have a concentration of *potential* customers. Unless you already have sky-high market share, those are the areas where you should direct your advertising efforts.

✔ **Follow your enquiries.** Enquiries are customers waiting to happen. They're consumers whose interest you've aroused and whose radar you're on. Your first objective should be to convert inquiry interest into buying action. Further, by finding out where enquiries are coming from, you may discover new geographic areas to target with future marketing efforts.

✔ **Locate new customer prospects in your local market area.** Identify people who match the profile of your current customers but who don't yet buy from you. By discovering where these prospects live, you also discover areas for potential market expansion.

   • Contact media outlets that serve your business sector. Ask for information regarding geographic areas with a concentration of people who fit your customer profile. Advertising representatives are often willing to share information as a way to convince you of their ability to carry your marketing message to the right prospects.

   • Contact your industry association. Enquire about industry market analyses that detail geographic areas with concentrated interest in your offerings. If you can export your offering beyond your regional marketplace, you may discover national or international market opportunities that you otherwise wouldn't have considered.

   • Visit your local library. It can provide access to books, databases and publications to help you research companies, markets and sectors.

Each time you discover a geographic area with easy access to your business and with a concentration of residents who fit your buyer profile, add the region to your list of prospective geographic target markets.

Demographics: Collecting customer data

After you determine *where* your customers are, the next step is to define *who* they are so that you can target your marketing decisions directly toward people who fit your customer profile.

Trying to market to everyone is a budget-breaking proposition. Instead, narrow your customer definition by using demographic facts to zero in on exactly whom you serve by following these steps:

1. **Use your own general impressions to define your customers in broad terms based on how you describe their age, education level, ethnicity, income, marital status, profession, sex and household size.**

   Answer these questions about your customers:

   - Are they mostly male or female?

   - Are they mostly children, teenagers, young adults, early retirees or senior citizens?

   - Are they students, graduates or PhDs?

   - What do they do – are they housewives, teachers, young professionals or doctors?

   - Are they mostly single, couples with no children at home, parents, grandparents or recent empty nesters?

   - How would you describe their ethnicity and the languages they speak?

   - Based on your observations, how would you define their income levels?

2. **Break your market into subgroups, perhaps categorised by the kinds of products the customers usually purchase or the time of year they typically do business with you.**

   A restaurant that analyses its weekday lunchtime clientele and patrons of its dinner business may discover that the two time frames draw customers with dramatically different demographic profiles. For example, perhaps the lunchtime clientele is comprised mostly of business people from the nearby area, whereas the dinner traffic is largely tourist families. This finding may lead to the development of two different and highly targeted promotions: a *50 minutes or it's free* lunch offer aimed at the nearby business community and promoted through the Chamber of Commerce newsletter and other low-cost, local business publications; and a *Kids under 7 eat free* offer aimed at tourists and promoted through hotel receptions and local visitor publications.

3. **Verify your answers by asking your customers.**

   Incorporate questions during inquiry and sales contacts by following the advice in the 'Do-it-yourself fact-finding' section, earlier in this chapter.

As you collect demographic information about your customers, realise that people who fit the same factual description may vary widely in their purchasing patterns. That's why you need to make sure that you also understand customer lifestyles and buying behaviours, covered in the next section on psychographics.

Psychographics: Customer buying behaviour

Knowing where and who your customers are allows you to select the right communication vehicles to carry your marketing messages. As you decide what to say and how to present your message, you also want to find out as much as you can about the attitudes, beliefs, purchasing patterns and behaviour of your customers. This information helps you create marketing messages that interest your prospects and motivate them to buy from you.

Defining who isn't a prospect for your product

Sometimes, the easiest way to start your customer profiling is to think about who *isn't* likely to buy from your business.

- ✔ A manufacturer of swings and climbing frames knows that most customers aren't young professional couples living in flats. It needs to talk to families whose homes have back gardens.

- ✔ A landscape and nursery business knows that it won't find many customers in city centre apartments.

- ✔ A manufacturer of architectural siding may decide that its buyer isn't the end user – or homeowner – at all. Rather, the customer is the architect who specifies the product in the initial building design.

Don't be afraid to target the audience for your marketing messages. You can still sell to anyone who enters your business or website, but your marketing investment should target only those who best fit your customer description.

Identifying the purchasing tendencies that customers have in common

Based on your personal impressions and also on information that you find through conversations and surveys (see advice earlier in this chapter), make a list of common traits shared by your best customers by answering the following questions:

- ✔ Do they buy on impulse or after careful consideration?

- ✔ Are they price-conscious or more concerned about the quality and prestige of the purchase?

- ✔ Are they loyal shoppers who buy from you on a frequent basis or are they one-time buyers?

- ✔ Do they buy from your business exclusively or do they also buy from your competitors?

✔ Do they reach you through a certain channel – for example, your office, shop or website – or do they contact you via referrals from other businesses or professionals?

A retailer in a tourist area may organise customers into the following subgroups:

✔ **Geographic origin:** Local residents, regional, national and international visitors.

✔ **Activity interest:** Golfers, skiers, campers and business travellers/convention guests.

By creating customer subgroups, you'll see patterns emerge. Certain customer groups account for higher sales volume, more frequent purchases, purchases of certain types of products, purchases during certain seasons or hours, purchases through your website rather than in person and so on. When you know the tendencies of various segments, you know what to offer to each target group.

Determining Which Customers Buy What

Marketing is a matter of resource allocation. No budget – not even those of mega-brands like General Motors or McDonald's – is big enough to do it all. At some point, every marketer has to decide to spend their budget on the markets and products that have the best chance of delivering results and providing a good return on the marketing investment.

Viewing your sales by market segment

The best marketers aim promotions precisely at target audiences that they believe have the interest and ability to purchase the featured product. Take these steps as you match segments of your market with the categories of your product line that they're most likely to want to purchase:

1. **Break down your sales by product categories to gain a clear picture of the types of products you sell, the sales volume each category produces and the type of customer each attracts.**

2. **Use your findings to determine which product categories offer the best potential growth opportunities and also to clarify which segments of your clientele are most likely to respond to marketing messages.**

3. **Weight your marketing expenditures and develop your marketing messages and media plans to achieve your targeted sales goals through promotions that appeal to clearly defined customer segments.**

A furniture manufacturer may divide its products into office, dining and children's lines – each meeting the demands of a different market segment and even employing a different distribution and retailing strategy. The manufacturer would follow three separate marketing-communications strategies, placing primary emphasis (and budget allocation) on promoting the line most able to deliver top sales volume over the upcoming period.

An accounting firm may sort its clientele both by type of service purchased and by client profile. For example, it may target individual clients for tax-returns in the month prior to the submission deadline .

After you're clear about which segments of your customer base are most likely to purchase which products, you have the information you need to develop and communicate compelling promotions and offers. You may also discover clues to new-customer development. For example, studying sales patterns may lead to the finding that certain products or services provide a good point of customer entry to your business, arming you with valuable knowledge you can use in new-customer promotions.

Table 2-1   Market Segmentation Analysis: Mountain Valley Hotel

	Home town	Rest of Home County	Neighbouring Counties	Other National/ International
Total Sales				
£712,000	£56,960	£462,800	£128,160	£64,080
	8%	65%	18%	9%
Sales by Length of Stay				
1-night stay	£48,416	£83,304	£19,224	£3,204
2-night stay	£2,848	£231,400	£70,488	£32,448
3–5 night stay	None	£101,816	£32,040	£28,428
6+ night stay	£5,696	£46,280	£6,408	none
Sales by Season				
Summer	£5,696	£277,680	£96,120	£54,468
Autumn	£11,962	£55,536	£12,816	£6,408
Winter	£4,557	£37,024	£6,408	none
Christmas	£22,783	£23,140	None	none
Spring	£11,962	£69,420	£12,816	£3,204

With detailed market knowledge, you can make market-sensitive decisions that lead to promotions tailored specifically to consumer patterns and demands. The following examples show how the hotel featured in Table 2-1 can use its findings to make marketing decisions:

✔ **Local market guests** primarily stay for a single night and mostly during the Christmas holidays, making them good targets for local year-end promotions. Additionally, 10 per cent of local guests stay for six nights or longer, probably while undergoing household renovations or lifestyle changes. This long-stay business tends to occur during non-summer periods when hotel occupancy is low, so the hotel may want to consider special offers to attract more of this low-season business.

✔ **Half of countywide guests** spend two nights per stay, although nearly a third spend three to six nights, which proves that the hotel is capable of drawing countywide guests for longer stays. This information may lead to an add-a-day promotion.

✔ **National and international guests** account for approximately one-quarter of the hotel's business. Because these guests are a far-flung group, the cost of trying to reach them in their home market areas via advertising would be prohibitive. Instead, the hotel managers may research how these guests found out about the hotel. If they booked following advice from travel agents, tour group operators or websites, the managers could cultivate those sources for more bookings. Or, if the guests made their decisions while driving through town, the hotel may benefit from well-placed outdoor ads and greater participation in travel apps and review sites that influence traveller behaviour.

Conduct a similar analysis for your own business:

✔ How do your products break down into product lines? (See Chapter 3 for more information about this important topic.)

✔ What kind of customer is the most prevalent buyer for each line?

Then put your knowledge to work. If one of your product lines attracts customers who are highly discerning and prestige-oriented, think twice about a strategy that relies on discount vouchers, for example.

Matching customers with distribution channels

Distribution is the means by which you get your product to the customer. A good distribution system blends knowledge about your customer (see the first half of this chapter) with knowledge of how that person ended up with your product (that's what distribution is about). This route can often be a surprisingly complex one.

To demonstrate, take a look at how visitors may arrive at a local museum. Suppose that 50,000 visitors walk through the turnstiles every year. Suppose that 10,000 of those visitors are school groups, 5,000 are tour groups, 5,000 pre-purchased tickets through local B&B's and hotels, 5,000 pre-purchased tickets through the websites of the museum and the regional tourist board, 5,000 have tickets distributed by partner businesses as part of special promotional programmes, and 20,000 are museum members or independent visitors.

Based on these numbers, the museum is distributing its tickets through the following channels:

- ✔ Educators (possibly influenced by curriculum directors)
- ✔ Tour companies (possibly influenced by regional or local travel agents)
- ✔ Lodging establishment front desks (probably influenced by hotel and hotel marketing departments)
- ✔ The Internet (possibly influenced by state or local travel agents)
- ✔ Partner businesses (influenced by museum networking)
- ✔ The museum entrance gate (influenced by museum marketing efforts)

By allocating guest counts and revenues to each of the channels, the museum would arrive at the distribution analysis shown in Table 2-2. By studying the findings, the museum can determine which channels are most profitable and which are most likely to respond positively to increased marketing efforts.

Table 2-2	Channel Distribution Analysis		
Distribution Channel	*Ticket Revenue*	*Number of Guests/ Per cent of Total*	*Sales Revenue/ Per cent of Total*
Educators	£5.00	10,000/20%	£50,000/16%
Tour companies	£6.00	5,000/10%	£30,000/10%
Hotels/hotels	£6.50	5,000/10%	£32,500/11%
Internet			
Museum website	£8.00	3,000/6%	£24,000/8%
Travel agent website	£6.50	2,000/4%	£13,000/4%
Museum entry gate			
Museum members	£3.00	5,000/10%	£15,000/5%
Independent visitors	£8.00	15,000/30%	£120,000/39%
Partnering businesses	£4.00	5,000/10%	£20,000/7%

Now create your own channel analysis, providing your business with information about how customers reach your business and the levels of sales activity that each channel generates. Put your findings to work taking these steps:

1. **Track sales changes by distribution channel.**

   If one distribution channel starts declining radically, give that channel more marketing attention or enhance another channel to replace the revenue loss.

2. **Compare percentage of sales to percentage of revenue from each channel.**

   Channels that deliver lower-than-average income per unit should involve a lower-than-average marketing investment or deliver some alternative benefit to your business. For example, in the case of the museum in Table 2-2, the tickets distributed through partnering businesses deliver lower-than-average revenue and likely require a substantial marketing investment. Yet they've an alternative benefit – they introduce new people to the museum and therefore cultivate membership sales, donations and word-of-mouth support.

3. **Communicate with the decision makers in each distribution channel.**

   When you know your channels, you know who to contact with special promotional offers. For example, if school groups arrive at a museum because the museum is on an approved list from the Department of Education, this department is the decision point, and is where the museum would want to direct marketing efforts. If school groups arrive because art or history teachers make the choice, the museum would want to get information to those art or history teachers.

As part of your channel analysis, consider whether your business can reach and serve prospective customers through new distribution channels, whether that means introducing online sales, off-premise purchase locations, new promotional partnerships or other means of reaching those who fit your target customer profile but who don't currently buy from your business.

Catering to screen-connected customers

In addition to everything you find out about your customers – who they are, where they live, how they buy and what they want – realise that one common denominator applies to all: They're all influenced by the Internet.

Even if your customers are among the rare few who aren't online, you can bet that their purchase decisions are affected by input from those who are.

Research shows that 89 per cent of consumers find online channels trustworthy sources for product and service reviews, and an even greater percentage use online media before purchasing products, even in their local market area. Go to Part III for information on preparing your business to connect with your customers online. Online is where they are, so online is where your business needs to meet and interact with them.

Chapter 3

Seeing Your Product through Your Customers' Eyes

*T*he best products aren't *sold* – they're *bought.*

You never hear a customer say he *bought* a banger at the used car showroom. Nope, someone *sold* him that banger – but hopefully not you or your business. If you're a good marketer, you aren't *selling* anyone anything. Instead, you're helping customers select the right products to solve their problems, address their needs or fulfil their desires. You're helping them *buy.*

As a result, you can devote the bulk of your marketing efforts to the steps that take place long before and after money changes hands. These efforts involve targeting customers, designing the right product line, communicating your offerings in terms that address customers' wants and needs, and interacting after the sale in a way that builds loyalty and repeat business. This chapter spotlights everything you need to know about your products and the reasons your customers want to buy those products from you.

Getting to Know Your Product

The first step toward stronger sales is to know everything you possibly can about the products you sell and the reasons why your customers buy.

Look beyond your primary offerings to consider the full range of solutions that your business provides. You're likely to discover that your offerings are more diverse than you first realise, a finding that can lead to stronger, more targeted marketing efforts.

Consider the products of a lakeside resort. The owners would list the number of cabins, seats in the restaurant and rowing boats for rent. Then they'd include the shopping opportunities in the resort's bait shop. Their list may also include summer youth camps, winter cross-country ski packages, all-inclusive corporate retreats and such intangibles as family memories, based on their finding that many reservations are motivated by an emotional response to the lakeside setting as an annual holiday site.

Similarly, a law firm may describe its products by listing the number of wills, estate plans, company formations, bankruptcies, divorces, adoptions and lawsuits it handles annually. And if they manage this list well, the lawyers know which of those product lines are profitable and which services are performed at a loss in return for the likelihood of ongoing, profitable relationships.

What about your business?

- ✔ What do you sell? How much? How many? What times of year or week or day do your products sell best? How often is a customer likely to buy or use your product?

- ✔ What does your product or service do for your customers? How do they use it? How does it make them feel? What problem does it solve?

- ✔ How is your offering different from and better than your competitors'?

- ✔ How is it better than it was even a year ago?

- ✔ What does it cost?

- ✔ What do customers do if they're displeased or if something goes wrong?

By answering these questions, you gain an understanding of your products and the ability to steer their future sales.

When service is your product

If your business is among the great number of companies that sell services rather than three-dimensional or packaged goods, from here on when you see the word *product,* think *service.* In your case, service *is* your product.

Today, the service sector is the dominant sector of the UK economy and contributes around 73 per cent of GDP. Services – preparing tax returns, writing wills, creating websites, styling hair or designing house plans, to name a few – aren't things that you can hold in your hands. In fact, the difference between services and tangible products is that customers can see and touch the tangible product *before* making the purchase, whereas when they buy a service, they commit to the purchase before seeing the outcome of their decisions, relying heavily on their perception of the reputation of your business.

Your product is what Google says it is

Chances are high that before people contact you or your business directly they check you out online. Close to a hundred million names are searched on Google every day. Before buying products, visiting businesses or meeting others, people look online to see which businesses dominate the first screens of their search results.

For help determining which terms people looking for businesses like yours use, use Google's Keyword Planner at `http://adwords.google.com/keywordplanner`. Enter the terms you think people will search to see which ones are most frequently used in your market area, and then optimise your online presence by using those keywords in your website and social media pages.

Customers also look online to see whether their search results turn up credible and trust-building information about your business, including links to positive and descriptive sites and, increasingly, Google +1 recommendations from people they know and regard highly.

See for yourself: Conduct searches for your business name, product name, product category, personal name and keywords that customers may use when seeking information about you and your business. Does your business appear prominently – with links to positive information – in search results for keywords that customers are likely to be using? If so, pat yourself on the back and keep up the good work on your online identity. If not, turn to the chapters in Part III for online image-development advice. For search tips, check out the sidebar, 'Tips for ego-surfers: Find out how you look online.'

Tips for ego-surfers: Find out how you look online

Ego-surfing, also known as *Googling yourself* or *vanity searching,* starts with typing your name into a search engine and often ends with you wondering how Google matched your name to the list of results you see.

'The first step is to search for yourself early and often,' says Janine Warner, founder of DigitalFamily.com and author of *Websites DIY For Dummies.* 'Then set up an alert at www. google.com/alerts so Google will email you every time it discovers your name online.'

When you go ego-surfing, Janine shares these insider tips:

✔ **Don't stop with Google.** Also check and optimise your search results in Bing, Yahoo and the many other search engines out there.

✔ **Look beyond the first results you see.** Use the search engine's filters to adjust results. Choose the News and Blog links to see whether you've been mentioned recently, or use the Images and Video links to find photos and footage linked to your name online.

✔ **Search online phone and address directories.** Also, plug your business street address into Google Maps to pinpoint the location and see a photo from street level. If you can prove that the information is incorrect, outdated or worse, Google and other sites will update the information.

✔ **Search social media sites.** Many allow you to change privacy settings to control how much information is available to people you haven't accepted as 'friends'. Visit http://namechk.com to check name availability on dozens of social media sites.

✔ **Check business directories.** ZoomInfo (www.zoominfo.com) lists more than 50 million people, searchable by name, company, title, industry keywords and location.

Create a profile to manage what appears when people search your name.

✔ **Realise that your own searches may deliver a distorted view of your search ranking.** Google factors in your location and search history when it delivers search results, so your past searches may influence your results. So, if you live in a different city to your friend, the two of you get different results for your name search, just as you'd both get different results if you search words like *accountant, restaurant* and *parks.*

✔ **Go incognito to get the best search results.** Internet Explorer, Google Chrome and Firefox web browsers allow you to surf the web without revealing your location, IP address, browser history and other identifiable information. As a result, you get clean Google search results that aren't affected by the search engine's ability to track your search history. You can turn 'In Private', 'Incognito' and 'Private Browsing' on in your browser settings.

'In case you think private searches are just for those who don't want others to know their nefarious online activities, think again,' Janine says. 'I've taught journalists and business executives all over the world to use free web proxy sites to surf anonymously, especially in places where your online activity can get you killed or kidnapped. The free web proxy service Hide My Ass (www.hidemyass.com) always gets a laugh when I mention it in a speech, but protecting your online identity and reputation is no joke.'

This sidebar is based on information by Janine Warner. For more about her books, speaking engagements and videos, visit http://jcwarner.com *and* www. DigitalFamily.com.

Illogical, Irrational and Real Reasons Why People Buy What You Sell

Online searches and customer opinion research results reveal what people believe about your product, your product category, what your offering means to them personally, and why they make what otherwise may seem like illogical buying decisions. Think about it:

- Why pay £3 for a loaf of bread at the out-of-the-way deli if you can buy bread for under a pound at the supermarket?

- Why pay nearly double for a Lexus than for a Toyota if some models of both are built with many of the same components?

- Why seek cost estimates from three service providers and then choose the most expensive bid if all three propose nearly the same solution?

Why? Because people rarely buy what you think you're selling.

People don't buy your *product*. They buy the promises, the hopes or the satisfaction that they believe your product can deliver.

They buy the £3 loaf of salt-crusted rosemary bread because they believe the loaf is worth it, perhaps because it tastes superior or maybe because it satisfies their sense of worldliness and self-indulgence. They opt for the high-end car for the feeling of safety, quality, prestige and luxury it delivers. They pay top price for services perhaps because they like having their name on a prestigious client roster – or maybe because they simply like or trust the high-cost service provider more than the lower-cost ones.

People may choose to buy from your business over another simply because you make them feel better when they walk through your door.

Don't fool yourself into thinking that you can win customers simply by matching your competitor's features or price. People decide to buy for all kinds of irrational reasons. They buy because they see some intangible and often impossible-to-define value that makes them believe the product is a fair trade for the asking price. Often, that value has to do with the simple truth that they like the people they're dealing with. Never underestimate the power of a personal relationship.

Buying Decisions: Rarely about Price, Always about Value

Customers decide to buy based on their perception of the value they're receiving for the price they're paying. Whatever you charge for your product, that price must reflect what your customer thinks your offering is worth. If nothing distinguishes your product, it falls into the category of a commodity, for which customers are unwilling to pay extra.

If a customer thinks that your price is too high, expect one of the following:

- ✔ The customer won't buy.

- ✔ The customer *will* buy but won't feel satisfied about the value, meaning you win the transaction but sacrifice the customer's goodwill and possibly the chance for repeat business.

- ✔ The customer tells others that your products are overpriced.

Before you panic over a customer calling you high-priced, keep in mind that the dissatisfied customer's negative word-of-mouth is only bad news if others respect the person's opinions regarding price and value. You're often better advised to lose the business of a cherry-picking bargain hunter than to sacrifice your profit margins by trying to price to that person's demanding standards. If your prices are on the high side, though, be certain that the quality, prestige and service – the *value* – that you offer is commensurate with your pricing. Also realise that you can definitely *under-price* your offering as well. If a prospect thinks that your product is worth more than its price tag, expect one of the following:

- ✔ You may sacrifice the sale if the prospect interprets the low price as a reflection of a second-rate offering.

- ✔ You may make the sale, but at a lower price (and lower profit margin) than the customer is willing to pay, leaving lost revenue and possibly customer questions following the transaction.

- ✔ The customer may leave with the impression that you're a discounter – a perception that may steer future opinions and purchase decisions.

Unless you aim to own the bargain-basement position in your market (a dangerous strategy because some other business can always go lower), you're better off providing excellent value and setting your prices accordingly.

Calculating the value formula

During the split second it takes for customers to rate your product's value, they weigh a range of attributes:

- ✔ What does it cost?
- ✔ What is the quality?
- ✔ What features are included?
- ✔ Is it convenient?
- ✔ Is it reliable?
- ✔ Can they trust your expertise?
- ✔ How is the product supported?
- ✔ What guarantee, promise or ongoing relationship can they count on?

These considerations start a mental juggling act, during which customers determine your offering's value. If they decide that what you deliver is average, they'll expect a low price to tip the deal in your favour. On the other hand, if they rank aspects of your offering well above those of competing options, they'll likely be willing to pay a premium for the perceived value.

Customers match high prices with high demands. Remember the sign you used to see in print shops and garages? 'Price, quality and speed – choose any two'? How times have changed. Today's customers expect the companies they buy from to offer price, quality *and* speed. But here's the good news: They expect you to be *competitive* in all three areas but *exemplary* in only one. Here are a few well-known examples:

- ✔ Costco = Price
- ✔ John Lewis = Service
- ✔ Tesco = Convenience
- ✔ FedEx = Reliability
- ✔ BMW = Quality

Riding the price/value teeter-totter

Price emphasises the money spent. Price is what you get out of the deal. Value is what you deliver to customers. Value is what they care most about and what your communications should emphasise.

Pricing truths

When sales are down or customers seem dissatisfied, small businesses turn too quickly to their pricing in their search for a quick-fix solution. Before reducing prices to increase sales or satisfaction levels, think first about how you can increase the value you deliver. Consider the following points:

- ✔ Your customer must perceive your product's value – or the worth of the solution your product delivers – to be greater than the asking price.

- ✔ The less value customers equate with your product, the more emphasis they put on low price.

- ✔ The lower the price, the lower the perceived value.

- ✔ Customers like price reductions way better than price increases, so be sure that when you reduce prices that you can live with the change, because upping prices later may not sit well.

- ✔ Products that are desperately needed, rarely available or one-of-a-kind are almost never price-sensitive.

Penny-pinching versus shooting the moon

Tell a person he needs angioplasty surgery, and he'll pay whatever the surgeon charges – no questions asked. But tell him he's out of dishwasher tablets, and he'll comparison shop. Why? Because one product is more essential, harder to substitute, harder to evaluate and needed far less often than the other. One is a matter of life and death, the other mundane. See Table 3-1 to determine where your product fits on the price-sensitivity scale.

Table 3-1	Price Sensitivity Factors
Price Matters Less if Products Are	**Price Matters More if Products Are**
Hard to come by	Readily available
Purchased rarely	Purchased frequently
Essential	Non-essential
Hard to substitute	Easy to substitute
Hard to evaluate and compare	Easy to evaluate and compare
Wanted or needed immediately	Easy to put off purchasing until later
Emotionally sensitive	Emotion-free
Capable of providing desirable and highly beneficial outcomes	Hard to link to a clear return-on-investment
One-of-a-kind	Ten a penny

Evaluating your pricing

Give your prices an annual check-up. Here are factors to consider and questions to ask:

- ✔ **Your price level:** Compared to competitors' offerings, how does your offering rank in terms of value and price? How easily can the customer find a substitute – or choose not to buy at all? (See Chapter 4.)

- ✔ **Your pricing structure:** Do you include or charge extra for enhanced features or benefits? What promotions, discounts, rebates or incentives do you offer? Do you offer quantity discounts? Does your pricing motivate desired customer behaviour, for example by offering a discount on volume purchases, contract renewals or other incentives that are factored into your pricing to reduce hesitation and inspire future purchases?

- ✔ **Pricing timetable:** How often do you change your pricing? How often do your competitors change their pricing? Do you anticipate competitive actions or market shifts that may affect your pricing? Do you expect your costs to affect your prices in the near future? Do you need to consider any looming market changes or buyer taste changes?

Raising prices

Customers resist or barely register price rises. Their reaction largely depends on how you announce the change. One of the worst approaches is to simply raise prices with a take-it-or-leave-it announcement. Far better is to include new pricing as part of a menu of pricing options, following these tips:

- ✔ **Accompany price rises with lower-priced alternatives.** Examples include bulk-purchase prices, happy hour or low-season rates and bundled product packages that provide a discount in return for the larger transaction.

- ✔ **Announce a new range of products instead of simply high- and low-priced options.** Research shows that, though customers often opt for the lower of two price levels, when three price levels are provided, they choose the mid-range or upper level rather than the least expensive.

- ✔ **Give customers choices by unbundling all-inclusive products.** By presenting product components and service agreements as self-standing offerings, customers can self-tailor a lower-priced offering.

- ✔ **Give advance notice of price increases.** In service businesses, don't make customers discover increases on their invoices. Allow them time to accommodate new pricing in their budgets. In retail businesses, give customers the opportunity to stock up before price rises take effect.

- ✔ **Believe in your pricing.** Especially when you raise prices, be certain that your pricing is a fair reflection of your product's cost and value. Then instil that belief throughout your business.

Presenting prices

The way you present prices can inspire your prospects – or confuse or under-whelm them. Use Table 3-2 and the following advice to show your prices in the most favourable light:

- ✔ **Don't let your price presentation get too complex.** Table 3-2 presents examples for presenting prices in a straightforward, visually attractive manner that communicates clearly without misleading consumers.

- ✔ **Do make the price compelling.** In a world of outlet shopping, online bargains and warehouse stores, '10 per cent off' isn't considered a deal.

- ✔ **Do support pricing announcements with the positive benefits your product promises to deliver.** Price alone is never reason enough to buy.

Table 3-2	Pricing Presentation Do's and Don'ts	
Do	*Don't*	*Why*
Announcing a new number to remember – £89 per night	We've just cut our nightly rates – £89 midweek; some restrictions apply	The first approach makes the deal sound noteworthy, whereas the second approach provides no positive rationale and implies that 'small print applies.'
Sofa and love-seat £1,995	Sofa and loveseat £1,995.00	When prices are more than £100, drop the decimal point and zeroes to lighten the effect.
50 per cent off second pair	25 per cent off two or more	Complicated discounts are uninspiring, and '50 per cent off' sounds like double the discount of 25 per cent off when you buy two.
Usually £995; now £695 while stocks last	30 per cent off	1/3 off sounds more compelling than 30 per cent off, but showing a £300 reduction is stronger yet. 'While stocks last' adds incentive and urgency.
£17.95 includes free delivery	£14.95 plus shipping/ handling	The word 'plus' alerts the consumer that the price is only the beginning. Calculate and include shipping and handling to remove buyer concern and possible objection.

The Care and Feeding of a Product Line

You have two ways to increase sales:

1. **Sell more to existing customers.**

2. **Attract new customers.**

Figure 3-1 presents questions to ask as you seek to build business from new and existing customers through new and existing products.

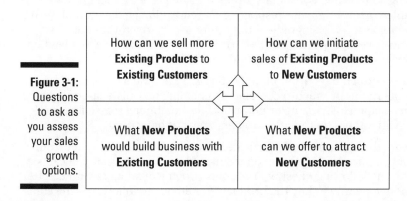

Figure 3-1: Questions to ask as you assess your sales growth options.

Products get old. They follow a life cycle (shown in Figure 3-2) that begins with product development and proceeds until the product reaches old age, at which time its growth rate halts and sales decline.

Figure 3-2: Sales follow a predictable curve throughout the product life cycle.

Enhancing the appeal of existing products

At least annually, small businesses need to assess whether their products still appeal to customers. When customers lose interest, a company needs to adjust features, services, pricing or packaging – or make other changes to sustain or reignite buyer interest. Here are some of your options:

- ✔ **Same product, new use:** Start by looking for ways that you can repurpose a product to win new purchases by established and new customers.

  A historic example of repurposing a product comes from Arm & Hammer baking soda. When consumers stopped baking, sales of baking soda tumbled. Arm & Hammer responded by reintroducing baking soda – this time not as a recipe ingredient but rather as a refrigerator deodoriser. Today, that repurposing has led Arm & Hammer into a role as a leading supplier of cleaning and household solutions.

- ✔ **Same product, new promotional offer:** Examine ways to update how you offer your product to customers, including new distribution, customer-responsive pricing or new packages combining top-selling products with others that your customers may not have tried.

  Be sure that your new offer provides advantages that address customer wants and needs. Before you offer a new 'deal', be sure that you can say yes to the following question: Does this provide customers with a better, higher-value way to buy the product? For advice to follow, see the sidebar, 'Innovation isn't for the self-absorbed', later in the chapter.

- ✔ **Same product, new customer:** Expand the market for existing products through low-risk, introductory trial offers or samples or through free seminars, guest lectures or events that attract the kinds of people you target as customers and develop their interest in your offerings.

Raising a healthy product

Sales follow a predictable pattern as a product moves through the life cycle illustrated in Figure 3-2. The following descriptions explain the marketing steps and sales expectations that accompany each phase of the product's life:

- ✔ **Introductory phase:** At the beginning of a product's life cycle, you want to build awareness, interest and market acceptance while working to change existing market purchase patterns. Use introductory offers to gain trial and drive sales to speed up your cost/investment recovery.

  Although prompting early sales through low pricing is tempting be careful, because how you introduce a product determines how its image is established. If customers link the product with a low price, that first impression sticks and limits your ability to increase prices later. Better to set the price where it belongs relative to your product value and to gain sales through heavy start-up advertising and, if necessary, carefully crafted promotional offers.

✔ **Growth phase:** The product enters this phase after it has been adopted by the first 10 to 20 per cent of the market, called the *innovators* or *early adopters*. The masses follow this pace-setting group, and when the masses start buying, growth takes off and competitors enter. Consider promotions and special offers to protect and build market share.

✔ **Maturity:** When the product reaches maturity, its sales are at their peak level, and sales growth starts to decline.

✔ **Saturation phase:** At this phase, the market is flooded with options. Sales come largely from replacement purchases. Use pricing offers and incentives to recruit new customers and win them from competitors.

✔ **Declining phase:** When the product reaches the point of deep sales decline, a business has only a few choices. One is to abandon the product in favour of new offerings, perhaps introducing phase-out pricing to hasten the cycle closure. Another is to let the product exist on its own with minor marketing support and, as a result, lowered sales expectations. A third option is to reinvent the product's usage, application or distribution to gain appeal with a new market; you need to take this revitalising step when a product reaches its maturity rather than after its appeal is in decline.

Developing new products

Whether you're doing it to seize a new market opportunity or to offset shrinking sales with replacement products, one of the most exciting aspects of business is introducing new products. It's also one of the most treacherous because it involves betting your business resources on a new idea.

As you pursue product development, ask these questions:

✔ What current product can we significantly update or enhance to address changing customer wants and needs?

✔ What altogether new idea can satisfy currently unaddressed wants and needs of our customers and prospective customers?

✔ What market trend can we address with a new product?

Companies develop many new products to address fads that may or may not become lasting trends. Before capitalising on a fad, consider these factors:

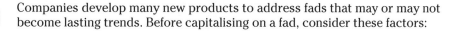

✔ Only a fraction of hot fads launch marketplace trends. Most come and go quickly, so have a plan to get in and get out of the market quickly if interest ebbs.

✔ Be sure that you aren't entering the market too late. Take a second to review Figure 3-2, the product life cycle. If other companies have already introduced offerings to address the fad, and if those products have already reached the saturation phase, then your new offering has to come with pricing and other incentives to win business from the lineup of competitors already in the field.

Here are questions to ask during the research stage of product development:

✔ Is it unique? Is another business already producing it, and, if so, is your product going to be materially different – and better?

✔ Does it deliver customer value? If this value is an upgrade of an existing product, how is it different in a way that matters to customers?

✔ Will it appeal to a growing market? What is its customer profile?

✔ Is it feasible? What does it cost to produce or deliver, and how much can you charge for it?

✔ Does it fit with your company image? Is it consistent with what people already believe about you, or does it require a leap of faith?

✔ Is it legal and safe? Does it conform to all laws? Does it infringe on any patents? Does it have safety concerns?

✔ Can you make and market it? Do you have the people and cash resources to back it? Can you get it to market? Do sales projections support the cost of development, introduction, and production?

✔ Can you find a unique niche in the marketplace for it? The topic of positioning and branding products is a chapter unto itself, so turn to Chapter 7 for more information.

As you study new product ideas, beware of the following:

✔ Features that don't inspire your customer

✔ Features that don't deliver clear customer benefit

✔ Product enhancements that don't add significant product value

✔ 'New' products that are really old products in some newfangled disguise that means nothing to customers

✔ Products that don't fit within your expertise and reputation

✔ Products that address fads or trends that are already starting to wane

One last caution: If you're introducing a product that's the very first of its kind, budget sufficiently to achieve customer knowledge and a fast following. Otherwise you may lose the advantage to a competitor who arrives second but with a better offering and marketing effort. As proof, consider how AltaVista was eclipsed by Google or how MySpace was overtaken by Facebook.

Innovation isn't for the self-absorbed

Businessweek magazine named Sohrab Vossoughi one of the top five innovation gurus in the United States. His innovation and design consultancy firm Ziba (www.ziba.com) is responsible for some of the world's biggest innovation success stories. During an interview for Business on Main, MSN's small business website, he shared this innovation advice for small businesses:

- Innovation is useful only when it results in meaningful value to consumers. Ninety per cent of products fail because they're not based on the grounded desires of consumers. Successful innovation makes a meaningful promise: 'I know what you value, and this is what I'm going to do for you.'

- Innovators need to understand their customers and have empathy for what they need, desire and value. Address those values to win their purchases. Move beyond their fundamental wants and needs to win their hearts and minds.

- Innovation must be consistent with the DNA of your business. It must be believable within the promise that customers already believe your business makes and keeps.

- As a brand, you can't be everything to everybody. Innovate for the customers you have and know.

- Trends affect value systems and open opportunities. You need to ask, 'Is this the right time for this offering?'

- Social media is a co-creation tool. It can allow you to get information about customer wants and needs so you can synthesise what you're hearing and what it means, making a connection between customer values and new product designs.

- There's a difference between extracting and adding value. Extracting value from another offering leads to incremental and superficial change – change that's literal versus fundamental. Consumers don't buy that as meaningful.

- The same thing that makes innovation successful gets innovators into trouble: excitement. If all the excitement is driven from inside the business, they don't have enough understanding of what excites the customers. That's how most innovators get their expectations off track and why they end up trying to sell to someone who doesn't value what they're offering.

Managing your product offerings

Product line management is less about what you're selling than about what the market is buying. Keep your focus on your customers – on what they value – not just today, but tomorrow.

Make a list of products you sell and the revenue that each offering generates. Concentrate only on the end products you deliver. For example, a law firm provides clerical services, but because those services are part of other products and aren't the reason people do business with the lawyers in the first place, they shouldn't show up on the firm's product list.

To get you started, Table 3-3 shows products for a bookstore.

Table 3-3	Independent Bookstore Product Line Analysis	
Product	*Product Revenue*	*Percentage of Revenue*
Books	£250,000	43.4 per cent
Magazines	£95,000	16.5 per cent
Coffee and cakes	£95,000	16.5 per cent
Greeting cards and gift items	£55,000	9.5 per cent
Audiobooks	£45,000	7.8 per cent
Audiobook rentals	£18,500	3.2 per cent
Stationery	£18,000	3.1 per cent

Follow these steps to prioritise and manage your product line:

✔ **Sell more of what customers are buying.** Study your list for surprises. You may find some products that are performing better than you realised. This knowledge can alert you to customer interests that you can ride to higher revenues. For example, nearly one-third of all revenues at the bookstore featured in Table 3-3 come from beverage, drinks, food and magazine sales (combined). This finding may support a decision to move the magazine display nearer to the café, giving each area a greater sense of space and bringing consumers of both offerings into nearer proximity (and therefore buying convenience).

✔ **Promote products that you've hidden from your customers.** You may have a product line that's lagging behind simply because your customers aren't aware of it. When the bookstore in Table 3-3 realised that only 3 per cent of revenues were from sales of stationery, the owners boosted the line by giving it a more prominent store location. The result? Sales increased. Had the line continued to lag, though, the owners were ready to replace it with one capable of drawing a greater response.

✔ **Move fast-selling items out of prime retail positions.** Give the spotlight to harder-to-sell offerings or give the slower-selling items visibility by placing them near top sellers. In the case of the bookstore in Table 3-3, moving a display of greeting cards closer to the popular pastry counter led to increased sales.

✔ **Back your winners.** Use your product analysis to track which lines are increasing or decreasing in sales and respond accordingly. If the bookstore in Table 3-3 is fighting a decline in book sales while sales of reading accessories and gifts are growing, the owners may decide to address the trend by adding lamps, bookends and even reading glasses.

✔ **Bet only on product lines that have adequate growth potential.** Before committing to new product strategies, project your return on investment. For example, Table 3-3 shows that a little more than 3 per cent of sales result from audiobook rentals. Doubling this business would increase annual revenues by only £18,500. Realising this, the owners asked: What's the likelihood of increasing this business – and at what cost? On the other hand, increasing café sales by 20 per cent would realise £19,000 of additional revenue, which the owners determined was a safer marketing bet and a stronger strategic move.

Chapter 4

Sizing Up Competitors and Staking Out Market Share

....

....

*N*o matter how unique your offering, you always have competition.

When Alexander Graham Bell called to Mr Watson through his new-fangled invention in 1876, he had competition already. He held in his hand the one and only such device in the whole world, yet from its moment of inception, the telephone had to fight for market share. It had to compete with all the existing and more familiar means of message delivery, and it was certain to spawn a crop of copycat products to vie for message delivery in the future.

Competition may not be obvious or direct, but is always present. The sooner you face it and plan for it, the better. Use the information in this chapter to gauge and grow your 'share' of business.

Playing the Competitive Field

Competition is the contest among businesses to attract customers and sales. The opposite of competition is a *monopoly,* where a single company has complete control of an industry or service offering.

Competition occurs whenever winning attention is necessary for selection and survival. In nature, the peacock's tail, the rose's scent and the apple's sweetness are the marketing tools. In business, the battle is fought and won with product innovations and marketing activities designed to attract customers to one business over another.

Thanks to the forces of competition, the free enterprise system is undergoing constant improvement. Here are a few examples of what competition does:

- ✔ It prompts product upgrades and innovations.
- ✔ It leads to higher quality and lower prices.
- ✔ It enhances selection.
- ✔ It inspires business efficiencies.

Speaking the language of competition

Your sales figures provide your first indication of how you're doing in your competitive arena. If they're strong and growing, your business is on the right track. If they're sliding downhill, you have your work cut out for you. This section defines the terms to know in order to evaluate and improve your position in the competitive field.

Market share

Market share is your slice of the market pie – or your portion of all the sales of products like yours that are taking place in your market area. For example, suppose that you manage a cinema in a market with a dozen other cinemas within a reasonable driving distance. Your market share is the percentage that your cinema captures of all the movie tickets sold by all 13 cinemas. See the 'Calculating Your Market Share' section later in this chapter for tips on how to determine and grow your market share.

Share of customer

Share of customer is the percentage that you capture of all the purchases that each individual customer *could* make at your business. Continuing with the cinema example, in addition to tickets, the cinema sells popcorn, drinks, sweets, movie posters, gift certificates and so on. Every customer who purchases a movie ticket – nothing else – represents an opportunity to seize a greater share of customer, also known as *share of wallet.* For tips on calculating and growing your share of customer, see Chapter 19.

Share of opportunity

Share of opportunity measures all those people who could but don't buy products like the ones you sell.

Years ago, Coca-Cola released research documenting that nearly 6 billion people in the world were consuming, on average, 64 ounces of fluid a day. Of that total intake, only 2 ounces of the liquid consumed was Coca-Cola. Coca-Cola officials used this information as the basis of an effort to increase what they termed their *share of stomach.*

An insurance company sells life insurance, which provides a solution for peace of mind. Its competition comes from competing insurers and all the other ways that people address their desire for financial security, including everything from investing in stocks to stashing money under the mattress to buying lottery tickets. The insurance company may want to think in terms of how to increase its *nest egg share.*

Find a 'stomach share' analogy for your business. What satisfaction does your product address? What solution does your business provide? You probably won't be able to arrive at a firm calculation of the total size of the opportunity your business addresses, but simply by thinking in terms of why people buy your offering and how they participate with your business, you may land on new promotional ideas that lead to a greater share of business.

Knowing what you're up against

Your business faces three kinds of competition:

- **Direct competitors that eat into your market share:** They offer the same kinds of products or services that you do and appeal to customers in the same markets that you do business. Your market share increases when you lure business from direct competitors to your business.

- **Indirect competitors that erode your share of customer:** For instance, if you sell paint but your customer buys a paintbrush somewhere else, that paintbrush seller is an indirect competitor because it's capturing your customer's secondary sale. Similarly, if you own a marketing company and your client also uses a sales coach to build business, the sales coach is your indirect competitor. To increase your share of customer, find a way to serve as a one-stop solution by offering your primary product and also the secondary, complementary or add-on products that customers currently obtain elsewhere.

- **Phantom competitors that block your share of opportunity:** One of the biggest obstacles to a purchase – and therefore the biggest phantom competition – is your customer's inclination to buy nothing or to find an alternative or do-it-yourself solution instead of buying what you're selling. Taking the paint shop example a step further, if you offer a choice between enamel and latex paint but your customers opt for vinyl cladding (which never needs paint), an outlet is a phantom competitor capable of blocking your business. For that matter, if customers decide that their houses can go another year without a paint job, the option to do nothing is your phantom competitor. To increase your share of opportunity, discover your phantom competitors and then make your product an easier, more satisfying and more valuable alternative.

Understanding how to compete

All else being equal, most customers opt for the product with the lowest price. If you want to charge more, make sure that everything else *isn't* equal between you and your lower-priced competitor. Most competitors fall into one of the following two categories:

- ✔ **Price competitors** emphasise price as their competitive advantage. To succeed as a price competitor, a business must be prepared to offset lower profit margins with higher sales volume. It also must be prepared to lose its only competitive edge if another business offers a lower price.

- ✔ **Non-price competitors** gain business through a distinction other than low price. They win business based on superior quality, prestige, service, location, reputation, uniqueness of offering or customer convenience. They must offer an overall value that customers perceive to be worth a higher price tag. They also need to be able to clearly communicate their quality distinction – for instance, *Zero defects, Phone calls returned in 4 hours* or *Delivery in 30 minutes or it's free.*

Winning Your Share of the Market

You win market share by taking business from your direct competitors, thereby reducing their slice of the market pie while increasing your own. Here's what you must do:

1. **Get to know your direct competition.**

   If prospects don't buy from your business, where do they go instead?

2. **Find out why your customers buy from competing businesses over yours.**

3. **Determine how to win business from direct competitors by enhancing or communicating the value of your offerings in a way that makes them more attractive than the competing alternatives.**

The following sections go into more detail on how to accomplish these steps.

Defining your direct competition

The first step toward gaining market share is to acknowledge that you have competition and to get real about which businesses are winning the sales that you're working to capture. On an annual or regular basis, ask yourself the questions outlined in this section.

With which businesses does your business directly compete?

When people consider buying your product or service, which other businesses do they think of at the same time?

Be realistic as you name your direct competitors. Just because a retailer sells jewellery in London, it doesn't necessarily compete with Tiffany & Co. Your direct competitors are businesses that provide your customers a similar offering and a reasonable alternative to your product or service.

If you have a service business, your direct competitors are those companies that you regularly go up against as you try to win contracts or jobs. If you're a retailer, your direct competitors are the businesses whose shopping bags your customers carry as they walk by your store or the business names you overhear while customers deliberate whether to buy your product or some alternative. Investigate by conducting customer research (see Chapter 2).

How does your business compare to its direct competitors?

Invest time finding out about the strengths and weaknesses of your competitors. Shop in their stores, call their offices, visit their websites or take any other steps to approach them in the manner your customers approach your business. Compare how their offerings, their presentations, their brand images (see Chapter 7) and the experience of dealing with their businesses compares with the offerings of your business.

Consider the following:

- ✔ What are this competitor's strengths?
- ✔ What are this competitor's weaknesses?
- ✔ What can your business do differently to draw this competitor's customers over to your business?

As you compare your business to your competitors, try using the Customer Satisfaction Analysis Form from www.dummies.com/extras/small busmarketinguk. It presents a list of the attributes and values that prospects consider when choosing among competing businesses.

Among your direct competitors, how does your business rank?

Are you the top-tier player in your competitive arena or are you on the low end of the spectrum trying to become a more dominant player? Here are approaches for pegging your place in your competitive field:

- ✔ Compare how your business ranks with competitors based on number of employees, sales volume or any other indicator you can measure.
- ✔ Compare your market share with the share of each competitor. (See the section 'Calculating Your Market Share' later in this chapter.)

✔ Evaluate your *top of mind* ranking – sometimes called your *mind share*. When prospects are asked to name three to five businesses in your field, does your name consistently make the list? If so, you can be pretty sure that your business has top-tier mind share in its competitive arena. Keep listening and you'll discover the names of the businesses your customers think are your direct competitors. And if you don't hear your business name, listen anyway, because when you know which businesses *are* in the top-of-mind category, you can begin to analyse what they do differently to achieve the prominence you seek.

Moving up the competitive ladder

Most businesses misdirect their time and energy by tackling the wrong competitors. They take on the biggest names in their market area instead of the biggest threats to their business. As you develop your competitive plan of attack, follow these steps:

1. **Start by winning market share from the businesses you're actually losing customers to** *today*.

   Do this even if it involves facing the harsh reality that your customers consider your business among a less prestigious group than you wish they did. After you name your current competitors, study their offerings, their marketing and the customer service they provide (see Chapter 20) as you honestly evaluate how your business compares.

2. **Make a list of the companies you** *wish* **you were running with.**

   Evaluate why you're not in that group. Is it because of your business's image or location? Does the nature of your clientele mark you as a lower-level player? Or do your products and pricing prevent you from competing with the biggest names in your business arena?

3. **Consider whether changing competitive levels is advantageous.**

   Assess whether your business is more likely to be successful at its current competitive level (think of the big-fish-in-a-small-pond concept) or at the next competitive level (where perhaps you can compete for more lucrative business but where competition may be stiffer and where customers may be fewer or more demanding).

If you decide that your business would be better off competing with more visible and prestigious businesses in your arena, commit to making the changes necessary to get the market to see you through new eyes. See Chapter 7 for information on how to influence market perceptions and win your chosen space in your marketplace.

Calculating Your Market Share

Having a sense of your market share provides a good indication of your competitive rank and a way to monitor your growth within your target market.

Sizing up your target market

To calculate your share of the market, first define the size of the market in which you compete.

The *total* market includes the entire nation or world – a market area that matters enormously to major global marketers like Nike or Levi's. But to a small business like yours, what matters is your *target* market – the one within the sphere of your business's influence. You can assess your target market's size by using the following criteria:

- **Geographic targeting:** Where are your customers, and how many are there? For example, a retailer may determine that its geographic target market consists primarily of people who live or holiday within a two-hour drive of the retailer's place of business. An accountant may determine that her geographic target market is concentrated within a city's boundaries. A consultant may target businesses in her local region.

- **Customer targeting:** How many people or businesses actually fit your customer profile? (See Chapter 2 for profiling information.) An office furniture manufacturer may target all the nation's office-furnishing retail establishments, along with architects and interior designers who specify office furnishings. An online florist may focus exclusively on wedding planners and brides-to-be within a single county or region.

- **Product-oriented targeting:** Sometimes, the most effective way to measure your target market's size is through an analysis of how many sales of products like yours occur in the market. For instance, a microbrewery may measure its share of a market as a percentage of all premium beer sold in its geographic target area. (The microbrewery wouldn't measure its sales against *all* beer sales; it would focus on premium beer sales, because that's the microbrewery's sphere of business influence.) Likewise, a lawyer who specialises in land-use planning would assess the number of land-use cases in the target market area before trying to calculate market share.

Doing the sums

When you've a good sense of your total target market's size, you can use several approaches to calculate your share:

- ✔ **Unit sales:** Some businesses can easily figure out the total number of products like theirs sold each year. A hotel manager, for instance, can divide the number of rooms it rents out by the total number of hotel rooms in an area and then multiply by 100 to arrive at their percentage share of the market.

- ✔ **Number of potential customers:** If you know that 30,000 adults are in your target market area, and if you can make an educated guess that one in ten of them – or 10 per cent – is a consumer of services like yours, you can assume that your business has a total potential market of 3,000 adults. If you serve 300 of those adults, you've a 10 per cent share of your target market.

To aid in your guesswork, visit your local library and search electronic databases like Key Note and Mintel for information on customers in your market area.

For instance, imagine a fabric and sewing supply store that serves a geographic area that includes 7,000 homes within a 15-minute drive of the store. The owners can find out from Key Note or Mintel that 18.5 per cent of the households in the area participate in home sewing. If they multiply their 7,000-household market area by 18.5 per cent, they'll discover that they've 1,295 potential customers in their geographic market area. If the owners currently serve 250 of these potential customers, they've a market share of just less than 20 per cent – meaning plenty of opportunity for growth.

- ✔ **Total sales volume:** Another way to estimate market share is to calculate how much people spend at businesses like yours in your market area each year and then divide that figure by your sales revenue. For example, if annually in your market area people spend a total of £1 million on products like those you sell, and if your business does £100,000 annually in sales, then you've a 10 per cent market share.

Regional business journals and newspapers compile lists that rank sales by businesses in specific industries or service sectors. Businesses submit their revenues (often slightly inflated, so read them with a realistic eye) as a basis for appearing in these lists. Study the lists for your industry to find clues to regional sales revenues in your field.

Market share: Sample calculation

Suppose that Green Gardens, a residential landscaping business, serves a market area that includes 20,000 houses, of which approximately 10 per cent use landscape services. Thus, the potential residential landscape service market is 2,000 homes. If Green Gardens serves 200 homes, it has a 10 per cent market share.

Another way to look at market share is by sales volume. Green Gardens can estimate the revenues of each of its competitors and then add those figures to the Green Gardens revenue figure to produce a rough estimate of total target market residential landscape service

sales. If target market sales total £4 million, and if Green Gardens has annual sales of £600,000, Green Gardens has a 15 per cent market share.

If Green Gardens combines its knowledge of market share based on unit sales (number of houses served) *and* market share based on sales volume, its owners would see that they've a 10 per cent share of all houses served, yet they've a 15 per cent share of total sales volume. This finding may lead them to conclude that they serve larger-sized accounts than some of their competitors. And based on that, they should have a small celebration!

Increasing Your Market Share

If you're in business and you're ringing up sales, you can rest assured that your business enjoys at least some level of market awareness and market share. But you can be equally certain that not everyone knows about or buys from your business. No brand in the world has 100 per cent brand awareness, let alone 100 per cent market share, so be reasonable with your market share goals and growth expectations.

Also, as you seek to increase market share, steer clear of these land mines:

✔ **Avoid 'buying' market share through price reductions.** Don't sacrifice your bottom line as you prepare to welcome new customers through the door. Before you go the price-slashing route, glance through the pricing advice in Chapter 3.

✔ **Be ready before issuing an invitation to new customers.** Don't procrastinate, but do give yourself time to be sure that you're ready to make a great first impression. Run through the following checklist before launching a new business development effort:

  • **Current customer satisfaction levels:** Are your current customers happy with your product? Are they happy with your business in general? Do they return to your business again and again, or do you have a high turnover rate? Do customers speak well on your behalf? Are your customer satisfaction levels sky-high? (If you're not sure, turn to Chapter 20.)

- **Customer service adjustments:** Before working to draw in new customers, make changes to enhance your customer experience and service levels (see Chapter 20), increasing the odds that you develop lasting and loyal customer relationships. Start by studying current customer reviews, ratings and input, looking for legitimate service or product complaints you can address before reaching out to new customers. Then, beyond righting wrongs, get proactive. Do you need to fine-tune your product offering – how you price it, how you package and present it or even how you guarantee it? Do you need to improve how you interact with customers? This may include everything from enhancing your business environment to revising your on-hold telephone message to improving the speed and user-friendliness of your website.

- **Business readiness:** Do you have the inventory (or, if you own a service business, the staff, talent and capacity) to deliver what you're offering? Are your staff well-informed and ready to help prospects become buyers when they respond to your marketing messages?

When market share means market saturation

The common rule is that a 25 per cent market share is considered a dominant market position. As you calculate your market share, watch closely as it reaches a dominant position. When it gets there, take time to celebrate, for sure, but also be aware that as your share edges further upward, it nears a level called market saturation.

Market saturation occurs when a business captures the sales of about 40 per cent of the potential customers within its target market, at which point one of several things tends to happen:

- ✔ **Competitors start to eat into market share.** After a business begins to saturate its marketplace, competitors realise the opportunity and enter to seize a share of the sales.

- ✔ **The dominant business gets complacent,** and often quality control gets lax and customers begin to stray.

- ✔ **Customers' interest or need wanes.** By the time a business gains dominant market share, often customers have bought the products they need and, other than replacements, their purchases grow few and far between.

- ✔ **The business seeks new opportunities.** With market saturation comes the need for change. Businesses that dominate their market areas seek growth by opening new markets or introducing new products. Most of all, they restore their emphasis on customer service and satisfaction – the very thing that made the business a success in the first place.

Don't turn from a growing market too soon, but don't cling exclusively to a saturated market too long. Use market share knowledge as your steering wheel.

Chapter 5

Setting Your Goals, Objectives, Strategies and Budgets

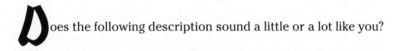

Does the following description sound a little or a lot like you?

You don't know where to start with your marketing efforts. You don't know how much you should spend. You don't know whether you need to hire someone to take on the marketing task. You aren't sure what you should be saying or to whom. In fact, you aren't even certain what you're trying to accomplish with your marketing efforts.

If that description sounds familiar, this chapter is for you, because getting clear about your marketing goals simplifies everything.

After you actually state what you want to achieve, marketing becomes a pretty reasonable task. For example, an accounting firm may determine that it wants to add three new corporate clients over the coming year. A retail establishment may want to gain £200,000 in new sales. A commercial cleaning business may want to take on five more business contracts.

When small business owners are clear about where they want to go, they nearly always get there. In huge companies, the process of getting all the departments focused on the same goal is like herding cats. But small businesses have fewer people to orchestrate, and the owner's will can more clearly affect the actions of the full business team. As a small business marketer, if you start with a goal, a plan and a reasonable budget for achieving your desired outcome, chances are that you'll get where you want to go.

Where Are You Going, Anyway?

Mission. Vision. Goals. Objectives. What's what?

Some consultants do nothing but lead corporations and organisations through the *visioning* process, helping them clarify why they exist, what they hope to achieve and how they intend to get where they want to be.

Small companies rarely have the funds to dedicate to this kind of strategic process. For that matter, they rarely have time to stop and think about what they're trying to accomplish beyond the survival objective of bringing in enough revenue to cover the expenses. That's why your business will have an edge – and a greater chance for success – if you devote some time upfront to setting your sights and aiming yourself and your business in the right direction.

The 'vision' thing

Well-run businesses set annual goals that are supported by the foundation of a business vision and mission. The terms *vision* and *mission* are often used interchangeably, but a fine-line difference does exist between them.

Your *vision* is a statement of what your company strives to be. It defines your desired future and is the big picture of where you're going. Your company's *mission,* on the other hand, is the path you plan to follow to achieve success.

A hallmark example of clearly defined vision and mission statements comes from the Oregon Trail, the 19th-century trek from Missouri to Oregon. If ever an organisation needed a vision to overshadow the mission's rigour and to guide all goals and objectives, it was this 2,200-mile journey across the United States.

> **Oregon Trail Vision:** To find a better life.

> **Oregon Trail Mission:** To travel by wagon to Oregon.

Even if your own challenges pale in comparison to those of the United States's pioneers (and with any luck, they do!), your organisation can still benefit from clarity about what you're working to achieve. You may come up with vision and mission statements, or you may combine the two in a single *statement of purpose*, following the examples of success stories in the upcoming section.

Either way, by defining what your business seeks to achieve you create a barometer by which to measure every planning and marketing decision your business makes.

Your statement of purpose

Your business will be stronger if you put into writing the ultimate reason that you come to work every day. Consider these questions as you work on your company's reason for being:

✔ Why did you get into this business in the first place?

✔ What need did you see that you feel you can fulfil better than anyone else?

✔ What makes your business different from others?

✔ What commitment do you make to those you deal with – from employees to suppliers to customers?

✔ What's the ultimate reason for your work?

Turning a profit is a desired result of your success, but don't let the bottom line become your purpose. Instead, articulate what positive change you want to create through your business. This defines the heart and soul of your company and the driving force behind all the decisions that you make. From there, success – and profits – should flow.

Success stories

Most successful companies display their statements of purpose throughout their workplaces and in their written communications. Check annual reports and websites to find the statements of purpose from the business world's well-known success stories.

Here are a few examples:

✔ **Google:** To organise the world's information and make it universally accessible and useful.

✔ **Microsoft:** To help people and businesses throughout the world to realise their full potential.

✔ **Coca-Cola Company:** To refresh the world. To inspire moments of optimism and happiness. To create value and make a difference.

Now it's your turn: Use the formula in Figure 5-1 to create a sentence that serves as the beacon for your business. As you develop your statement, think in terms of your vision (what positive change you want to achieve) and your mission (how you'll make your vision real).

Formula for a Purpose Statement

BEGIN WITH

A verb that describes the change you want to make

THEN ADD

A clause summarizing the need your business addresses

AND YOU HAVE

The Purpose Statement for your company

Figure 5-1:
How to develop a statement of purpose.

Defining Goals and Objectives Simply

More than just business buzzwords, *goal, objective, strategy* and *tactic* fit together to take your small business from ideas to action.

- ✔ **Goal:** The overall sales or professional target that your marketing programme seeks to achieve. Your goal is an expression of a realistic and clearly defined target, usually accompanied by a time frame.

- ✔ **Objective:** The measurable result that is necessary to achieve the goal. A plan usually has several objectives that define the major means by which you'll meet the goal.

- ✔ **Strategy:** The plan for achieving each measurable objective.

- ✔ **Tactic:** An action that you take to enact your strategy.

Figure 5-2 shows how these elements come together.

Figure 5-2:
The planning pyramid.

THE ACTIONS WE WILL TAKE — Strategy

HOW WE WILL ACHIEVE IT — Objectives

WHAT WE WANT — Goals

WHY WE DO THIS — Vision, Mission and Core Values/Purpose

Setting goals and objectives

The line between goals and objectives is razor thin, and many marketers spend undue time trying to differentiate between the two. The truth is that you can run a perfectly successful company without drowning in goal-versus-objective details. Yet sure enough, the minute you decide to skip the whole exercise, your bank, investor or major partner will ask you to define how you've set your goals and objectives, and you'll be left tongue-tied in the meeting. If that happens, the following descriptions can bail you out:

- ✔ **Your goal** is what you want to achieve during the upcoming marketing period to move toward the vision you've set for your company.

- ✔ **Your objectives** define how your business is going to achieve its goal over the upcoming year.

A local newspaper may set an annual goal to increase readership by 5 per cent in order to more fully achieve its vision to serve as the region's most trusted information vehicle. The goal defines *what* the newspaper wants to achieve, but not *how* it will achieve it. Here are some objectives a newspaper may set to increase readership by 5 per cent:

A Verb	A Noun	A Precise Description of the Desired Change
To introduce	a new section	aimed at young, affluent, urban professionals
To gain	5 per cent	market share from Competitor X
To improve	delivery time	by one hour daily

Planning strategies

Strategies are the plans for achieving business objectives. They're practical, achievable and action-oriented. Strategies generally detail changes that a business intends to make to the four marketing functions called the *marketing mix* (or the *four p's*): pricing, product, promotion and place (also known as distribution).

Cast your goals and objectives in cement when you create your marketing plan each year, but keep your strategies flexible so you can adjust them in response to competitive forces, economic realities or new opportunities. Just remember that the only strategy worth pursuing is one that directly supports your goals and objectives.

Putting goals, objectives and strategies into action

After you're clear about your marketing goal, every action becomes a building block toward achieving that ultimate desired end.

Small businesses sometimes confuse goals and strategies. Opening a new office, beginning to sell a new product or increasing prices in June are strategies, not goals. Knowing your strategies without being clear about the goal you're trying to reach is like wandering in the woods wearing a blindfold.

In Figure 5-3, you can see how all parts of the business programme fit together in the plan for a microbrewery.

Following the fail-safe planning sequence

Successful marketers follow the same steps:

1. **Conduct market research.**

   Doing so ensures that you know everything you can about your customer, your product, your competition and your business environment. Follow the steps outlined in Chapters 2, 3 and 4.

2. **Establish marketing goals and objectives.**

   The previous sections of this chapter are full of instructions on this step.

3. **Set the marketing strategies and determine the marketing mix that you'll employ to achieve your objectives.**

   The preceding section guides you through this step.

4. **Choose your marketing tools and tactics.**

   That's what the rest of this book is about.

Never, ever start with Step 4. In other words, never decide on your tactic – whether to run an ad or hire a new distributor or take on a new partner – until you know your strategies. Because when you know your strategies, you know your objectives, which means that you know your goals, which means that you know where you want your business to go. After that, all that's left is to establish interim milestones and measure results along the way, fine-tuning your tools and tactics as necessary until you reach your goal.

Tactics *follow* strategies – not vice versa.

Purpose: To make a difference by creating great beer to drink in the warm, lively atmosphere of our brewpub, contributing to the success of events and celebrations, and supporting important causes in the community that surrounds us.

Annual Goal:
Increase gross revenues by 10%.

Objectives:
Increase brewpub business by 20%.
Increase case sales by 8%.
Increase revenue from ancillary products and services by 20%.

Strategies:

Place or Distribution Strategy

- Broaden retail distribution to increase taps in regional bars and restaurants.
- Broaden wholesale distribution to increase grocery and convenience store sales.
- Establish a retail outlet in the brewpub for sale of logo items.

Pricing Strategy

- Increase prices by 3–5% to adjust for cost increases and to align better with premium labels.
- Establish bulk pricing for multi-keg or multiple-case orders.

Product Strategy

- Create a mobile pub unit that can be loaned to event hosts.
- Establish a line of logo items to be sold online and in a new brewpub outlet.
- Create beer-brewing classes to drive business during slow seasons and daytime hours.

Promotion Strategy

- Use broadcast and social media advertising to build brand awareness.
- Use social media to promote beer-brewing classes and mobile pub events.
- Link all communications to a website landing page featuring logo items and mobile pub events.
- Sponsor community events and participate in community fundraisers that align with our mission and the mission of our key retail partners.

Figure 5-3:
A brewpub's marketing purpose, goal, objective and strategies.

Budgeting to Reach Your Goals

Small business marketing budgets include two variables: time and money. You can reach customers with paid advertising and marketing communications or you can reach them through personal contacts, which requires time but little if any cash outlay.

Networking and sales calls have long served as an alternative to costly advertising outreach. But in today's marketplace, those who can devote time to marketing have powerful additional tools in their arsenal: social media and digital communications.

Turn to Part III for three chapters that cover connecting with customers online. If your customers are online, and if you're willing to commit the time to meet and interact with them through your website, social media channels and other sites, then your need for marketing spend can be offset by your investment of time. This section helps you weigh the balance.

Realistic talk about small business marketing budgets

The most important commitment you can make to your marketing programme is to establish and stick to a budget. Whether you're budgeting time, money or both, cover these four points:

- ✔ Establish a marketing budget.
- ✔ Spend the allocated time or funds on a planned marketing programme.
- ✔ View the allocation as an important business investment.
- ✔ Manage the programme well.

If you cut back on marketing, you put your business on a dangerous downhill slide. Sure, you recoup some money – or time – when you make the budget cut, but following that one-off saving, look at what happens. With the reduction comes fewer communication efforts. With fewer communications, sales decline. Declining sales reduce your overall revenues, which means you've even fewer resources to allocate for future marketing.

Think long and hard before trimming your marketing budget because this budget is the one expense item designated specifically to attract and keep customers.

How much should you be spending?

How much money you spend on marketing depends on the type of business you have and the marketing tools you employ. Everyone wants a magic formula, but there isn't one, especially today when so much marketing happens online rather than through paid advertising.

- Mature businesses in established markets with low growth goals can get away with low marketing investments of as little as 2–5 per cent of sales. Companies that target high growth must invest far more.

- Businesses whose sales come primarily from subcontracting can spend almost no cash on marketing, while businesses that need to win the attention of a broad cross section of retail customers must budget enough to gain visibility through paid media ads, online communications and promotions.

- Businesses with customers who are active online and in social media networks can establish communication and ongoing interaction with little or no cash investment, though don't fool yourself into believing that social media and online marketing is free. At the least, you need to allocate time, which may translate to money if you hire staff or outside resources to establish and manage a truly effective online presence.

Only a decade ago, marketing success – especially for business-to-consumer marketers – relied heavily on how much money a business could invest in efforts to push its message into the marketplace. Today, success results not from merely pushing marketing messages but from forming two-way interactions with customers, both personally and through the Internet.

Cash no longer makes or breaks marketing effectiveness. Today's marketers need to budget both money and time to communicate with *and* listen to customers – interacting, responding and developing two-way relationships as a result.

As you determine how much to allocate for marketing, consider the following:

- **The nature of your business and your market:** Businesses that market to other businesses tend to allocate a lower percentage of sales to marketing than businesses that market to a wide range or number of consumers. The difference is the proverbial rifle versus shotgun. The business-to-business marketer can set its sights and reach its customers directly, whereas the business-to-consumer marketer must reach a broader audience, usually involving costly investments of time and money.

✔ **The maturity of your business:** Start-up businesses need to invest more heavily than established businesses, in part to cover extraordinary one-time costs that existing businesses have behind them and in part to accelerate communications to gain first-time prospect awareness.

✔ **The size of your market area:** Businesses that serve customers who are primarily located within a short drive or walk from the business location can target marketing communications into a concise market area. As a result, they can probably allocate a lower investment than businesses that have to build awareness and interest in regional, national or even international markets.

✔ **Your competition:** Businesses with a monopoly have to enhance their marketing efforts if several competitors suddenly open nearby. And businesses that are the underdog and want to take on the leaders must invest accordingly.

✔ **Your objective and task:** The most important consideration in setting your budget is to understand your growth goals. The more aggressive they are, the more time and money you need to budget for marketing. For example, if you're planning to launch a new product or open a new location, you need to increase your marketing efforts to gain awareness, interest and action and to fund the training, marketing support and additional advertising required to make your plan possible.

You can find many forms to help you allocate funding for your marketing programme if you search online for 'marketing budget templates'. The template best-suited for your marketing budget depends on the nature of your programme – whether you're marketing business-to-business, business-to-consumer, primarily through events and networking, primarily using online and social media communications, or primarily through paid advertising. Websites that offer free templates for you to choose from include:

✔ **Google Spreadsheet Marketing Budget Template for Start-ups:** http://davidcummings.org/2011/11/25/google-spreadsheet-marketing-budget-template-for-startups/

✔ **Microsoft Marketing Budget Planner Template:** www.microsoft templates.org/microsoft-excel-templates/marketing-budget-planner-template.me html

✔ **Marketing Donut: Marketing budget template** www.marketingdonut.co.uk/tools/marketing-budget-template

Your money or your time? How companies decide

Some businesses decide *not* to invest significant money in advertising. Instead, they direct their resources at sales presentations, networking efforts, community and industry trade shows and events and online communications, through which they can establish contact and interact with customers and prospective customers.

That doesn't mean that they aren't investing in marketing. They're investing time (and supporting cash) rather than relying exclusively on costly and traditional advertising vehicles. Here are examples of businesses that rely more heavily on an investment of time than money:

✔ A lawyer who wants to attract regional corporate clients may serve as a board member and volunteer counsel for a community non-profit organisation, knowing that doing so can generate working relationships with fellow board members who fit the target client profile.

✔ A regional holiday resort that wants to attract more families from the local market area may decide to offer outdoor activity lessons to all Year 6 pupils in local schools as a way to establish relationships directly with teachers and parents rather than via paid marketing communications.

✔ A hair salon that wants to build business may shift its emphasis from paid ads to pay-per-click search ads and social networking, aiming to reach customers at the moment they're considering salon services. The salon can direct online interest to a landing page that features a special offer and reservation invitation, converting leads to customers with no cash investment beyond initial site setup. See Part III for information on how to connect with customers online.

Part II
Laying the Foundation for Marketing Success

Product Reaches Maturity

Increased Promotion

Growth Rate Slows

Competitors Enter

Similar Products Introduced

Repeat Purchase and New Sales

Price Wars

New Product Sales

Sales Decline

Development

Product Withdrawal or Reinvention

Introduction   Growth   Maturity   Saturation   Decline

In this part . . .

- ✔ Uncover gaps that may exist between what people think of your business and what you *think* they think.

- ✔ Learn how what you've been saying (or not saying) can lead to misconceptions.

- ✔ Define your business position and brand.

- ✔ Create top-notch marketing communications.

- ✔ Know when to bring in professionals to help you implement your marketing programme.

Chapter 6

Taking Stock of Your Business Image

In This Chapter

▶ Taking steps to ensure that your business makes a consistent, positive impression

▶ Compiling an inventory of the impressions your business makes

▶ Assessing and strengthening your marketing communications

Right now, your business is making an impression. Somewhere, someone is encountering your ad, seeing your logo, calling your company, visiting your website, reading a review or article about your business or walking through your door. Maybe someone is driving by the sign on your locked-up shop at night or running across your business name in a web search.

As a result, right now people are drawing conclusions about your business. Based on what they're seeing or hearing, they're deciding whether your business looks like a top-tier player, an economical alternative or a struggling start-up – all based on impressions that you may not even be aware that you're making.

This chapter is about where and when your business makes impressions and how you can align your communications so that people form the opinion you want them to have.

Making First Impressions

You've heard the saying a thousand times: 'You never get a second chance to make a first impression.' The advice is self-evident and sounds easy enough to follow until you realise that your business most often makes its first impressions when you're nowhere to be found. In your place is your website, your Facebook page, your voicemail message, your ad or direct mailing, your business sign, your employees, some customer's review or rating or maybe your logo on a leaflet or flyer.

Ask yourself the following questions as you assess whether the impressions you're making on customers represent you well:

✔ When people receive multiple impressions of your business, do they see and hear evidence of a consistent, reliable, well-managed, successful enterprise?

✔ Do your communications look and sound like they all represent the same company?

✔ Does your logo always look the same? What about your use of typestyles and colour scheme? How about the sound and smell of your business? And the tone or voice of your communications? People form impressions through all senses. Be sure that you're consistent through all encounters.

✔ If you use a tag line or slogan, is it always the same or does it change from one presentation to the next?

✔ Do search engines deliver results that are consistent with the image you want customers to see and believe about your business?

To evaluate what kinds of impressions you're making, begin by tracking the ways that customers approach your business. Then work backwards to determine what marketing efforts led to their arrival. After that, work forwards to determine what kinds of impressions customers form when they actually 'meet' your business, whether that first contact is made in person, over the phone or online.

Encountering your business through online searches

What customers see online is fundamental to their impressions of what you and your business are and offer. The chapters in Part III are all about connecting with customers online. This section is about assessing what customers see when they search online and whether their search results align with what you want them to believe about your business.

Study search results for your name and the name of your company and products. First, Google your name and then search with Bing, Yahoo!, and other search engines. (For advice on how to get the best results, see Chapter 3.) Here's what to look for:

✔ Does the name you're searching for appear prominently in the first few pages of results, which is as far as most people look?

✔ Are you happy with what you see? Do links to your name lead to sites with information that's relevant to the brand image you want to project? (For more on the topic of brand images, turn to Chapter 7.)

✔ Do top results lead straight to your business website or to a map or phone number for your company?

✔ When you search your name in online images and videos, are you happy with what you see or are results inconsistent with the image you want your business to project?

If your search results are underwhelming, take action. Turn to Chapter 10 for advice on how to gain online prominence. Then use Chapters 11 and 12 to leverage the power of social media and blogs to heighten your online presence and your showing in search engine results.

Arriving at your website

To people shopping online, your website *is* your business. To everyone else, your website is a gateway to your business.

Chapter 10 is full of information to help you achieve your online marketing objectives. Here are a few quick points to keep in mind as you develop an online presence that supports your business image:

✔ **You have to work to be found online.** In 2011, experts estimated that the web hosted at least a trillion pages, with the number of URLs or site addresses increasing by more than 150,000 a day. Any business in this day and age needs the following:

- A website with its own name in the site address

- Social media pages

- A network of online links that point web users to the business site

- A commitment to optimising the site's visibility in search engine results

- A communication effort that features links to all major online locations in all ads and marketing materials

Turn to Part III for advice on getting online and attracting traffic to your website and online pages.

✔ **People arriving at your site may not know where they are.** They may be coming from search engine results or online links that send them to an internal page of your site, so be sure that every page features your name or logo, along with a link to your home page. Better yet, whenever possible, direct online clicks to customised landing pages (see Chapter 15) that address the customer's interest and allow you to capture the new-business lead.

✓ **Realise that most customers are channel agnostics.** They migrate between online and off-line encounters and expect continuity as they travel. Whether they see your Facebook page, your website or blog, your traditional media ads, your display windows or you and your staff members in person, they expect a single business image. Be sure that your online identity meshes with your off-line identity, right down to the style of typeface you use, the kinds of messages you present and the way you display your business name and logo. For more information on establishing and maintaining a consistent image, see Chapter 7.

Google+ Local: Your key to being found through Google

If you serve a local market, your customers are searching for you online. Improve your position in their search results by establishing a free Google Places listing that appears to consumers as a Google+ Local page. Google+ Local pages integrate business-provided information with information from other Google properties such as Search, Maps, Zagat ratings and reviews and recommendations from friends, family and colleagues. What's more, Local pages are indexed by Google to appear in search results, and customers can reach them through the Local tab on their Google+ pages.

Start by going to `www.google.com/places` to claim and create your free listing, following these tips:

✓ **Be sure that your listing is complete, with your business name, street address, town or city, county, postcode, phone number, email address, website address and 200-character description.**

✓ **Enhance your listing to improve search results by adding photos, videos, a list of services (such as free parking) and vouchers or offers.** Be sure that all visuals on your page are titled using relevant keywords and are tagged with descriptive words that people searching online may use.

✓ **Optimise your page title by including frequently searched keywords so long as they're part of your business name.** For example, Patient Paul's Bait Shop can feature ' bait shop' in its page title because those words are actually part of the business name. But another shop can't just add ' bait shop' to its title without being penalised by search engines for keyword stuffing.

✓ **Use keywords in your business description.** In your free, 200-character description, include the keywords that customers are likely to search for when looking for businesses or products like yours, but don't duplicate keywords presented by your business name. The business description for Patient Paul's Bait Shop shouldn't repeat 'bait shop' but may include 'fly-fishing trips' or 'fly-tying classes' if customers typically seek those offerings. It may also include the business location if it serves a local market area (for example, 'offering the freshest bait in the Lake District'). Use Google's Keyword Planner (`http://adwords.google.com/keywordplanner`) to see which terms on your website are most frequently searched globally and locally.

The findings can help you determine which keywords to feature in your description.

✔ **Create a page for each location of your business, and always use street addresses because Google often rejects P.O. box addresses.**

✔ **Encourage customers to add reviews.** Reviews, especially if they're spaced to appear from time to time rather than all at once, help your page appear more prominently in results. Just be sure not to offer reviewers incentives, which Google considers a conflict of interest.

✔ **Establish listings in other online directories.** Those listings make your business more findable online and therefore improve your position in search results (see Chapter 13 for advice).

From time to time, log on to your Google Places page to study which keywords users are searching and how many clicks your site received as a result. Also, visit `http://support.google.com/places` to get the latest tips. You can also stay on top of ongoing changes by following the official Google blog at `http://googleblog.blogspot.com`.

Don't ignore the fact that more than eight out of ten smart phone owners search from their phones while they're shopping, travelling or otherwise away from their computers, even when they're in their own homes. See Chapter 10 for advice on 'mobifying' your site so that it looks good on mobile devices.

Managing email impressions

Sometime in the late 1990s (sounds like ancient history, doesn't it?), the number of email messages eclipsed the volume of traditional letters sent by businesses. By 2010 estimates, 294 billion emails were sent daily, amounting to more than 100 trillion a year, a quarter of which were sent by businesses.

Yet while businesses routinely format, proofread, print and file traditional correspondence, they send email messages spontaneously, often with no standard policy and rarely with a company record for future referral. Such an informal approach to email is fine for thank-you notes or quick updates to customers, but what if the message includes a fee estimate or a notice that client-requested changes will result in an additional thousand pounds of expense? And what if the staff member who sent the email is no longer with your company when the customer questions the bill?

For the sake of your business, set a few email guidelines:

✔ **Unify all company emails by use of a common signature.** A *signature* or *sig* is a few lines of text that appears at the end of every email message. The signature usually includes

- The name of the person sending the message

- Your business logo

- A tag line that tells people what your business does

- Your business address, phone number and website

- Often a promotional message or offer

You can create a signature in almost any email program. Go to the help function for instructions.

✔ **Set a tone and style for email messages.** In well-managed businesses, traditional letters go out on company letterhead, use a consistent type-face and style and employ clear, professional language. Consider email a dressed-down version of your formal correspondence. It can be more relaxed and more spontaneous, and it can (and should) be more to the point – but it can't be impolite or unprofessional.

✔ **Respond to email within four hours, even if your response is simply an auto-reply that offers a complete answer within days.** An email that isn't answered promptly falls into the same category as phone calls that are placed on endless hold or long, slow-moving queues at the tills. The customer service impact is devastating.

✔ **Back up email messages so they're accessible should an employee quit or not be available when a customer questions a price, or other promise made through email communications.**

✔ **Consider establishing business-wide email standards.** Keep email messages short, encourage the use of greetings and standard punctuation and limit the use of emoticons. Also avoid coloured backgrounds or graphics that make messages slow to download on customer computers or mobile devices.

Arriving by telephone

Often, with no prompting at all, callers tell you how they found your number. 'John Jones suggested I call,' or, 'I'm curious about the new whatchamacallits I see in your ad', or, 'I was on your website, but I couldn't tell whether your business is open on a Sunday.' If the conversation doesn't naturally disclose how the person obtained your phone number, take a few seconds (but only a few seconds) to ask something like, 'I'm glad you called us. We're always working to improve our communications, and I'd love to note how you got our phone number.'

The responses help you see what is and isn't working to generate phone calls. They also help you determine which first impression points bring qualified prospects into your business and which ones reel in people who are ' just looking'. In the latter case, realise that the problem is rarely with the caller and most often with the impression point.

An estate agent that specialises in high-end residential properties continuously fields calls from house hunters trying to buy homes in a much lower price bracket than those listed by the agency. Upon questioning, the estate agents discover that most of the mismatched callers found the phone number in a regional property guide in which the company's ad read, 'We have your dream home.' The agents realise that their ad message is appealing to the wrong target market. As a result, they amend their ad to read, 'Specialists in fine properties and luxury homes.'

To get the right prospects to call your business, be sure to target your communications carefully, help customers understand what you offer, make your phone number appropriately large and bold, give people a reason to dial it and then be ready to treat every call as a valuable business opportunity.

All marketing communications – whether through advertising, direct mail, email, networking, presentations, social media or website visits – aim to achieve a single goal: a personal contact and the opportunity to make a sale.

When the hard-earned call comes, don't squander the opportunity:

- ✔ **Answer calls promptly.** Pick up after the first or second ring whenever possible. Even if you have a receptionist, train others to serve as backups, answering any call that reaches a third ring.

- ✔ **Transfer calls as quickly as you answer them.** Be prompt about getting the caller to the appropriate person in your business. If that person isn't available, say so immediately. Offer to take a message, put the caller through to voicemail or find someone else to help.

    On hold is a dangerous and costly place to leave valuable prospects.

- ✔ **Get everyone in your company to answer the phone in a consistent and professional manner.** 'Hello, this is John' is an appropriate business greeting only when the caller is specifically calling John. Otherwise, answer with the business name in addition to a personal name.

- ✔ **Keep voicemail messages brief and friendly.** Use wording that conveys your business purpose and personality and offer no more than three options so callers can quickly jump to the option they seek.

    'Thank you for calling 20/20 Vision. We're focusing on eye exams and frame selections right now, but please press 1 for our hours and location or press 2 to leave a message. We promise to call you back within the hour.'

> ✔ **Ask your phone company to monitor and report on your hang-up rate.** Multiple rings, lengthy hold times and voicemail responses are reasons for callers to abandon their efforts to reach your business.

Consider placing mirrors near the phones if your business relies heavily on telephone contact. People instinctively smile at themselves in mirrors because it makes them look more attractive, and a smile also makes a voice more attractive – more natural, friendly and enthusiastic. You'll be able to hear the difference, and so will the person on the other end of the line.

Approaching your business in person

If a person walks into your business, looks around and asks, 'What kind of a business is this?' you can make an educated guess that the drop-in was unplanned and triggered only by a look at your signage or window displays. (You may want to improve these impression points to better address this obvious question.)

Making your voicemail more personal

A personal greeting, a meaningful message and a commitment to prompt, personal follow-up are all it takes to turn voicemail from a personality-free and sometimes annoying fact of life to a pleasant and efficient means to present yourself and your message. Follow these tips:

✔ Record a greeting that accurately reflects your company's image, update it regularly and check for messages faithfully.

✔ Make sure that your greeting includes your company name (or your own name if the phone in question is a personal phone), indicates when you'll return the call and invites the caller to leave a message.

✔ Encourage detailed messages. 'Please leave a message of up to three minutes, and we'll get back to you by the end of the day.' If you encourage a lengthy message, the caller is more likely to convey complete information, reducing the need for telephone tag after the call.

✔ If possible, include the option of pressing zero to speak with a real, live person.

✔ If you can't fully respond to the caller's request within the specified time period, call with a polite explanation and say when you'll have a response.

✔ Voicemail boxes have limited storage capacity. Delete messages regularly to ensure that new messages can be stored.

✔ Regularly call your own voicemail to see that it's working and that the message is current.

The minute that your voicemail starts to sound like that of a big, faceless corporation, move quickly to put your small business personality back into it. Customers choose small businesses in large part for their personal touch. Don't let voicemail or other systems encroach on that small business advantage.

Many businesses boast that their signage is their most effective means of attracting first-time visitors. But before banking on your sign to draw people in, realise that when people respond only to your signage, they're making spur-of-the-moment, drop-in visits – perhaps at a time when they're short on both time and money. Instead, work to achieve *destination visits* by making impressions and cultivating interest well in advance of prospects noticing your sign and walking through your door.

Leading people to your business

If your business relies on consumer visits, convey directions on your website and in ads, mailings and other advance communications. Build a mobile version of your website (see Chapter 10) to quickly help on-the-go customers reach your location. Invest in directional road signs or outdoor ads if appropriate. Establish a Google+ Local page, a free Google service that helps your business appear in local search results along with a map showing your location (see the sidebar earlier in this chapter, 'Google+ Local: Your key to getting found on Google'). Also, be sure that when visitors arrive at your business, whether you're located in a high-rise building or a home office, they see a sign with your business name and instructions on how to reach your front door.

Parking

Is your business's parking area clean, well-marked, well-lit and capable of making a good impression? If a parking charge is involved, do you have a parking permit scheme that customers know about in advance? Have you saved the nearest spaces for customers rather than for your car or your employees' cars? (How many times have you driven into a car park only to see the space nearest to the door marked 'Reserved for Manager' ? And what do those three simple words tell you about your standing as a customer?)

Nearing your front door

As a prospect approaches your entrance, does your business look open and inviting? Here's a list of questions to consider:

- ✔ Is your signage visible, clean and professional?
- ✔ Do signs and window displays clearly indicate what your business does?
- ✔ Is your business well-lit?
- ✔ Is the entrance easy to find?

- ✔ Is your entryway signage welcoming or is it papered with negatives such as 'No UPS,' 'No Smoking,' 'Deliveries Use Back Door,' or 'No Outside Food or Beverages'? With just a little editing, you can state your rules in a positive way. 'Let us hold your umbrella and bags while you shop' is better than 'No backpacks.'

✔ If your business success relies on foot traffic, do your windows have show-stopping capacity? Stand back and look hard. If necessary, adjust lighting to improve visibility or to cut glare. Replace small objects with big, bold items that are magnets for attention. Use mirrors to slow people down and also to help them adjust their dispositions (remember, people automatically put on a friendly face when they look in the mirror), both of which are likely to benefit your business.

The moment of arrival

Walk through the process of approaching and entering your business. Forget for a minute that this business is *your* business. Imagine how it feels to a stranger. Does it convey the right set of impressions? Consider the following:

✔ Is your entry area impeccably clean?

✔ Is the entry area decorated to make a strong statement about the nature of your business, its customers and its products?

✔ Do your surroundings present and promote *your* company or do they inadvertently promote other companies whose logos happen to appear on calendars, posters, coffee cups and other items that sneak their way into your environment? Rather than making your lobby a display for others, turn it into a showcase of your own products, your clients or your staff. If you want customers to be proud to associate with your business, proudly highlight your offerings.

✔ Does your business have a clear 'landing area' – a place where a visitor can pause upon entry and receive a good first impression?

✔ Does your business offer an obvious greeting, by a person or a welcoming display?

✔ If you have a customer waiting area, do people head straight for it or do they pause and look for an invitation before entering? In some businesses, a coffee maker, a stack of logo ID cups and a welcoming sign are all it takes to break the ice. Other times, you may need to remodel or at least redecorate to break down obstacles and enhance the sense of welcome.

If customers consistently stop in a certain area or study a particular display, consider that area as a prime marketing spot and think of ways that you can enhance it to deliver the strongest possible statement on behalf of your business.

What it's like to be a customer in your business

In designing your business environment, balance your operations and internal needs against the wants and needs of your most important asset: your customers. Follow the path that customers take through your business to figure out where you need to make adjustments to improve their experience. Take the following steps, and then repeat the process in fact-finding visits to a few of your competitors, if such visits are possible:

✔ **Stop where customers stop.** Stand in an inconspicuous spot and watch what people do when they enter your business.

- How long do they wait until someone greets them?

- Do they look around for a clue regarding what to do next?

- If you're a retailer, do they see a bottleneck at the till as their first impression?

- How many people make a U-turn and leave before they make a purchase, and where do they seem to most frequently lose interest?

✔ **Shop like they shop.** Study what a customer experiences when they purchase your product. How many different people or departments do customers deal with, and does each contribute value rather than require an annoying duplication of customer input? Where do points of concern or resistance arise? How can you eliminate obstacles that hinder your customers' decisions to buy or their ability to enjoy dealing with your business?

- If you have a service business and customers want to know how your charges add up, be ready with answers. Create a brochure or handout describing your services and fee structure.

- If they want to touch the merchandise, build appropriate displays.

- If they need to try before they buy, offer samples, fitting rooms, before-and-after photos or other ways to experience your product.

- If they want to browse, display products at eye level and give them room to stop and shop, realising that narrow aisles and tight spaces drive people – especially women – right out the door.

✔ **Wait where they wait and for as long.** Test your customer service from a customer's viewpoint. Look at how customers react to the way your company serves and treats them.

- Have you provided chairs in areas where they end up waiting?

- In areas where customers pause, have you placed displays that move them toward buying decisions?

- If spouses, children or friends accompany customers, have you created entertainment areas and appropriate diversions?

- If their visits consistently last longer than an hour, do you provide some form of refreshment?

- Watch for non-verbal complaints about a lack of attentiveness. Do customers glance at their watches or fidget while waiting for employees to handle phone calls, deal with other customers, complete paperwork? Be aware that customers use waiting time as the single most important factor in gauging your customer service, so plan accordingly.

Auditing the Impressions Your Business Makes

The only way you can be sure that you're making consistently good impressions in your marketplace is to take stock and assess every contact with prospects, customers and others who deal with your business.

Surveying your marketing materials and communications

Start by gathering samples of stationery, ads, signs, brochures, coffee cups, T-shirts, online communications and any other items that represent your business. Line them all up and evaluate them using these questions:

- ✔ Does your business name and logo look the same every time you make an impression?

- ✔ Do you consistently use the same colours?

- ✔ Do you consistently use the same typeface?

- ✔ Do your marketing materials present a consistent image in terms of look, quality and message?

Study your samples and isolate those that don't fit with the others, perhaps because they use outdated or inaccurate versions of your name or logo. Or maybe the colours are wrong or the tone is inconsistent. Possibly the message is witty or silly when the rest of your communications are fact-filled and serious. Or the calibre may be unprofessional compared to the rest of your materials.

Cull the inappropriate items and then look at what's left.

- ✔ Does the consistent portion of your marketing materials accurately reflect your business?

- ✔ Do your marketing materials adequately appeal to your target market?

    - • For example, if you know that your customers value top quality, do your marketing materials convey a top-quality company? Do your ads convey quality? Do you apply your logo only to prestigious advertising items? If you're a retailer, are your shopping bags the finest you can afford? If you're a service company, do you present your proposals in a manner that reinforces the calibre of your firm while affirming your customer's taste level?

- If your customers value economy, do your materials look too upmarket? If so, they may send out the wrong message.

- If your customers choose you primarily for convenience, do your materials put forth that assurance? Or, if customers value your reliability, do you convey that attribute through a flawless commitment to a reliably consistent projection of your identity?

REMEMBER

In forming opinions about your company, your market relies on the impressions it gets from your communications.

Creating an impression inventory

Your business makes impressions in person, online, in ads and marketing materials, in correspondence . . . the list goes on and on. Every contact is capable of contributing to or detracting from the image that you want people to hold in their minds about your business.

Create an Impression Inventory and Audit, listing ways that your business makes impressions in the market place following these directions:

- ✔ **Define your company's impression points.** Using the provided entries, check all impression points that apply to your business, and add any additional ways that your business comes into contact with customers and prospective customers. No item is too small to include. If your ad is a work of art but your proposal cover is flimsy, the negative impact of one cancels out the positive impact of the other. Every impression counts.

- ✔ **Define the target market for each impression point.** Is it to develop a new prospect or to communicate with an existing customer – or maybe a little bit of both? If your business has a number of customer types or product lines, you may want to get even more specific. For instance, one ad for an insurance broker may target property insurance prospects and another may target life insurance prospects. By defining the different purposes, the brokerage is able to gauge how much it invests in the development of each product line.

- ✔ **Rate the quality of each impression your business makes.** Give each of your marketing materials a grade of Good, Average or Poor, based on your assessment of how well it conveys your business image, message, look and style.

- ✔ **Who's in charge of each impression point?** Many impressions that affect a company's image are made by those who don't think of themselves as marketers. Nine times out of ten, no one is thinking about marketing when a cost estimate is presented, a bill is sent or a purchase order is issued. The key is to think about the marketing impact far in advance so that you create materials, processes and systems that advance a positive image for your company.

✔ **Evaluate the costs involved.** What does each communication cost in terms of development, media, printing or other expenses? After you know the answer, you can add up what you're spending on business development, customer retention and marketing of each product line. You may be surprised to find that you're over-supporting some functions and under-supporting others, and you can adjust accordingly.

Improving the impressions you're making

After defining all the impressions that your business makes on its customers, ask the following questions to assess the quality and effectiveness of the impressions that your business makes:

✔ Are you allocating your efforts well? Are you spending enough on efforts to keep current customers happy or are your efforts too heavily weighted toward getting new people through the door – or vice versa?

✔ Do your communications fit your image and objectives? Answer this question for every item, whether the item is an ad or a logo-emblazoned coffee cup. Be sure that each contributes to the image you're trying to establish in your marketplace rather than to some decision made long ago based on the powerful presentation by a sales representative.

✔ Is your image consistent, professional and well-suited to the audiences that matter most to your business?

Use your inventory as you fine-tune your communications, then keep it to hand. Then, if you ever decide to change your name, logo or overall look, this list can remind you of all the items that you need to update.

Use your impression inventory to guide changes as you strengthen the image you project to your market. Work to phase out and replace any impression points you rate as poor and to adjust and improve the quality of any impression points you rate as average. As you make necessary changes, turn to Chapter 7 for everything you need to know about managing your image, setting a creative strategy to guide your communications, and writing an image style guide to set your image rules in stone.

Chapter 7

Forging Your Brand

. . . .

In This Chapter

▶ Defining what brands are and why they're important

▶ Beginning to build your brand

▶ Positioning your brand in your market

▶ Using taglines to enhance your brand

▶ Developing your brand message, creative strategy and consistent style

. . . .

*W*e're just a small business,' you may be thinking. 'We're not Coca-Cola or Nike, with a multi-million pound ad budget and a global market. We're just 12 people trying to build half a million pounds in sales. We hardly need a brand.'

Guess what? A brand isn't some mysterious, expensive treasure available only to the rich and famous. And a brand isn't just for mega-marketers, though they all have one.

Branding simply (well, maybe not all *that* simply) involves developing and consistently communicating a set of positive characteristics that consumers can relate to your name. If those characteristics happen to fill a meaningful and available position in their minds – a need they've been sensing and trying to fill – then you just scored a marketing goal, and that half a million pound sales target becomes much easier to reach.

What Brands Are and Do

Keep in mind two facts about what brands are and aren't:

✔ A brand is a set of beliefs, a promise that customers believe.

✔ A brand isn't a logo. A logo is a symbol that identifies a brand. When people see your logo or hear your name, a set of images arises. Those images define your brand in their minds.

Your brand isn't what *you* think it is. Your brand is whatever mental image those in your target audience automatically unlock when they encounter your name or logo. Your brand is what they believe about you based on everything they've ever seen or heard – whether good or bad, true or false.

If you make impressions in your marketplace, whether proactively or unconsciously, you're building your brand. In fact, you're probably building two brands at once – a business brand for your company and a personal brand for yourself, a brand balancing act featured in a section later in the chapter.

Something as basic as your street or online address contributes to how people perceive your brand. For that matter, customers, prospective customers, job applicants, reporters, bankers, suppliers and those who refer people to you and your business form impressions every time they walk through your front door, visit your website, meet an employee, see your ad or scan an online review or search results.

All those impressions accumulate to become your brand image in your customer's mind, which is where brands live.

Unlocking the power and value of a brand

If you need a motivating fact to kick start you into branding action, here's one: Branding makes selling easier because people want to buy from those they know and like, and those they trust to deliver on commitments. A good brand puts forth that promise.

With a well-managed brand, your company hardly needs to introduce itself. Within your target market, people already know your business, its personality and the promise it makes to customers – all based on the positive set of impressions you've made and they've stored in their minds.

Without a well-managed brand, you spend a good part of every sales opportunity trying to introduce your business, while some well-known brand down the street can spend that time actually making the sale.

Brands fuel success in three ways:

- ✔ **Brands lead to name awareness**, which sets your business apart from all the contenders that your audience has never heard of.

- ✔ **Brands prompt consumer selection** because people prefer to work with those they've heard of and heard good things about.

- ✔ **Brands unlock profitability** because people pay premium prices for products (or, in the case of personal brands, for people) that they trust can deliver higher value than less-known and less-trusted alternatives.

As a result of the advantages they deliver, brands increase the odds of business success, which makes them especially valuable in a world where half of all businesses fail in the first five years, nine out of ten products don't make it to their second anniversary, and too many people are vying for the same jobs, sales and opportunities.

Tipping the balance online

Without a brand, you have to build the case for your business before every sale. Doing that is tough work in person and even tougher online, because you can't be there to make introductions, inspire confidence, counter resistance or break down barriers.

Brands are essential to online and off-line success for different reasons.

✔ **For those who sell online, brands are necessary for credibility.**

People buy everything online – from contact lenses to cars – all without the benefit of personal persuasion, hands-on evaluation or test drives. Why? Because customers arrive at websites with confidence in the brands they buy. When they see a brand they know and like, they check the price and terms, click to buy, and move on to checkout. If your business takes place primarily online, your brand is your key to sales.

✔ **For those who sell off-line, brands are necessary for findability.**

These days, nearly every brand needs to be findable, prominent and credible online. The rare exceptions are those that serve a target market that never goes online and that's never influenced by those that do. For every other brand, Chris Anderson, author of *The Long Tail* and *Wired* magazine editor-in-chief, says, 'Your brand is what Google says it is.' If customers can't find your business in an online search, they conclude that you don't exist or aren't a top player in your arena. Turn to Part III to remedy the situation.

Branding facilitates sales and spurs success, whether your cash register is online or on the high street.

Building a Powerful Brand

Your small business will probably never have a globally recognised 'power brand' simply because you don't have (and for that matter don't need) the marketing muscle that would fuel that level of awareness.

But you *can* be the most powerful brand in your target market. All it takes is

- Knowing the brand image that you want to project
- Developing a distinct point of difference that's relevant and beneficial to your target audience
- Having commitment and discipline to project your brand well
- Spending what's necessary to get your message to your target market
- Managing your marketing so that it makes consistent impressions that etch your desired brand image into the mind of your target prospect

---

Adding horsepower to your brand

Branding expert Liz Goodgold knows what it takes to power up a brand. She's done it for herself and for her business, Red Fire Branding (www.redfirebranding.com). The result: features on more than 500 media outlets, including ABC, NBC, CBS, PBS, CNBC, CNN, *The Wall Street Journal* and *The New York Times*.

Her branding advice includes these steps:

1. Set a goal and follow your passion.

2. Start your brand-building effort by developing a core competency.

3. Find and leverage your 'cool quotient', the aspect of you or your business that's unique, memorable and interview-worthy.

If you're not sure about your 'cool quotient', Goodgold recommends duplicating the successes of huge brands to build your own branding success story. As examples, she turns to celebrities in this five-question brand-strength quiz:

- Do you have street cred? Do you have depth in your field and knowledge of key trends? Are you continuously improving your expertise and offerings? Becoming a brand without any core competency places you in the category of Paris Hilton or Kim Kardashian.

- Do you have *je ne sais quoi*? Simon Cowell may call it the 'X Factor': the unique brand DNA that makes you interesting, exciting and unforgettable. Carrie Underwood and Josh Krajcik definitely have it.

- Do you have a signature phrase? If you use the same expression at the end of a talk, you're on your way to a proprietary brand vocabulary.

- Do people know you by a single name? Is your moniker so unique and known in your arena that using your full name isn't necessary? Examples: Seal, Bono, Beyoncé and Adele.

- Is your brand visually consistent? A unique and consistent look builds brand recognition. People want to know that what you look like today you'll look like tomorrow. Bruno Mars, for example, isn't putting away his fedora any time soon.

Being consistent to power your brand

To build a strong brand, project a consistent look, tone and level of quality through each point of customer contact, whether in person or through marketing and whether online or off-line.

Then stick with the brand you build. People in your target audience are exposed to thousands of images every day. To manage the marketing clutter, they filter out all but the messages and images that are relevant and familiar. The quickest route to making your brand image one they recognise and trust is to present it consistently – without fail.

Don't try to change your brand image unless you're certain that this image no longer appropriate for the market. (And if that's the case, you better be prepared to change your business, because your brand is the public representation of your business.) Imagine how tired the people at Campbell's Soup must be of their label, but imagine what would happen to their sales if they abandoned it simply because a fickle marketing manager said, 'Let's try something new.'

Consistency builds brands, and brands build business.

Taking six brand-management steps

Building a well-managed brand follows certain steps:

1. **Define why you're in business.**

   What does your business do? Or, if you're building a personal brand, what do you do? How do you do it better than anyone else?

   Refer to Chapter 5 as you put into writing the reason that your business exists and the positive change you aim to achieve.

2. **Consider what you want people to think when they hear your name.**

   What do you want current and prospective employees to think about your business? What do you want prospects, customers, suppliers, associates, competitors and friends to think?

   You can't be different things to each of these groups and still have a well-managed brand. For example, you can't have an internal company mind-set that says 'economy at any price' and expect consumers to believe that no one cares more about product quality and customer service than you do.

Figure out what you want people to think when they hear your name. Then ask yourself whether that brand image is believable to each of the various groups with whom you communicate. If it isn't, decide how you need to alter your business to make achieving your brand image possible.

3. **Think about the words you want people to use when defining your business.**

   Ask your employees, associates and customers this question: 'When people hear our name, what images do you think come into their minds?' If everyone says the same thing, and if those words are the words you *want* associated with your name, you've a well-managed brand. If gaps occur, you've your brand-management work cut out for you.

   List words that you want people to link to your business and be certain that you live up to that desired image. Then lead people to the right conclusions by presenting those characteristics – that brand image – consistently and repeatedly in your marketing communications. Choose messages and graphic symbols that support the image you want to project. For example, Rolex maintains its luxury brand image by featuring a crown as its logo and by giving its signature watch collection the name *Oyster*.

4. **Pinpoint the advantages you want people to associate with your business.**

   Figuring out these distinctions leads to your definition of the position you want to own in consumer minds. (For more about this topic, see the next section, 'Your Market Position: The Birthplace of Your Brand'.)

5. **Define your brand.**

   Look at your business through a customer's or prospect's eyes as you define your brand. What do people say and think about your company and the unique benefits they count on it to deliver? Why do they choose your business and prefer to buy from you again and again? How would they define your brand and the promise it makes?

   Boil your findings down to one concept – one brand definition – that you honestly believe you can own in the minds of those who deal with your business. The following are examples of how three widely known brands are generally perceived by the public:

   - Volvo: The safest car

   - BBC: The most trusted news source

   - Google: The top Internet search engine

6. **Build your brand through every impression that you make.**

   Flip back to Chapter 6 for advice as you audit your brand's impression points. Consider whether each impression enhances or detracts from the brand you're building, depending on how well it projects your brand with clarity and consistency.

Your Market Position: The Birthplace of Your Brand

Brands live in consumer minds. But just like you need to find a vacant plot if you want to build a home to live in, you need to find an empty mind space if you want to embed your brand in your customer's brain.

Positioning involves figuring out what meaningful and available niche in the market – and in your customer's head – your business is designed to fill, and then filling it and performing so well that people have no reason to allow anyone else into the space in their minds they hold for your brand.

Seeing how positioning happens

When people find out about your business, they subconsciously slot you into a business hierarchy composed of the following:

- **Me-too businesses:** If the mind slot – or position – that you want for your business is already taken, you have to persuade consumers to switch allegiances on your behalf, and that's a tough job. The best advice for a 'me-too' business is to find a way to become a 'similar-but-different' business (see the next bullet) by targeting an un-served market niche or providing a differentiating benefit.

- **Similar-but-different businesses:** These businesses market a meaningful difference in a crowded field. Depending on the nature of your business, your positioning distinction may be based on pricing, inventory, target market, service structure or company personality. For example, instead of simply opening your town's umpteenth pizza takeaway, open the only one in a trendy new neighbourhood, the only one that offers New York-style pizza by the slice or the only one that uses recipes from Southern Italy in a trattoria setting. Your distinction better be compelling, though, because you have to convince people the difference is worth hearing about, sampling and changing for.

- **Brand-new offerings:** If you can be the first to fill a market's needs, you have the easiest positioning task of all. Just don't expect that marketing to seize that brand-new position is going to be a piece of cake. First-in-market businesses need to educate consumers about what the new offering is and why the consumer should care. Then they have to pro-mote skilfully and forcefully before competitors enter the fray.

First-in-a-market businesses and first-of-a-kind products have to market fast and fastidiously because, in the end, being first isn't as important as being first to seize a positive position in the consumer's mind.

Determining your positioning strategy

The simplest way to figure out what position you hold is to determine what your business offers that your customers would have a hard or impossible time finding elsewhere. Questions that can lead to your positioning statement include the following:

- ✔ How is our offering unique or at least difficult to copy?
- ✔ Is our unique offering something that consumers really want?
- ✔ Is our offering compatible with economic and market trends?
- ✔ How is our offering different – and better – than available options?
- ✔ Is our claim believable?

Don't aim for a position that requires the market to make a leap of faith on your behalf. If a restaurant is known for the best burgers in town, it can't suddenly decide to try to jump into the position of 'the finest steakhouse in the city.' Leapfrogging doesn't work well when the game is positioning.

Develop your position around the distinct attributes that have made your business successful to date. For example:

> *Small Business Marketing For Dummies* is a friendly guide packed with advice and tools to help small business leaders plan, launch, and manage low-cost, high-impact marketing success stories.

See how it works? A positioning statement is easy to construct – just apply the formula you see in Figure 7-1.

Figure 7-1:
This formula helps you build a positioning statement.

| Your Name | + | Your Business Description | + | Your Point of Distinction | + | Your Market Description | = | Your Positioning Statement |

As you write your statement, avoid these traps:

- ✔ **Don't try to duplicate a position in an already crowded category.** Opening the third shoe repair shop in a small town requires more than a location and announcement. You need to convince customers who are already committed to the other shops that your store is better – because of its location, service or other distinguishing attributes.

✔ **Don't base your distinction on a pricing or quality difference that a competitor can take from you.** For instance, you're only egging on your competitors if you position yourself as 'the lowest priced' or 'the most creative'. With effort, a competitor can beat you on both fronts.

✔ **Don't hang your hat on a factor you can't control.** Too many hotel resorts have ended up red-faced after positioning themselves as 'the region's only five-star hotel', only to lose a star or have a competitor gain one. Instead, communicate distinctions that matter to your customers and then back them up with definitions and promises. For example, instead of making a vague promise about 'best service,' Alaska Air says it's the first major US airline with a 20-minute baggage service guarantee.

✔ **Don't settle for a generic positioning statement.** Be sure that you can answer no to this question: Can another business say the same thing?

Conveying Your Position and Brand through Taglines

Your *tagline* or *slogan* is a quick, memorable phrase that helps consumers link your name to your business brand and position. Your positioning statement describes the unique market niche and mind space you aim to occupy. Your tagline converts that statement to a line that matters to consumers.

You need a tagline if your brand name benefits from some explanation. For instance, Kwik Fit doesn't need a tagline but BMW does, because if you'd never heard of BMW, its name alone wouldn't tell you what it is and does.

For a little tagline inspiration, go to `www.adslogans.co.uk/hof` for a list of famous taglines compiled by the Advertising Slogan Hall of Fame.

As you develop a tagline for your brand, follow advice from Eric Swartz, who calls himself a *verbal branding professional* and *master wordslinger*, and who lives up to his self-description on both counts. He's created thousands of brand expressions, including corporate taglines, city mottos, campaign slogans, company and product names, headlines and other short-form messages.

His business, TagLine Guru (`www.taglineguru.com`), is summed up by the tagline, 'It's your brand on the line.' Here's what he says you need to know as you write a tagline for your brand:

✔ **A tagline should say something essential about who you are, what makes you special, and why the world should care.** It should add value to your brand and illustrate the appeal of your organisation. Think of your tagline as a final exclamation that wraps up your 30-second elevator pitch.

✔ **Because taglines aren't written in stone, you can easily update or replace them if your organisation or message undergoes a shift.** Use your tagline to reflect a change in positioning, launch a marketing or brand-awareness campaign, forge a relationship with a new audience, define a new direction or highlight a key benefit or attribute.

Swartz lists the following 12 characteristics of great taglines:

✔ **Original:** Make it your own.

✔ **Believable:** Keep it real.

✔ **Simple:** Make it understandable.

✔ **Succinct:** Get to the point.

✔ **Positive:** Elevate their mood.

✔ **Specific:** Make it relevant.

✔ **Unconventional:** Break the mould.

✔ **Provocative:** Make them think.

✔ **Conversational:** Make it personable.

✔ **Persuasive:** Sell the big idea.

✔ **Humorous:** Tickle their funny bone.

✔ **Memorable:** Make a lasting impression.

Not all taglines incorporate all 12 characteristics – obviously, a legal or accounting firm wouldn't aim to convey humour – but this list can help during the tagline brainstorming process.

Need help? Swartz says that a pro can help you shape a tagline from 'mundane to memorable' and from 'a bland statement to brand statement'.

After you adopt a tagline, include it in all marketing communications so that when people see your brand name, they also see the tagline that translates your brand promise into a descriptive and memorable phrase.

Balancing Personal and Business Brands

Most people build two brands at once: one for their business and one for themselves, personally. Both have a value but you need to maintain balance between the two.

To rate your personal/business brand balance, answer these questions:

✔ Online and within your personal and business community, is one of your brands – your personal brand or your business brand – significantly more visible and credible than the other?

✔ If you sold your business or left your current position tomorrow, is your personal brand strong enough to transport you into new business opportunities?

✔ If you own your business, is your business brand strong enough to survive without the weight of your personal brand behind it?

Based on your answers, you can take one of two steps:

✔ **Strengthen your personal brand if this brand is weak in comparison to your business brand.** Especially if you own your company, your personal brand helps you humanise your business and take it places where only people go, such as into networking events and community or industry leadership positions.

- Follow the six brand management steps in this chapter to develop your personal brand in addition to your business brand.

- Develop heightened personal-brand awareness within your business, industry and community, and especially online, which is where most brand research starts.

- Create and maintain a personal online home base – your own website, a blog or pages on social networks such as LinkedIn. (See Part III for help with this step.)

✔ **Strengthen your business brand if this brand is eclipsed by your personal brand.** Doing so is especially important if you hope to one day sell your business or develop it into an enterprise that can survive without you.

- If your business doesn't have a website, get one (see Chapter 10 for advice). And if it doesn't rank well in search results, broaden its online presence to improve its visibility (see Chapters 11 and 12).

- If your personal brand is monopolising your business image, make way for others on your team to get more visible with clients, on projects, in media and within your community and industry. Online, instead of personally representing your business, create separate social media accounts for yourself and your company. Then invite members of your team to add their voices (with guidance) to your business blog and social media pages so people view your company as an enterprise larger than one visible person.

- Make a conscious effort to direct interest in you, personally, to your business. Feature your business prominently in your personal communications and introductions. Even consider using your business logo instead of a personal photo on your personal online pages, where business contacts may be searching.

Especially if you're planning to grow or sell your business, strengthen your business brand. If you want to pursue personal career opportunities or to humanise your business, strengthen your personal brand. In between, the best approach is to keep your two brands nicely in balance.

Maintaining and Protecting Your Brand

For something so powerful, brands are surprisingly vulnerable. They thrive with consistency and they wither under the attack of zigs and zags in message, experience and management. The best way to grow a healthy brand is to follow two steps:

- ✔ Establish your brand message and creative strategy.
- ✔ Put controls in place to protect your brand and ensure its consistent presentation.

Staying consistent with your brand message and creative strategy

Your *creative strategy* is the plan that directs the development of all your marketing communications. It defines

- ✔ Your target market
- ✔ The believable and meaningful benefit that you offer to your market
- ✔ The way you present your personality in your communications

Writing your creative strategy

You can write your creative strategy in three sentences that define the purpose, approach and personality that will guide the creation of your marketing communications, following this formula:

1. **'The purpose of our marketing communications is to convince** [insert a brief description of your target market] **that our product is the most** [describe the primary benefit you provide to customers].'

2. **'We will prove our claim by** [insert a description of why your distinct benefit is believable and how you'll prove it in your marketing].'

3. **'The mood and tone of our communications will be** [insert a description of the personality that your communications will convey].'

Following is a sample strategy for a fictitious business:

> **Glass Houses, a window-cleaning service:** The purpose of our marketing communications is to convince affluent homeowners in our hometown that our service is the easiest and most immediately gratifying way to beautify their homes. We will prove our claim by guaranteeing a same-week and streak-free service, by promising four-month call-back reminders, and by offering special, three-times-a-year rates so that homeowners never have to think about window cleaning after their first call to us. The mood and tone of our communications will be straightforward and clean – like our service.

Using your creative strategy

Every time you create an ad, a mailer, a voicemail recording or even a business letter or an employee uniform or dress code, be 100 per cent certain that your communication is consistent with the creative strategy that you've established to guide your business personality. Here are some ways to do so:

- ✔ **Use your creative strategy to guide every representation of your business – and your brand.** Start by looking around your business to see that your physical space projects the tone and develops the image you want for your business. If your creative strategy stipulates a discreet image for your business, you don't want prospects to encounter a rowdy atmosphere with music blaring when they walk into or call your business. Carry that same discipline into every marketing communication.

- ✔ **Create each new marketing communication with your creative strategy in mind.** Whether you're developing a building sign, a website or a major ad campaign, insist that the final product adheres to your creative strategy.

- ✔ **Fine-tune your creative strategy annually.** Each year as you update your marketing plan (see Chapter 23), review your creative strategy. You may decide to reach out to a different target market or to present a different marketing message based on your assessment of market opportunities. But hold tight to your definition of the mood and tone of your communications. (Flip back to the section 'Being consistent to power your brand' for a reminder of why your look and tone need to be reliable indicators of your brand image.)

Controlling your brand presentation

Well-branded organisations have rules – called *style guidelines* – that determine how their logos may be presented, what typestyles and colours may be used in marketing materials, how certain words are used and when and how taglines, copyrights and trademark indicators apply.

Create style guidelines to protect the consistency of your brand image, too. Then, before a print shop, specialty-advertising producer, staff designer, outside marketing firm or any other supplier creates marketing materials on your behalf, share your style guidelines to steer the outcome of their efforts.

Managing your logo presentation

Your logo is the face of your business on marketing materials. Ensure that this logo is presented cleanly and without unnecessary alteration by asking and answering the following questions in your style guidelines:

- ✔ When your logo appears in black ink, what colour backgrounds may be used?

- ✔ When your logo appears in white ink (called a *reverse*), what colour backgrounds may be used?

- ✔ When your logo appears in colour, what ink colour or colours may be used?

- ✔ What's the smallest size that can be used for your logo?

Indicate in your guidelines that your logo must be reproduced from original artwork or a professionally produced reproduction and never from a photocopy or previously printed piece, because the quality will be inferior. If a professional designed your logo, be sure to request the EPS or vector art files. JPG and PNG files may look fine online, but they appear fuzzy when stretched for large-scale use. Also, get professional guidance on which colours to use, whether your logo translates well in reverse treatments, and other presentation advice.

Deciding on your typestyle

A quick way to build consistency is to limit the typestyles you use in your ads, web pages, brochures, signs and all other communications. Choose one typeface (also called a *font*) for headlines and one for ad copy. If your company prints technical materials (instruction guides, warranties, operating or assembly instructions or other copy-intensive pieces), you may designate a third, easy-to-read font for small print and long-text applications or for online use where your selected brand fonts may not display well.

When choosing fonts for your marketing materials, aim to reflect your brand's personality. If you want to convey an old-fashioned or traditional tone, you probably need a *serif* type, which is also the best choice for use in large bodies of type. But if you want your materials to appear informal or clean and straightforward, *sans serif* type is an appropriate choice. (See Chapter 13 for more on selecting and using type.)

In addition to specifying fonts, you may want to define usage preferences, taking the following points into consideration:

✔ Type featuring both uppercase and lowercase letters is easier to read than copy printed in all capital letters. For legibility, avoid using all capital letters unless the headline or copy block is extremely short and easy for the eyes to track.

✔ If your target market has ageing vision, keep text or body copy no smaller than 10 points in size.

✔ Avoid reversed type – white type on black or dark backgrounds – if you expect people to read your words easily. If, for design purposes, you decide to reverse type, keep the type size large.

✔ Use only two fonts in any single marketing piece, unless you're trying through your design to create a cluttered look.

Establishing copy guidelines

Copy refers to the words, text or content of your marketing materials. As you establish style guidelines, also define how you want your copy prepared, taking these points into consideration:

✔ If certain words in your marketing materials require copyright (©), trademark (™) or registered trademark (®) symbols, list these words in your style guidelines.

✔ Indicate in your guidelines whether you want your marketing materials to carry a copyright notice in small (usually 6-point) type. For example: ©2005 John Smith. (Go to www.ipo.gov.uk for more information.)

✔ If you plan to send printed materials over national borders, ask your solicitor whether you need to include a line reading 'Printed in the UK'. If so, include the instructions in your guidelines.

✔ Decide which words you prefer to have capitalised. For example, perhaps your style preference is to say that your business is located in 'Southern Scotland' and not 'southern Scotland.' Or maybe you want your business to be 'The Candy Factory' and not 'the Candy Factory'.

✔ Determine whether you want to ban certain words. For example, a property developer may prohibit the word _plots_ in favour of the word _homesites._ A public relations firm may insist that the term _PR_ be spelled out to read _public relations._ A business with a down-to-earth image may rule out any word that ends in '-ise', saying 'see' instead of 'visualise' or 'make the most of' instead of 'maximise'.

Finally, protect the ownership of your brand by filing national or international trademarks, following the advice in Chapter 21.

Chapter 8

Creating Marketing Communications That Work

*C*reative. The very word turns confident people queasy and rational people giddy. It prompts marketers to say such outrageous things as, 'Let's dress up like chickens', or such well-intended but pointless things as, 'Let's cut through the noise' or, 'Let's think outside the box'. Far less often do you hear the conversation turn strategic, with statements like, 'Let's talk in terms that matter to our customers' or, 'Let's define what we're trying to accomplish'.

This chapter helps you set communication objectives and steer past the mistakes that shoot too many ad efforts into the great abyss, where wasted budgets languish.

Note: The first three sections of this chapter help *all* marketers, whether you present your marketing communications in person, online, with print or broadcast ads or through direct mail. If you place ads in traditional mass media outlets such as newspapers, magazines and TV or radio stations, stick with this chapter to the end for information on scheduling and evaluating your ads. Then turn to Chapters 13 and 14 as you make media selections and produce your ads. For info on using digital communications, including social media, turn to Part III and especially to Chapter 11. For advice on the effective use of direct mail and direct email, flip to Chapter 15.

Starting with Good Objectives

Copywriters and designers are talented and creative, but they're rarely telepathic. They can't create marketing materials that meet specific objectives if their instructions don't include what they're expected to accomplish.

So who is supposed to define the objective, set the strategy and steer the creative process? Well, get ready, because that task falls to the person responsible for marketing, which is probably, well, *you*.

Defining what you want to accomplish

You can hit your marketing target almost every time if you take careful aim. Consider the following examples of creative instructions and note the differences:

> **Example 1:** 'We need to build sales. Let's run some ads.'

> **Example 2:** 'We need a campaign to convince teenagers that by shopping after school on weekdays they'll enjoy our best prices in a club atmosphere because we feature live music, two-for-one café specials and weekday-only student discounts.'

Example 1 forces those creating the ad to guess what message to project – and toward whom. This kind of instruction is likely to lead to round after round of revisions as the creative team makes best guesses about the target market, promotional offer and creative approach.

Example 2 tells the ad creators precisely which consumers to target, what message and offer to project and what action to prompt. It guides the project toward an appropriate concept and media plan – probably on the first try.

As the chief marketer for your business, your job is to give those who produce your marketing communications the information they need to do the job right the first time.

An old saying among marketers concludes that half of all ad spend is wasted, but no one knows which half. You can move the dividing line between what works and what doesn't by avoiding three wasteful errors:

> ✔ **Mistake #1:** Producing marketing materials without first defining your marketing objectives, leading to materials that address neither the target prospect nor the marketing objective.

> ✔ **Mistake #2:** Creating messages that are too 'hard-sell' – asking for the order without first reeling in the prospect's attention and interest.

> ✔ **Mistake #3:** Creating self-centred communications that focus more on what your business wants to say about itself than on the benefits that matter to a prospective customer.

A good ad can inform, persuade, sell or connect with consumers, but it can't do all those things at once, nor is it likely to move the right target audience to the desired consumer action if the audience and objective aren't clearly established before the ad creation begins.

Before you undertake any marketing effort, define the audience you aim to influence, the action you're working to inspire, the message you want to promote and the way that you'll measure effectiveness, whether by leads, web or store traffic, enquiries, social media likes or follows or other actions you can prompt and monitor.

When setting the objective for your marketing communication, use the following template by inserting the appropriate text in the brackets.

> *This* [ad/brochure/sales call/speech/trade stand display] *will convince* [describe the target market for this communication] *that by* [describe the action that you intend to prompt] *they will* [describe the benefit the target audience will realise] *because* [state the facts that prove your claim, which form the basis of the message you want the communication to convey].

Putting creative directions in writing

Your communication objective defines *what* you're trying to accomplish. A *creative brief* provides the instructions for *how* you'll get the job done.

Who is your target audience for this communication?

Start with everything you know about your prospective customers (see Chapter 2 for more information) and then boil down your knowledge into a one-sentence definition that encapsulates the geographic location, the lifestyle facts and the purchasing motivators of those you want to reach.

The target audience is comprised of Surrey residents, age 40+, married with children living at home, with professional careers, upper-level income and an affinity for travel, outdoor recreation, status brands and high levels of service.

What does your target audience currently know or think about your business and offering?

Use research findings (if available), your own instincts and input from your staff and colleagues to answer the following questions:

- ✔ Have prospects heard of your business?

- ✔ Do they know what products or services you offer?

- ✔ Do they know where you're located or how to reach you?

- ✔ Do they see you as a major player? If they were asked to name three suppliers of your product or service, would you be among the responses?

- ✔ How do they rate your service, quality, pricing, accessibility, range of products and reputation?

- ✔ Do you have a clear brand and market position or a mistaken identity in their minds?

Be candid with your answers. Only by acknowledging your real or perceived shortcomings can you begin to address them through your marketing efforts. If your prospects haven't heard of your business, you need to develop awareness. If they're clueless about your offerings, you need to present meaningful facts. If they hold inaccurate impressions, you need to persuade them to think differently. Here's an example:

The majority of those in our target audience aren't aware of our existence, but among those familiar with our name, we're known to provide an experience competitive with the best contenders in our field. We need to reinforce the opinions of our acquaintances while also developing awareness and credibility with prospective customers and especially with opinion leaders whose recommendations are most valued by our affluent and socially connected target market.

What do you want your target audience to think and do?

Don't get greedy. In each communication, present one clear idea and chances are good that you'll *convey* one clear idea. If you try to present two or three messages, you'll probably communicate nothing at all.

Four out of five consumers read only your headline, absorb no more than seven words off of an outdoor ad and take only one idea away from a broadcast ad – provided they don't tune out or skip over the ad altogether.

What single idea do you want prospects to take away from this particular marketing effort? As you answer, follow this process:

1. **Step out of your own shoes and stand in those of your prospect.**

2. **Think about what your prospect wants or needs to know.**

3. **Develop a single sentence describing what you want people to think and what motivating idea you want them to take away from this communication.**

Here's the desired outcome for a computer retailer targeting senior citizens:

> We want senior citizens to know that they're invited to our Computer 101 open days every Wednesday afternoon this month, where they can watch computer and Internet demonstrations, receive hands-on training and learn about our special, first-time computer owner packages.

Be careful what you ask for. Be sure that you're prepared for the outcome you say you desire. If you aren't geared up to handle the online traffic, answer the phone, manage the footfall or fulfil the buying demand that your ad generates, you fail strategically even though you succeeded – wildly – on the advertising front.

Consider this example: A one-man painting company decides to rev up business by placing a series of clever, small-space newspaper ads touting impeccable service, outstanding quality, affordable estimates and prompt response. The ads win attention, action and advertising awards. The problem is, the painter can't keep up with the phone calls, the estimates or the orders. Prospects – who had been inspired by the great ads – end up signing contracts with the painter's competitors instead.

The moral of the story is to expect a miracle from good advertising and to be prepared to get what you ask for.

Why should people believe you and take the proposed action?

To be believable, your marketing materials need to make and support a claim.

- ✔ **The easy way** is to list features: the oldest moving company in the North East, under new management, the only manufacturer featuring the X2000 widget, the winner of our industry's top award.

- ✔ **The effective way** is to turn those features into benefits that you promise to your customers. The difference between features and benefits is that features are facts and benefits are personal outcomes.

Table 8-1 shows you exactly what this crucial difference means.

Table 8-1		Features versus Benefits	
Product	*Feature*	*Benefit*	*Emotional Outcome*
Diet cola	One calorie	Lose weight	Look and feel great
Flower arrangements	Daily exotic imports	Send unique floral presentations	Satisfaction that your gift stands out and draws attention
Car	Best crash rating	Reduce risk of harm in accidents	Security that your family is safe

Every time you describe a *feature* of your product or service, you're talking to yourself. Every time you describe the *benefit* that your product or service delivers, you're talking to your prospect. Consumers don't buy the feature – they buy what the feature does for them. Here are a few examples:

✔ Consumers don't buy V-8 engines. They buy speed.

✔ They don't buy shock-absorbing shoes. They buy walking comfort.

✔ They don't buy the lightest tablet computer. They buy the freedom to get online wherever they want.

Follow these steps to translate features into benefits:

1. **State your product or business feature.**

2. **Add the phrase 'which means'.**

3. **Complete the sentence by stating the benefit.**

For example, a car has the highest safety rating (that's the feature), *which means* you breathe a little easier as you hand the keys over to your teenager (that's the benefit).

What information must your communication convey?

Be clear about your must-haves. Those who create ads, websites, mailers and other communications call it 'death by a thousand cuts' when marketers respond to every creative presentation with, 'Yes, but we also have to include. . . .'

If you know that you need to feature a certain look, specific information or artwork, say so upfront – not after you see the first creative presentation. And keep the list of requirements as short as possible. Here are some guidelines:

✔ **Must-have #1:** Every communication has to advance your brand image (refer to Chapter 7 for information about defining your image). Provide your image style guide whenever you assign a member of staff or outside professional to help with the development of marketing materials.

✔ **Must-have #2:** Be sparing with all other 'musts.' Every time you start to say, 'We have to include . . .' check yourself with this self-test:

- Is this element necessary to protect our brand?

- Is it necessary to protect our legal standing?

- Is it necessary to prompt the marketing action we want to achieve?

- Is it necessary to motivate the prospect?

Let necessity – not history – guide your answers. Any ad designer can tell you that less is more. The more stuff you try to cram into an ad, the less consumer attention it draws. Include no more information than is necessary to arouse interest and lead people to the next step in the buying process.

How do you measure success?

Small business leaders are critical of their marketing efforts – after the fact. Instead, before creating any marketing communication, set your expectations and define your measurement standard in your creative brief.

After an ad has run its course, you hear such criticism as, 'That ad didn't work, it didn't make the phone ring and it certainly didn't create footfall.' Yet if you examine the ad, you often find that it includes no reason to call, no special offer, a phone number that requires a magnifying glass and no address whatsoever.

What's your time frame and budget?

Know the specifications of your job before you start producing it, especially if you assign the production task to others.

✔ **Set and be frank about your budget.** Small business owners often worry that if they divulge their budgets, the creative team will spend it all – whether it needs to or not. But the never-reveal-the-budget strategy usually backfires. If suppliers *don't* know the budget, they *will* spend it all – and then some – simply because no one gave them a not-to-exceed figure to work within. The solution is to hire suppliers you trust, share your budget with them (along with instructions that they can't exceed the budget without your prior approval) and count on them to be partners in providing a cost-effective solution. (See Chapter 9 for advice on how to work with outside talent.)

✔ **Know and share deadlines and material requirements.** If you've already committed to a media buy, attach a media rate card to your creative brief so your designer can obtain the specifications directly rather than through your translation.

✔ **Define the parameters of non-media communication projects.** For example, if you ask for speechwriting assistance, know the length of time allocated for your speech. If you request materials for a sales presentation, know the audio-visual equipment availability and the number of handouts you want to distribute.

What the creative team doesn't know can cost you dearly in enthusiasm and overspend if you have to retrofit creative solutions to fit production realities. Communicate in advance for the best outcome.

Whether you're creating an ad, writing a speech, making a sales presentation, planning a brochure, posting on an online network or composing an important business letter, start by running through the questions on the creative brief to focus your thinking. For all major projects – or for any project that you plan to assign to a staff member, freelancer or advertising agency – take the time to put your answers in writing. Pass them along so they can serve as a valuable navigational aid. Then monitor success by counting inquiries, click-throughs to landing pages, voucher redemptions or other measurable actions prompted by your communications – and share your findings so your creative team can benefit from the knowledge of what worked well.

Developing Effective Marketing Communications

Whether delivered in person, through promotions or via traditional media, direct mail or email, all marketing communications need to accomplish the same tasks:

✔ Grab attention.

✔ Impart information that the prospect wants to know.

✔ Present offers that are sensitive to how and when the prospect wants to take action.

✔ Affirm why the prospect would want to take action.

✔ Offer a reason to take action.

✔ Launch a relationship, which increasingly means fostering interaction and two-way communication between you and your customer.

Good communications convince prospects and nudge them into action without any apparent effort. They match the copy to the visuals and the message with the messenger so the consumer receives a single, inspiring idea.

Creative types can tell you that making marketing communications look easy takes a lot of time and talent, and they're right. If you're spending more than £10,000 on an advertising effort or developing a major marketing vehicle such as a website, ad campaign or product packaging, bring in pros to help you out. Turn to Chapter 9 for information on hiring assistance.

Steering the creative process toward a 'big idea'

After you establish your objectives and prepare your creative brief (see the earlier 'Putting creative directions in writing' section), it's time to develop your creative message.

No matter which target audience you're reaching out to, the people in that audience are busy and distracted by an onslaught of competing messages. That's why great communicators know that they need to project big ideas to be heard over the marketplace din.

The *big idea* is to advertising what the brake, accelerator and steering wheel are to driving. (See why they call it *big?*) Here's what the big idea does:

- ✔ It stops the prospect.
- ✔ It fuels interest.
- ✔ It inspires prospects to take the desired action.

Advertising textbooks point to Volkswagen's 'Think Small' ad campaign as a historic example of a big idea. Volkswagen used it to stun a market into attention at a time when big, lane-hogging gas guzzlers ruled the roads. 'Think Small' – two words accompanied by a picture of a squat, round Volkswagen Beetle miniaturised on a full page – stopped consumers, changed attitudes and made the Bug chic.

More recently, 'Got Milk?' was the big idea that juiced up milk sales in the US and 'Smell like a man' worked like magic for Old Spice.

But big ideas aren't just for big advertisers. In my hometown of Portland, Oregon, quirky Voodoo Donut's big idea that 'The magic is in the hole' has gained international appeal for a two-outlet (though expanding) enterprise.

Big ideas are

✔ Appealing to your target market

✔ Attention-grabbing

✔ Capable of conveying the benefit you promise

✔ Compelling

✔ Memorable

✔ Persuasive

An idea qualifies as a big idea only if it meets *all* the preceding qualifications. Many advertisers quit when they hit on an attention-grabbing and memorable idea. Think of it this way: A slammed door is attention-grabbing and memorable, but is far from appealing, beneficial, compelling or persuasive.

Brainstorming

Brainstorming is an anything-goes group process for generating ideas through free association and imaginative thinking with no grandstanding, no idea ownership, no evaluation and definitely no criticism.

The point of brainstorming is to put the mind on automatic pilot and see where it leads. You can improve your brainstorming sessions by doing some research in advance:

✔ Study websites and magazines for inspiration. Pick up copies of *The Drum* or *Marketing* magazine (available at newsagents and libraries) for a look at the latest in ad trends. Also include fashion magazines, which are a showcase for big ideas and image advertising.

✔ Check out competitors' ads and ads for businesses that target similar audiences to yours. If you sell luxury goods, look at ads for high-end cars, jewellery or designer clothes. If you compete on price, study ads by Primark and Asda.

✔ Look at your own past ads.

✔ Think of how you can turn the most unusual attributes of your product or service into unique benefits.

✔ Doodle. Ultimately, great marketing messages combine words and visuals. See where your pencil leads your mind.

✔ Widen your perspective by inviting a customer or a front-line staff member to participate in the brainstorming session.

If you're turning your marketing project over to a staff member or to outside professionals, you may or may not decide to participate in the brainstorming session. If you do attend, remember that a brainstorming session has no boss, and every idea is a good idea. Bite your tongue each time you want to say, 'Yes, but . . .' or, 'We tried that once and . . .' or, 'Come on, that idea is just plain silly.'

At the end of the brainstorm, gather up and evaluate the ideas:

- ✔ Which ideas address the target audience and support the objectives outlined in your creative brief?
- ✔ Which ones best present the consumer benefit?
- ✔ Which ones can you implement with strength and within budget?

Any idea that wins on all counts is a candidate for implementation.

Following simple advertising rules

The following rules apply to *all* ads, regardless of the medium, the message, the mood or the creative direction:

- ✔ Know your objective and stay on strategy.
- ✔ Be honest.
- ✔ Be specific.
- ✔ Be original.
- ✔ Be clear and concise.
- ✔ Don't overpromise or exaggerate.
- ✔ Don't be self-centred or, worse, arrogant.
- ✔ Don't hard-sell.
- ✔ Don't insult, discriminate or offend.
- ✔ Don't hand the task of ad creation over to a committee.

Committees are great for brainstorming, but when it comes to developing headlines, they round the edges off strong ideas. They eliminate any nuance that any committee member finds questionable, and they crowd messages with details that matter more to the marketers than to the market. An old cartoon popular in ad agencies is captioned, 'A camel is a horse designed by committee'.

Making Media Selections

Even when advertisers only had to choose from three TV channels, a couple of local radio stations and a single local newspaper, deciding where to place ads was a nail-biting proposition.

Now add in satellite TV channels, dozens of digital radio stations, hundreds of consumer magazines (and thousands of online magazines), newspapers and constantly emerging online advertising options, and you can see why placing ads sometimes feels like a roll of the dice.

The next two sections help tip the odds in your favour with an overview of today's advertising channels and advice about how to select the best vehicles for your advertising messages.

Selecting from the media menu

Marketing communications are delivered in one of two ways:

- ✔ *Mass media* channels, which reach many people simultaneously.

- ✔ *One-to-one marketing* tools, which reach people individually, usually through direct mail or email. (Chapter 15 is all about direct mail.)

When people talk about *media,* they're usually talking about mass media, which traditionally has been divided into three categories, with a new category recently added:

- ✔ **Print media:** Includes newspapers, magazines and print directories.

- ✔ **Broadcast media:** Includes TV and radio.

- ✔ **Outdoor media:** Includes outdoor ads, murals and signage.

- ✔ **Digital media:** Just a few years ago, the digital-media category was usually called 'new media', but this category is not new anymore, and its usage, popularity and effectiveness increase almost by the moment. Exactly as its name implies, digital media includes any media that's reduced to digital data that can be communicated electronically. To you and me that means Internet advertising, webcasts, web pages, mobile and text ads and interactive media, including social media networks, all of which I address in Part III.

Each mass-media channel comes with its own set of attributes and considerations, which are summarised in Table 8-2.

Table 8-2	Mass Media Comparisons	
Media Channel	*Advantages*	*Considerations*
Newspapers, which reach a broad, geographically targeted market	Involve short timelines and low-cost ad production	You pay to reach the total circulation, even if only a portion fits your prospect profile
Magazines, which reach target markets that share characteristics and interests	Good for developing awareness and credibility through strong visual presentations	Require long advance planning and costly production; ads are viewed over long periods of time
Directories, which reach people at the time of purchase decisions	Increasingly available for free in digital versions; good for prompting selection over unlisted competitors	Print versions are impossible to update between editions and increasingly eclipsed by digital directories
Radio, which reaches targeted local audiences (if they're tuned in)	Cost is often negotiable; good for building immediate interest and response	You must air ads repeatedly to reach listeners; airtime is most expensive when most people are tuned in
TV, which reaches broad audiences of targeted viewers (if they're tuned in)	Well-produced ads engage viewer emotions while building awareness and credibility	Ad production is costly; reaching large audiences is expensive; ads must be aired repeatedly; 'TV On Demand' services like Sky+ and Freeview erode effectiveness
Digital media, which reaches people on-demand via any digital device	Allows two-way communication with customers; allows convergence of content by linking among digital sources; low cash investment	Requires targeting of customers and keywords and a significant time investment to create, monitor and evaluate online visibility and interaction

Deciding which media vehicles to use and when

Face it: Sorting through pitches from local newspapers, local radio stations, daily-deal coupon sites and industry-specific publications can consume entire days if you let it. Plus, you also have the elephant in the room: social media.

Your media options are seemingly infinite, but your time and budget aren't. So before considering media proposals for any given communication or campaign, answer the following questions:

✔ **What do you want this marketing effort to accomplish?**

If you want to develop general, far-reaching awareness and interest, use mass-media channels that reach a broad and general market. If you want to talk one-to-one with targeted prospective customers, bypass mass media in favour of targeted online communications (see Chapter 10) and direct mail or other one-to-one communication tools (see Chapter 18).

✔ **Where do the people you want to reach turn for information?**

When it comes to purchasing ad space and time, trying to be all-inclusive is a bankrupting proposition. The more precisely you can define your prospect (see Chapter 2), the more precisely you can determine which media that person uses and, therefore, which media channels you should consider for your marketing programme.

When in doubt, ask customers how they like to be reached with marketing messages. Ask whether they read the local newspaper, tune in to local radio stations or notice outdoor ads. Ask whether they use social media networks and which ones. Ask whether they like or dislike marketing messages sent by text message or email. Talking directly with customers is your great advantage as a small business. Ask directly if you can or use free survey tools available through sites like SurveyMonkey (www.surveymonkey.com) to poll customers.

By finding out the media habits of your established customers, you get a good idea of the media habits of your prospective customers because they likely fit a similar customer profile (see Chapter 2 for more on this topic). After you're clear about who your customers are and how they use media, you know which media channels to target.

✔ **What information do you want to convey, and when do you want to convey it?**

Be clear about your message urgency and content, and then refer to Table 8-2 to match your objectives with media channels. For example:

• If you're promoting an offer with a close deadline, such as a one-week special event, you obviously want to steer away from monthly magazines that are in circulation long after your offer is history.

• If you want to show your product in action, you want to feature video in TV ads or on your website or YouTube channel, to which you can lead customers by including the link in your promotional materials, ads and social media posts.

> ✔ **How much money is in your media budget?**
>
> Set your budget before planning your media buying. Doing so forces you to be realistic with your media choices and saves you an enormous amount of time because you don't have to listen to media sales pitches for approaches that are outside your budget range.

The Making of a Mass Media Schedule

When advertising on all mass media except digital media (see Chapter 10), the amount of money you spend and how you spend it depends on how you balance three scheduling considerations: *reach, frequency* and *timing.*

Balancing reach and frequency

Your ad schedule needs to achieve enough reach (that is, your message needs to get into the heads of enough readers or viewers) to generate a sufficient number of prospects to meet your sales objective. It also needs to achieve enough frequency to adequately impress your message into those minds – and that rarely happens with a single ad exposure.

> ✔ *Reach* is the number of individuals or homes exposed to your ad. In print media, reach is measured by circulation counts. In broadcast media, reach is measured by gross rating points (see Chapter 14 for information on broadcast ad terminology).
>
> ✔ *Frequency* is the number of times that an average person is exposed to your message.

If you have to choose between frequency and reach – and nearly every small business works with a budget that forces that choice – limit your reach to carefully selected target markets and then spend as much as you can on achieving frequency within that area.

The case for frequency

Ad recall studies prove that people remember ad messages in direct proportion to the number of times they encounter them. Here are a few facts about frequency:

> ✔ **One-off ads don't work, unless you opt to spend more than 3 million dollars to air an ad during the Super Bowl.** Even then, part of the audience will be away from the TV, putting the kettle on or grabbing a beer from the refrigerator.

- **On most broadcast channels, you need to place an ad as many as nine times to reach a prospect even once.** That means you need to place it as many as 27 times in order to make contact three times – the number of exposures it takes before most ad messages sink in. If your ad airs during a programme that people tune into with regular conviction, the placement requirement decreases, but especially in the case of radio ads, the 27-time schedule generally holds true.

  Why? Because each time your ad airs, a predictably large percentage of prospects aren't present. They're tuned out or distracted, or maybe your creative approach or offer failed to grab their attention.

- **Multiple exposures to your ad results in higher advertising effectiveness.** By achieving frequency, you increase the number of people who see your ad, resulting in increased recognition for your brand, increased consumer reaction to your message, and increased responsiveness to your call to action.

Reach creates awareness, but frequency changes minds.

The case for limiting reach by using only a few media channels

Frequency and limited-reach, concentrated ad campaigns go hand in hand. A *concentrated campaign* gains exposure using only a few media outlets.

Instead of running an ad once in each of six magazines that reach your target market, a concentrated campaign schedules your ad three times each in two of the publications. Or, instead of running a light radio schedule and a light newspaper schedule, a concentrated campaign bets the full budget on a strong schedule that builds frequency through one medium or the other.

Reversing the forgetting curve

Here's some information to remember – if you can.

In the late 1880s, German researcher Hermann Ebbinghaus quantified the rate at which people forget. You may not need formal statistics to confirm that most people forget 90 per cent of what they learn in the classroom within 30 days.

Get this: Most of the forgetting takes place in the first hour after contact with new information, and by the time two days have passed, people retain only 30 per cent of the information.

This *forgetting curve* is why ad repetition is so important to marketers. Through schedule frequency, prospects encounter your message and just when they're about to forget it, they encounter the information again . . . and again.

A concentrated ad campaign offers several benefits:

- ✔ It allows you to take advantage of media volume discounts.
- ✔ It can give you dominance in a single medium, which achieves a perception of strength and clout in the prospect's mind.
- ✔ It allows you to limit ad production costs.
- ✔ It ensures a higher level of frequency.

Timing your ads

No small business has enough money to sustain media exposure 52 weeks a year, 24/7. Instead, consider the following mass media scheduling concepts:

- ✔ **Flighting:** Create and sustain awareness by running ads for a short period, then go dormant before reappearing with another *flight* of ads.
- ✔ **Front-loading:** Announce openings, promote new products and kick-start sales by running a heavy schedule of ads before pulling back to a more economical schedule that aims to maintain awareness.
- ✔ **Heavy-up scheduling:** Synchronise ad schedules with seasonal business or market activity using schedules that include heavy buys several times a year during what's called *ad blitzes.*
- ✔ **Pulsing:** Maintain visibility with an on-and-off schedule that keeps your ad in media channels on an intermittent basis with no variations.

After setting your schedule, leverage your buy by using email and social media to alert customers to watch for your ads, or post the ad on your website and pages to make your investment go further.

Evaluating Your Efforts

Armchair criticism is a popular and pointless after-the-ad-runs activity. Instead, set objectives and plan your evaluation methods early on – not after the ad has taken place.

The quickest way to monitor ad effectiveness is to test a couple of great headlines online and measure the clicks they generate (flip to Chapter 10 for tips). The next-easiest way to monitor ad effectiveness is to produce ads that generate responses and then track how well they do, following this advice:

✔ Give your target audience a time-sensitive invitation to take action, a reason to respond and clear, easy instructions to follow. For example, if you're measuring phone calls, make your phone number large in your ad and be ready for call volume; if you're measuring website visits, present an easy-to-enter site address that leads to a landing page tied to your ad message (see Chapter 10).

✔ Measure media effectiveness by assessing the volume of responses that each media channel generates compared to the investment you made in that channel. Also measure ad effectiveness by tracking the volume of responses to various ad headlines.

✔ Produce your ads to make tracking possible by including a *key,* which is a code used to differentiate which ads produce an inquiry or order. Here are ways to key your ads:

- Direct calls to a unique phone extension keyed to indicate each medium or ad concept. Train those who answer the phone to record the responses to each extension so you can monitor media and ad effectiveness.

- Add a key to vouchers that you include in print ads and direct mailers. For direct mailers, the key may indicate the mailing list from which the inquiry was generated. For print ads, the code could match up with the publication name and issue date. For example, EC1402 may be the key for an ad that runs on Valentine's Day in *The Evening Chronicle* newspaper.

- Feature different PO box numbers or email addresses on ads running in various media channels. When receiving responses, attach the source as you enter names in your database so you can monitor not only the number of responses per medium but also the effectiveness of each medium in delivering prospects that convert to customers.

✔ Test headline or ad concepts by placing several ads that present an identical offer. Track responses to measure which ads perform best.

✔ Compare the cost effectiveness of various media buys by measuring the number of responses against the cost of the placement.

Chapter 9

Hiring Help When You Need It

. . . .

In This Chapter

▶ Checking out your options for marketing assistance

▶ Selecting and contracting with outside talent

▶ Getting help for your online marketing efforts

. . . .

*Y*ou're a small business marketer. You're probably not a trained marketing strategist, a media buyer, an award-winning designer or a stop-'em-in-their-tracks copywriter. You're also human. You've24 hours in every day, and perhaps you've realised that even by giving up sleep, you don't have enough time to run your company, develop your products and services, build your customer base, maintain your business relationships *and* produce and place your ads. Or maybe you've the time but lack the professional touch or talent to create great ads, brochures, websites or promotions on your own.

Perhaps all you need is occasional help from a graphic artist, copywriter, website designer or media buyer. Or maybe it's time to graduate to client status by hiring an agency to help polish and project your image. Either way, you need to know where to find marketing professionals, how to manage the selection process, and how to participate in a relationship that works to your immediate and lasting advantage. That's what this chapter is all about.

Reaching Out to Marketing Pros

Whether to call on marketing professionals depends on what you're trying to accomplish, the audience you're targeting, the talent available within your company, the size and scope of the effort you're about to undertake, and the communications tools you need to create.

Sometimes, especially with lower-budget or short-life materials, the help you need may be available through print shops, media outlets or online resources. Turn to Chapter 10 for website-building advice, Chapter 13 for ad-creation tips and Chapter 16 for help creating printed marketing materials.

When to bring in marketing experts

Seeking outside help is like most business investments – you can't afford to dive in too soon or wait too long. Here's when to bring in the pros:

- **When you're creating a long-life marketing piece.** If you're creating a logo, ad campaign, website or any other major marketing piece that will represent your business for years to come, invest in professional assistance if you're not certain that your own talents are up to the task.

- **When doing your own marketing takes you or your staff away from more profitable activities.** Focus on doing what you do best and contract with marketing professionals to do what they do best.

- **When the budget for a single marketing effort exceeds $10,000.** If you're putting significant amounts of money behind a marketing activity, don't risk your investment by trying to do it yourself unless you're certain of your capabilities.

- **When your annual budget for marketing communications reaches $50,000.** Don't wait until you reach this spending level to call on pros for help in creating important brand and marketing materials, but when your budget for brochures, advertising, web presence, direct mail and other outreach efforts reaches a mid-five-figure total, it's time to form a creative partnership with an advertising agency or a marketing firm that can help you direct your cash into a strong message and image for your company.

Who to call for help

When you're ready to call in the pros, here are some resources you may need:

- **A copywriter** writes ad headlines and text – called *copy* in print communications, *content* online and *scripts* in broadcast communications. Good copywriters know how to write simply, clearly and directly to target prospects, using a single-minded approach to grab and hold attention and to achieve the ad objective.

- **A designer** – also called a *graphic artist* – arranges headlines, text and art elements so they're visually appealing, using a layout that draws the viewer's eye to the correct starting point before guiding it with effortless movement through the ad.

- **A producer** is necessary if you're creating a broadcast ad, a video or a multimedia presentation. The difference in quality and impact between do-it-yourself and professional productions is big and identifiable. Radio stations can produce ads, but in return for their low production costs, you often have to supply your own creativity. If you're not up to the task, you may end up with an ad that looks unremarkably like all other station-produced creations.

✔ **A web designer** adds talent and expertise to the development of website visuals, content and navigation. Chapter 10 is all about websites. Ideally, choose someone who's both a web designer involved with the visual aspects of a site and a web developer involved with the necessary coding. The result: someone who can design a site that's aesthetically pleasing, user-friendly and efficient for your business.

✔ **An agency or marketing firm** handles entire campaigns, from strategic and concept development through design, copywriting, production management and implementation of printing, advertising and digital communications. Agencies have teams of professionals they can assign to your job, along with systems to handle multifaceted tasks. They also serve as brokers – screening, selecting and managing marketing specialists for you. Most assign a liaison, usually called an *account executive* or *account manager,* to serve as your primary contact and the person who holds the agency team members accountable on your behalf. The management function comes at a price, which is why most businesses don't hire an agency until their budgets are large enough to warrant management fees in addition to design, production and media charges. Until that time, small businesses often turn to marketing consultants to provide strategic planning and programme management on a more limited-budget basis.

What kind of expertise to hire

Many small business marketers call on the talent of staff members or rely on media or online resources as they produce low-budget marketing materials without investing in professional expertise. (Conduct web searches for 'online logos' or 'online brochures', for example, to find useful sites.)

Others hire professionals on a per-job basis to create more customised and professionally produced material. Usually referred to as *freelancers,* these experts work for a number of clients at a time. They usually perform tasks under *work-for-hire* agreements stipulating that copyright ownership of work commissioned and paid for, including credit and control, belongs to the company and not the freelancer who created the work.

As needs and budgets increase, businesses move up the professional-assistance ladder to hire a company that specialises not so much in projects as in campaigns or large-scale productions. Included in this category are public relations firms, web design firms, social media marketing firms and full-service ad agencies that get involved in all aspects of developing your marketing image, message and materials.

How do you choose your approach? Follow these tips:

- ✔ **Scale your resources to your needs.** If you want a photo of a new employee to send with a news release to the local paper, you hardly need to hire a photographer who charges £1,000 a day to take the mug shot. And you don't need to pay a public relations consultant £150 an hour to write a two-paragraph news release.

- ✔ **Hire the level of talent that fits the task you face.** If you need a single solution – say, a logo design or website development – a freelancer may be a great fit. But if your project requires management as well as creative expertise, you may be better off turning to an agency that's set up to offer full service and to assume the coordination role.

Most leaders of well-marketed businesses can tell you that when you can afford it, hire help from those who on a daily basis do what you're trying to accomplish. You end up with a more professional and more effective product that benefits from a depth of experience and knowledge about what works and what doesn't.

Choosing and Working with an Agency

Agencies aren't just producers; they're marketing partners. Before beginning the agency selection process, answer these questions:

- ✔ **What do you want the agency to help you accomplish?** Put your objectives in writing. Are you trying to establish and build a brand? Do you want to introduce a product? Do you need to reverse a sales decline or kick start stagnant sales? Is your objective to launch a long-term effort to build market share?

- ✔ **What do you value in an agency?** Are you looking for an agency that specialises in a certain kind of media – such as broadcast, print, online advertising or direct mail? Do you want an agency that specialises in the production of brochures and printed material? Do you primarily seek publicity assistance? Are you seeking an agency known for its award-winning creative work or its expertise with social media campaigns?

- ✔ **What do you bring to the table?** To get and keep the attention of a good agency, you need at least one and preferably two or all three of the following attributes:

  - **A budget:** You need a budget big enough to do the job and to allow the agency a decent profit.

  - **A product or service around which an agency can create high-visibility communications:** Agencies vie for clients who give them a chance to produce work that other clients will notice. Many throw in non-billable time and even forgo some profits to produce ads that build both your reputation and theirs. So if your work happens to win awards and visibility for the agency, the prominence of your campaign may compensate for a less-than-stellar budget.

- **A client mind-set that allows for creative excellence:** Agencies lose enthusiasm quickly when clients over-manage and stifle the creative process. If you want to attract an agency's enthusiasm, allow the agency the creative freedom to do great and noteworthy work on your behalf.

Requesting agency proposals

Start the agency selection process with a short list of firms that you believe fit your needs and provide a good match for the attributes you seek in an agency. In creating your list, follow these steps:

1. **Decide how many agencies you want to interview.**

   If your budget is in the low five figures, start with a list of only one. You've a good chance of getting the agency's attention by telling the agency that it's your top choice and by eliminating its need to compete for a budget in which they can probably earn little profit. If your budget is larger, start with a list of no more than four agencies.

2. **Get recommendations for agencies that match your needs.**

   Contact owners or marketing managers at companies that resemble yours in size and that have particularly strong advertising. Ask who produces their work. Advertising managers at media outlets are also good resources, as are sales representatives at major print shops and respected broadcast production companies. They know which agencies consistently submit professional work on time.

3. **Pre-qualify your finalists using the following questions:**
   - Do they handle accounts of our type and size?
   - Do we have confidence in their expertise and experience?
   - Does their creative style fit our brand and company culture?
   - Do they have the talent we need? Small businesses sometimes hire small agencies in the belief that smaller firms have lower overhead and therefore lower costs. But if your agency has to subcontract to get your job done, you may end up paying marked-up costs for services that it buys on your behalf.

Contact the CEO of each agency on your short list to invite the agency to present its capabilities and to discuss working with your business. Follow these dos and don'ts when requesting a proposal:

✔ Do describe your marketing objectives, target market and whether you're seeking help on a finite project or an ongoing relationship.

✔ Do ask to review samples of agency work, biographical sketches of key staff, a client list, a description of expertise in your industry or market area, and information about billing policies.

✔ Do decide when you'd like to interview the agency, and ask the CEO to confirm within a certain number of days whether the agency will participate in your agency search.

✔ Don't get overly prescriptive as you describe your needs. Explain *what* you want to accomplish through the agency relationship but not *how* you want to accomplish it. Leave room for the agency to bring its point of view and expertise to the task.

✔ Don't ask the agency to submit speculative work (in other words, free sample solutions). Doing so isn't fair, and speculative work isn't a good indication of an agency's abilities. Agencies work *with* clients, not *for* them. If you want to sample the firm's style, propose a small-project budget and be ready to play your role as the client – working with the agency on a solution to your marketing need.

✔ Don't unnecessarily withhold information. If an agency asks whether you're considering others for your account, share your list. If the agency asks what has and hasn't worked in the past, provide a summary.

Keep track of how you feel about the way the agency interacts with your business. Your impressions will be useful as you weigh the issues of chemistry and compatibility.

Interviewing agencies

When arranging agency interviews, first put together your agency review committee, being sure to include the person who will work most closely with the agency. Choose one member of your committee to field queries from all agencies to ensure that they all receive the same information. Then make sure that the committee takes these steps:

✔ Schedule interviews so that no more than a week elapses between the first interview and the final analysis and decision.

✔ Tour each agency to get a sense of how it works and a feel for the atmosphere. Ask to meet the people who will be assigned to your account and the account person who is to be your primary point of contact. Make sure that you feel comfortable with the team.

✔ Keep the interviews as relaxed as possible, aiming to find out about the agency's expertise and how it interacts with your team.

✔ Evaluate agencies on the capabilities that are important to your business. For example, if broadcast advertising is important to your business, rank each agency from one to ten on how well it convinced you of its expertise in this area. Then compare your impressions of capabilities to determine which agency seems to best address your needs.

Preparing the client-agency agreement

Most agencies prepare and submit a contract that defines the agency's role, the compensation arrangement, ownership of work produced under the contract, and ways that the relationship may be terminated. If your agency doesn't offer you such a contract or memo of agreement, ask for one, and be certain that you both sign and keep a copy on file.

You won't find a single standard contract, but all contracts define certain issues and agreements, including but not limited to the following points:

✔ **The services that the agency provides and the responsibilities that the agency assumes:** The contract may list specific services that the agency are to provide or it may cover the issue with a broad brush by stating that the agency is to provide 'services customarily rendered by an advertising agency'.

This section of the contract also defines agreements that protect your interests, such as stipulations regarding work for competing businesses, confidentiality agreements, and the agency's responsibility in obtaining rights to photographs, artwork, copyrights and other proprietary materials that it uses on your behalf.

✔ **Your obligations to the agency:** This part of the contract covers such points as your agreement to provide information as needed to allow the agency to do its job, agreement to pay for work in progress if you cancel a job prior to completion, and agreement that your business is responsible for determining accuracy and ownership of materials provided to the agency.

✔ **Agency compensation:** The contract should define how you pay the agency, including fees, reimbursements for purchases the agency makes on your behalf, and whether those purchases will be billed with mark-ups or commissions (which I explain in the following section). The contract also describes when payments are due, how you can qualify for prompt payment discounts offered by media or suppliers, and how you pay the agency for work that exceeds the scope of agreed-upon projects.

✔ **Project accountability:** Many contracts stipulate that the agency must submit and gain written approval of a timeline and cost estimate for each project, which must be met unless you authorise otherwise. This section also states that you agree to pay for cost overruns incurred as a result of changes to agency work that you had previously approved.

✔ **Ownership of materials:** Just because you pay for advertising materials that an agency produces for your company doesn't mean that you automatically own them. Ideally, you want the contract to say that any material the agency presents to your company becomes your company's property upon payment for the services rendered. Be aware, though, that even if you own the agency's work, you don't necessarily own unlimited rights to the artistic materials included in that work. You usually purchase photos, illustrations, original artwork and voice and acting talent with limited usage rights. If the agency buys outside art or talent on your behalf, ask whether the purchase covers limited usage rights, unlimited usage rights or outright ownership.

✔ **The term of the relationship:** The contract may remain in existence until 'cancelled by either party' or it may cover a finite period.

✔ **Ways that the contract can be terminated:** This is the 'prenuptial' part of the contract. It tells how the agency is paid during the termination period, how contracts that can't be cancelled are handled and how client materials are returned from the agency.

As you sift through all the legalese, keep repeating the mantra, 'An ounce of prevention is worth a pound of cure.'

Understanding agency fees

Most agencies are compensated by a combination of fees for time expended and commissions or mark-ups on purchases made on your behalf. A growing number of agencies and freelancers are moving toward a straight fee-based method of compensation, and others are willing to negotiate the amount by which they mark up expenses. Regardless, the following explanations describe what are still the most common calculations on agency invoices.

Commissions

When an agency buys a £1,000 newspaper ad for a client, if the newspaper allows the agency a 15 per cent commission, then the agency bills the client £1,000, pays the newspaper £850 and keeps the £150 commission as part of its compensation.

Newspaper ad charge billed to client	£1,000
Less 15% commission to recognised agency	–£150
Agency payment to media	£850

Mark-ups

When an agency makes a purchase from a supplier that doesn't offer a commission, the agency generally marks up the expense instead. To make the sums work, though, the agency marks up the charge not by 15 per cent, as you'd guess, but by 17.65 per cent in order to get the same level of compensation. Following is an example for an £850 printing job.

Printing charge to agency	£850
Plus 17.65% agency mark-up	+£150
Printing charge to client	£1,000

When reviewing contracts or approving estimates, ask agencies and freelancers to define their mark-up structures so that you're clear on the percentages they charge, and negotiate if the numbers seem too high.

Working with your agency

The best advice for building a great client-agency relationship is to give clear instructions and then trust your agency with your marketing plan, your budget and your hopes. In everyday terms, building a great relationship means that you do the following:

- ✔ Provide your agency with all the information it needs to do the job right the first time around.

- ✔ Boil down your input. Don't make your agency read encyclopedia-length documents to figure out your marketing plan, advertising strategy or positioning statement.

- ✔ Be frank about your budget. Don't act like a high roller (money is *always* an object). At the same time, don't withhold funds for fear the agency will spend them all unnecessarily.

- ✔ Spend your time understanding upfront project estimates rather than arguing over the bills after the event.

- ✔ Pay on time and expect to pay for your changes. If you wait until the final proof of your marketing materials to make alterations, expect to pay for the last-minute additional expenses involved. (Speaking of proofs, remember that it's your responsibility to proofread, proofread, proofread before issuing your final approval on any piece.)

- ✔ Be open to ideas and be constructive with your criticism.

- ✔ Set up a decision-making process and then stick to it. Eliminate the words 'let's just run it by so-and-so' from your vocabulary. Ads never get better as they go through a committee process.

- ✔ Stay involved. A direct correlation exists between great agency work and great interest at the top levels of the client organisation. That doesn't mean that you should be co-creating ads. It does mean that you should care about the objective, the strategy and the creative rationale.

✔ Be the agency's best client. How? Follow the preceding advice and send over an occasional gift or note of thanks.

Hiring Help for Website Creation

Chapter 10 is all about developing an online presence for your business. This section focuses on hiring the help that you need as you establish and develop web visibility. Keep in mind that hiring a web design firm entails most of the steps involved in hiring an agency (refer to the previous section), plus a few more.

Looking for help

When businesses look to hire an ad agency, they contact ad agencies. In contrast, when they look to hire help for their website, too often they contact friends, relatives or the guy down the street. Advice: Seek help from someone who not only has experience but also has a business doing the kind of work you need done. Here's how to begin the selection process:

✔ **Search online for web designers in your local area.** If you're considering a business that doesn't appear in the results, move on to another candidate. If the business you're considering can't optimise its own online presence, it probably can't optimise yours. Instead, contact companies that appear high in results. Even if they handle projects bigger than the one you're undertaking, chances are good they can refer you to smaller businesses or freelancers they know and trust.

✔ **Check out the website of any firm you're considering.** Is it fast to load, attractive to look at, easy to navigate and capable of making a great impression? These are qualities that you want in your own website, so it makes sense that your web design firm should execute them well.

✔ **Review a range of sites produced by the business.** A good web design firm's site features a portfolio of work. Click through the samples, looking for consistent quality and a range of unique site designs. Also, look to see what kinds of clients are represented. If the clients concentrate in your business sector, you're likely to benefit not only from technical expertise but also from awareness of how companies like yours use their sites to grow their businesses and interact with their clients – all important factors to a successful web presence.

Getting clear about your needs

Before contacting website design firms, know what you're looking for.

✔ **What kind of site are you building?** Do you want a site that presents information as a complement to your bricks-and-mortar business or are you planning to invest in an interactive site that features an online store, email subscription forms, a blog, an online catalogue, photo galleries, product videos or other features?

✔ **How many pages do you think your site needs to include?** Search engines don't require site maps for indexing small sites, but you'll still find it helpful to create a rough map that you can share with designers for planning purposes. Figure 9-1 provides a simple example.

✔ **Do you want to be able to update and edit your site's content yourself without relying on outside expertise?**

✔ **What do you want your site to do?** Do you want to make sales? Do you want to be able to easily store and retrieve information from a database?

✔ **How would you describe those you expect to visit your site, and how do you envision them reaching and using the site?**

✔ **How do you plan to drive traffic to the site?** Whether your site is primarily for use by established customers or for reaching new prospects affects how it's designed and optimised for search engines.

✔ **What sites are similar in look and complexity to the one that you'd like to create?**

Figure 9-1:
Sample of a
simple web-
site map.

```
            Home
            Flower Arrangements
                    Catalog
                    Prices
                    How to Order
            Wedding Center
                    Wedding Ideas
                    Prices
                    Sample Packages
                    Ordering Guide
            Blog
            About Us
            Contact Us
                    Phone, E-mail, Fax, Street Address
                    Map
```

Interviewing website designers

When interviewing website designers, include the following questions:

- ✔ **Do they know how to code HTML or PHP?** If not, they'll rely on web development software, which limits the design and complexity of the sites they can produce.

- ✔ **Do they use templates when creating websites?** If you're looking for an economical site, a firm that uses templates can provide efficient solutions. Today, WordPress and other content-management systems provide a wide range of themes that you can customise, along with pre-written plug-ins that deliver great features without the cost of custom code. Another advantage: If you ask other designers to work on your site in the future, chances are that they'll know how because the systems are in such common use.

- ✔ **Do they follow a structured planning process that's outlined in a document that helps you understand key steps and decision points?**

- ✔ **How do they address search engine optimisation (SEO), and is that service included in their fee estimates?**

- ✔ **Do they handle, and how do they charge for, site updates?**

- ✔ **What other services do they provide?** Do they provide domain name registration, search engine submissions, SEO services, web content writing services, social media marketing services, blog promotion, online advertising, web hosting, site maintenance and marketing services?

- ✔ **When and how do they charge?** And when do they require payment?

  Expect a request for an upfront deposit but run – fast – if they require full payment in advance.

- ✔ **Can they meet your deadline?** Put differently, how long does it typically take them to complete a site?

- ✔ **Will you own your domain name and the administrative rights to your site?** Will you also own all the code on your website so you can modify it in the future without charge? Will you be able to move the site to a different hosting company? You want the answer to each of these questions to be, unquestionably, 'yes'.

Finalising your choice

When you think you've found your website designer, take two more steps. First, ask for and contact past clients to hear how they evaluate the expert. How did the development process go? Were they happy with the results? Did the project stay on budget? Would they hire the designer again?

If you hear all the right answers, the final step is to hire the designer, but not before obtaining a firm quote, in writing, and signing a contract.

Most web design firms provide a contract for you to sign, but if they don't, ask for one. The contract should cover the following:

- ✔ **An estimated cost of the site design:** This should include a breakdown of design time and outside costs involved.

- ✔ **What the estimate covers:** Has the firm based its estimate on the total number of hours it thinks the project will require? Has it provided a breakdown of estimated costs regarding such elements as graphics, navigation, testing and other site-creation tasks so that you can go down the list and be sure that all necessary tasks are covered? Are time and costs for travel, if any, included? Is a round of changes included, or will changes lead to additional costs?

Include a clause stating that the cost estimate can't be exceeded without your prior written authorisation. As you work with the designers to construct your site, you may make decisions that alter the scope and therefore the cost of the project. This clause assures that you understand how your requests impact the price of creating your site – *before* you see the surprise on a supersized invoice.

- ✔ **The payment due date:** Many web design companies require a partial payment at the project's onset. This payment schedule is standard, but you shouldn't have to pay the balance until the site is live, tested and fully functioning. Put into writing the fact that final payment is based on your acceptance of the site.

- ✔ **What happens if the site doesn't work:** Stipulate in the contract whether the design firm has to absorb the cost of alterations required to fix dead links and site crashes within a specified period.

- ✔ **Penalties for non-performance:** State that you should pay less if the firm doesn't meet the deadlines or the expectations.

- ✔ **Performance milestones:** Include a timeline that sets dates for major steps in the process, including your deadline for providing content (and in what format).

- ✔ **Ownership:** Make sure that the contract stipulates your ownership of the site and all its components. Many small businesses overlook this point, only to find out later that they don't own the site and that they have to start all over if they choose to revise the site using a different designer.

Handing off the content

Content includes the website storyboard, text for each page, pictures and any other graphics to be included in your site. Because you're the expert on your business, you'll most likely provide the content or at least oversee its development. The process should go smoother if you follow these suggestions:

- ✔ Create and provide content in an electronic format that meets the agreed-upon specifications so that you eliminate unnecessary costs and errors.

- ✔ The closer you get your content to finished, edited form, the less time (and therefore money) the designer spends building your site. Don't provide your content in dribs and dabs.

- ✔ Be concise and clear with your instructions regarding how you want the content to appear.

Part III
Marketing in a Screen-Connected World

THE **ACTIONS** WE WILL TAKE — Strategy

HOW WE WILL ACHIEVE IT — Objectives

WHAT WE WANT — Goals

WHY WE DO THIS — Vision, Mission and Core Values/Purpose

For Dummies can help you get started with a huge range of subjects. Visit www.dummies.com/extras/smallbusinessmarketing for free bonus content, including forms designed to help your marketing efforts.

In this part . . .

✔ Ensure that your online profile is the best it can be.

✔ Make your business accessible to online users.

✔ Find out how to establish and expand your web presence.

✔ Understand how to leverage blogs for business success.

✔ Discover how to use social media to pull customers to your business.

Chapter 10

Establishing an Online Presence

●●

In This Chapter

▶ Realising the importance of inbound marketing

▶ Creating your online identity

▶ Deciding what kind of site to build

▶ Making your website findable and easy to navigate

▶ Reaching customers with online ads

●●

According to the Office for National Statistics, 43.5 million UK adults used the Internet in the first quarter of 2013 and 57 per cent of these said they used social networking sites like Facebook or Twitter (the highest in the EU), However, while all that online searching, shopping and buying was going on, just a third of small and medium businesses have a website and only 14 per cent sell their products online. If your business is among the 'unfindables', it's time to establish a web presence.

If you're in business – almost *any* business – your customers are online. They're finding out about people before meeting them face to face. They're researching products and services worldwide and in their hometowns. They're checking reviews and ratings. And they're looking for you and your business.

Pulling People to Your Business Online

In today's marketplace, pull marketing rules, especially online.

You've probably heard (and maybe wondered about) the terms *push marketing* and *pull marketing:*

▸ **Push marketing** involves pushing messages and products at customers by interrupting them and prompting them to take the action you're promoting. Push marketing is one-way communication: You talk and your customer listens and, ideally, takes action. Most often, push marketing takes place through mass-media advertising, direct mail, online banner ads and cold calls to prospective customers.

✔ **Pull marketing** involves developing consumer interest by providing entertaining or educational messages that pull attention toward your business, often via your website. In today's screen-connected marketplace, pull marketing is interactive; a two-way communication that begins with information, usually referred to as *content,* that you originate and customers encounter through search engines, referrals and social media. From there, customers take over by clicking a provided link, reaching out by phone or in person and, best of all, passing your message on to others through online or off-line sharing.

Online marketers call push marketing *outbound marketing* and pull marketing *inbound marketing.* HubSpot (www.hubspot.com), a repository of inbound marketing software, research and free tools, puts it this way: Outbound marketers buy, beg or bug their way in, while inbound marketers earn their way in with valuable content that customers find, share and act upon online.

Online marketing: Numbers seal the deal

HubSpot (www.hubspot.com) offers marketing software to help businesses generate leads online. The HubSpot website is a gateway to inbound marketing resources too many to list and too important to miss, including e-books, infographics, blog posts and a free 'Marketing Grader' tool at http://marketing.grader.com (see Figure 10-2 near the end of the chapter) that provides a free report on how well your website and online marketing is working – or isn't.

The need to be active and magnetic online isn't based on hype; the numbers keep adding up. Here's a set of statistics that HubSpot compiled in 2011, which tip even further in favour of online, inbound marketing with each passing month.

✔ 78 per cent of Internet users conduct product research online. If you're absent, you're missing out.

✔ Online email is being eclipsed by text, instant and social media messaging, especially among 12 to 17 year olds, but even among older groups.

✔ 78 per cent of businesspeople check email on their mobile devices, so be sure that your email messages and newsletters are optimised for mobile viewing.

✔ 40 per cent of smartphone owners use their devices to compare prices while they're in a store shopping for an item.

✔ 200 million Americans – two-thirds of the nation's citizens – are off-limits to telemarketers because they've registered on the Federal Trade Commission's National Do Not Call Registry. A good many of the others probably no longer have land-line phones. (In the UK, an estimated 19 million numbers have now been registered on the Telephone Preference Service (TPS) to stop unsolicited marketing calls).

✔ 90 per cent of email recipients have unsubscribed from business email they previously opted in to, and nearly half of all direct mail is never opened.

✔ 84 per cent of 25 to 34 year-olds have left a favourite website because of intrusive or irrelevant ads.

✔ 57 per cent of businesses have acquired a customer through their company blog.

✔ 41 per cent of business-to-business companies and 67 per cent of business-to-consumer companies have acquired a customer through Facebook.

✔ The number of marketers calling Facebook 'critical' or 'important' to their business increased 83 per cent between 2009 and 2011.

✔ Companies with blogs get 55 per cent more web traffic because the more you blog, the more pages search engines index and the more inbound links you're likely to have – which leads to a higher search engine rank.

And the most mind-blowing fact on the HubSpot list:

✔ Inbound marketing costs two-thirds less per lead than traditional, outbound marketing.

To stay on top of online statistics and inbound marketing advice, follow the HubSpot blog at `http://blog.hubspot.com`.

Setting Your Goals for Online Visibility

How findable is your business online, and what kind of results do people get when they search for your business or personal names? Type your name into a search engine to see for yourself. What you discover from your self-search can guide you straight to one or several online marketing goals:

✔ **Awareness:** If your name search shows that you're pretty much invisible online, generate awareness by establishing an online presence – pronto.

✔ **Credibility:** If your search shows that you've an online presence but that results lead to outdated or irrelevant information, make it your goal to dilute the visibility of weak or damaging information by creating a website and social media profiles with current, positive information that you control and can keep updated and accurate.

✔ **Connections:** As soon as your business achieves good online visibility and credible, positive search results, leverage your online presence by setting goals to develop valuable interactions with your target audience. See Chapters 11 and 12 for information on how social media, blogs and online participation unlock relationships online.

✔ **Sales:** Sales is the final goal. Before you can make a sale, you need to achieve and maintain the first three goals of awareness, credibility and connections with customers. Sales is the end result of all the other goals.

Out-and-out selling repels rather than attracts people in all online channels except retail environments. Online, the best approach is to deliver entertaining or educational messages of value and let customers find their way (through prominent links) to your point of purchase.

Claiming Your Online Identity

In the bricks-and-mortar world, people in small business get away with handing out more than one business card. Marketers advise against this approach because it shows a lack of commitment and credibility in any single arena, but it happens without great consequence because all cards have the same contact information, and they're all presented by a person whose name and face the customer recognises. None of those constants applies online.

Online, you need to claim, protect and consistently present a single identity for your business and a single identity for yourself. Otherwise, you'll never achieve the kind of online visibility necessary for marketing success. If you haven't already done so, take these steps:

✔ Register a *domain name* – a website address – for your business.

✔ Stake claim to a single user name for your business across all social media channels you may ever want to use. If you own your business, develop a strategy that links your personal name with your business name online, so that a search for either delivers results for both.

Registering for a domain name

Your *domain name* is the string of characters a person types into a search engine to reach your website, such as yourname.com. If you don't already have one, get one – the sooner the better.

Start by researching name availability on a domain name registration site such as www.123-reg.co.uk or www.godaddy.com. Domain name searches are free and registration costs next to nothing, so don't wait.

First try to register your business name plus *.com*. That sounds easier than you'll probably find it to be, however, because nearly every word in the English dictionary is already taken as a *.com* domain name. Unless your business has an unusually unique name, chances are slim that the name you want is available. If it is, grab it.

If the domain name you want isn't available, you can try to purchase the name from the existing owner, but this process is typically expensive and time-consuming. As an alternative, consider a name that describes your business offerings. This approach also works for businesses with long, difficult-to-recall names. For example, the domain name for the trip-planning site of the Hawaii Visitor and Convention Bureau is gohawaii.com.

Filing online change-of-address instructions

If all this talk about websites makes you realise that your current domain name is a marketing albatross, here's what to do: Establish a new domain name and reroute traffic from your old to new location by setting up what's called a *301 redirect,* which is the web's equivalent of a change-of-address form. Enter '301 redirect' in a search engine to reach how-to tutorials, including instructions from Google and other search engines.

While you're in the traffic-management mood, here's another point to consider: If people are likely to type in a misspelling of your domain name, try to buy the domain name for the incorrect version. If you can, do so, and then set up a 301 redirect so typos don't result in lost traffic.

Finally, if you're baffled by web address terminology, you'll like these definitions from Lorraine Ball, the owner of web design and social media marketing company Roundpeg:

✔ Your **domain name** is the address of your website. Like a mobile phone number, if you change service provider, you can take your domain name with you.

✔ Your **website** contains the graphic and data files that display when someone reaches your web address. The website is kind of like a mobile home or static caravan in that you need to hook it up to services in order to make it functional.

✔ Your **web host** is like a mobile home and caravan park that provides the hookups necessary to make your website visible to those trying to reach you online.

WARNING!

If you can't get the *.com* domain name you want, consider these warnings:

✔ Think twice before taking yourbusinessname.net instead. Domain names involve two parts – your name on the left and a *top-level domain* (such as *com, net* or *org*) on the right, separated by the now-famous 'dot'. Out of instinct, most people type .org for organisations, .edu for schools, and *.com* for business web addresses. If you take a .net address because the .com address you want is already reserved, a percentage of those looking for your site instinctively go to the other site.

✔ Be cautious about using hyphens or unusual spellings to turn an established business name into one that's available as a domain name. Unless you come up with an easy-to-recall solution, your domain name will suffer from confusion and typos that lead to lost traffic.

Reserving your social media user name

No matter how deeply you dive into social media (which is the focus of Chapter 11), take one free step right now by staking claim to your name on every network your business may ever use. The online world is moving fast.

Go to a social media name registration site, such as `http://knowem.com`, `http://checkusernames.com` or `http://namechk.com`. For free and within seconds, each of these sites lets you know whether the name you want to reserve is widely available or largely taken.

If results show that the name is unavailable on major networks such as Facebook, YouTube, Twitter and Google+, research alternative names. Otherwise, you're setting your business up for social media mayhem.

When selecting a name to use on social media, follow this advice:

✔ **Use your domain name if possible.** For example, if your domain name is `www.yourbusinessname.com` and if your business name is short and easy to spell and remember, see whether the name is available across social media channels. That way people search for the identical name everywhere, resulting in the best visibility and recall.

✔ **If your domain name isn't available or isn't a good fit for social media use, create a social media user name, called a *moniker*, to use instead.** When coming up with a moniker, keep these points in mind:

- **Commit to only one name that you use across all social media networks.**

- **Keep your moniker short.** Twitter limits user names to 15 characters (for example, @ForDummies). To achieve web-wide continuity, apply the 15-character limitation to the name you decide to use across all networks.

- **Avoid names with odd hyphenation or characters that people forget or mistype.**

- **Choose a name and provide a description that reflects your business arena or unique niche so it captures target market interest and appears in keyword searches.**

The only time to vary your social media user name is when a site requires personal rather than business participation. In those cases, use a single presentation of your personal name and feature your business name in your personal description (see Chapter 7 for more information).

Establishing Your Online Home Base

This section is for the nearly half of all small businesses (and I hope that number has gone down by the time you read this sentence) without a website. You can't pull people to your business if you don't have an online location for them to reach. To be credible, you need the following:

- ✔ A site that you control. A listing in a chamber of commerce or industry directory doesn't count because you can't control what's there or interact with customers through that listing.

- ✔ A site that's findable and reachable by a search for your business name.

- ✔ A site that accurately establishes your business and brand image, with a great 'About' section where media types and those seeking everything from speakers to industry resources can access professional, reproducible material. For information on this website component, turn to Chapter 17.

- ✔ A site that you can easily update with information about your business.

Your website is the gold standard for online home bases. Your blog is a good alternative – or a great complement – as both provide an updatable online location where you can share expertise, present offerings and invite customer interaction. (Chapter 12 is all about blogs.)

Until you establish your website or blog, set up business pages on Facebook and Google+ as an alternative or a placeholder. Both are free, easy to establish, great for customer interaction and highly findable in web searches.

Website basics

When creating a website, you can start with anything from a one-page site from a company like `www.one-page-website.co.uk`, to a larger site you can construct on your own or (far better) with help from a professional web designer.

Regardless of how simple or elaborate you want your site to be, the essential elements remain the same. You website must

- ✔ Convey what your business is and does.

- ✔ Display contact information, including open hours and directions if you serve consumers from a bricks-and-mortar location, and mail, phone or online contact information for everyone else.

✔ Showcase product information.

✔ Give reasons for site visitors to take the actions you want to prompt.

✔ Make liberal use of keywords or terms that people looking for businesses like yours type into search engines. A multiple-page site featuring the right terms gives your business a chance of landing in search results.

Contact sites

A *contact site* is easy and economical to create and maintain. It allows prospects – who increasingly seek business information through search engines or online local directories rather than through printed Yellow Page directories – to reach your business.

A simple contact site includes your business name and description, your products and services, your open hours and your contact information and location, preferably with access to a single-click phone call or map. Contact sites also often include an email address or a contact form that readers can fill out to get in touch with you. The contact form is less convenient than email for users, but it protects your email address from spam harvesters who collect addresses to use in ways you'd like to avoid.

Brochure sites

Similar to printed brochures, online brochures educate prospects about your products and services in a way that convinces them that they want to do business with your company, or at least that they'd like to receive more information about becoming a customer. (See Chapter 16 for tips on writing brochures and other company materials.)

This type of site requires a design that incorporates your brand look (see Chapter 7) while delivering information that's clear and easy to access. Costs depend on the design's complexity, amount of content, number of pages and whether the site can be built using an existing template.

Support sites

Support sites provide online customer service and communication. They offer information about product installation, usage and troubleshooting; share industry trends and product news; and help customers put products to use. Sometimes, support sites include e-commerce components as well, allowing site visitors to make a purchase after having their questions answered.

Lead-generating sites

More complex than brochure sites, *lead-generating sites* aim to establish relationships and interaction with target audiences. They typically include regularly updated unique content that customers can access and possibly download, often after registering to become part of your online community. Lead-generating sites often include a blog that's updated at least several times weekly, providing timely, relevant information to frequent visitors. Many lead-generating sites offer e-books and other free content designed to attract interest and lead registrations. (See Chapter 11 for more information.)

Mobile websites

Get ready: Those in the know project that by 2015, more people will access the web with mobile devices than with personal computers. Yet studies confirm that nine out of ten websites are currently mobile-unfriendly.

On mobile devices, your traditional site has three strikes against it if

- ✔ It takes too long to load.
- ✔ People find it difficult to view and navigate.
- ✔ It contains too much bothersome information and functionality for mobile users, who have a higher level of urgency and who are twice as likely to 'buy it now' than reach your site from their computers.

Consumers don't wait around for a traditional site to load on a mobile device. They instinctively and quickly leave in search of a mobile-friendly option in their search results, taking your business opportunity with them.

Building a mobile-friendly website doesn't require starting from scratch. Instead, make your mobile site a companion to your regular website but with features designed to be viewed on a tiny screen and to meet these standards:

- ✔ Within seconds, your site needs to load onto mobile devices as a single page featuring your logo and representing your business by reflecting the style, colours, fonts and other identifying elements of your company's brand image (see Chapter 7 for more branding tips).
- ✔ Your mobile site should feature easy-to-read type and easy-to-navigate links that are immediately available to press with no need to zoom or scroll vertically or horizontally.

✔ You should strip away all non-essential functionality and information from your main website, allowing on-the-go mobile customers to quickly access the 'need-it-now' information they seek, including

- Click-to-call access to your business

- Google Maps directions to your business

- High-demand information such as opening hours, prices and a brief description and menu of your products and services

✔ Your mobile site can link to your standard website for additional information, photos and details that only a small percentage of mobile customers require and that interfere with the immediate access desired by most customers trying to engage with your business from smartphones.

✔ Technology that detects an Internet search coming from a mobile device and automatically redirects that search to your mobile site rather than your standard or main website. Redirect service allows your business to promote (and your customers to remember) only one URL that automatically takes customers to the right version of your site.

Online payment options

Credit cards are the most popular form of online payment, but not everyone has a credit card or uses it online. To market online, you need to consider these payment alternatives as well:

✔ PayPal (www.paypal.com) is a money-transfer system that nearly all online retailers support and is most famous for its connection to eBay, which now owns it. Sage Pay (www.sagepay.com) is now 'the UK's most recommended payment gateway provider' and a close rival to PayPal. Google Checkout (http://checkout.google.com) is another trusted third-party payment processor.

✔ Shopping cart software provides programs that serve as a gateway to customer payments, processing credit cards, checks and third-party payments. Volusion.com, Shopify.com and 3dcart.com are among the leading shopping cart solutions.

Protect your customers and yourself from fraud before handling online sales transactions. When building your site, request a Secure Sockets Layer (SSL) that encrypts data as it comes through from customers.

E-commerce sites

No surprises here: The purpose of an *e-commerce site* is to sell goods online. Building an e-commerce site is complicated because of the many features that you must include. Customers need to discover your products, place orders, pay in a secure way and submit personal information to allow delivery. In most cases, e-commerce site creation falls far outside the realm of the computer novice. However, sites like `www.magentocommerce.com` enable you to create a shopping cart to embed on your website, blog or Facebook page.

Building Your Site

You generally build websites in one of two ways: As from-scratch custom sites or as template-based do-it-yourself sites. If you're planning to build a custom site, unless you're an experienced designer, technically adept and really know what you're doing, hire a pro. Chapter 9 helps guide your search and selection process. Hiring a pro costs you time and funds – that's the downside. The upside is that you end up with a site that conveys your unique brand image, with a viewing and navigation system precisely tailored to your unique business offering, all built on a platform that can grow with your business.

If you're planning to build your site yourself, the resources available to you just keep getting better. To start, check out the following free site design and layout services online:

- ✔ WordPress (`http://wordpress.com`) is a blog platform increasingly used as a website builder. You may need help from a freelance web expert, but for close to nothing (except time), you can get a site with good, basic functionality up and running. Go to `http://codex.wordpress.org` for tips and advice on how to get more from your WordPress site. Also check out *WordPress For Dummies* by Lisa Sabin-Wilson (Wiley).

- ✔ Weebly (`www.weebly.com`) lets you use drag-and-drop functions to create a site with no cash outlay that you can have up and running within days. Figure 10-1 shows a screenshot of a site in process.

  Whether you create a simple and functional site on your own or a customised, branded site with help from a pro, use the following sections to familiarise yourself with considerations to weigh and steps to take.

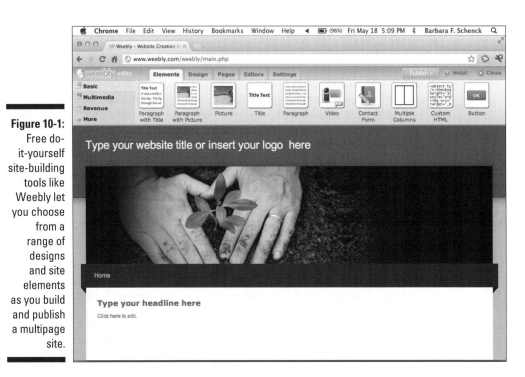

Figure 10-1:
Free do-
it-yourself
site-building
tools like
Weebly let
you choose
from a
range of
designs
and site
elements
as you build
and publish
a multipage
site.

Cracking the site-building code

Site builders use a language common in their field and foreign to most of the rest of us. Here are terms you'll encounter:

- ✔ **HTML,** or Hyper Text Markup Language, is the code that underlies most web pages and the common language of the web. HTML tells your browser what's what on a web page – what's a heading, where a picture goes and everything else you see on your screen. Part of the appeal of site design tools such as those offered by WordPress and Weebly is that they eliminate your need to learn HTML by building the code for you. If you do decide you want to use HTML, I recommend the latest version of *HTML 4 For Dummies* by Ed Tittel and Mary Burmeister (Wiley).

- ✔ **Content** describes electronically delivered information. Text (copy), photos, graphics and videos are all part of content.

- ✔ **Keywords** are words or phrases that describe a page's content. When people seek information online, they enter keywords into search engines. If the search request matches your keywords, your pages appear in their search results. How high on the list your site appears is a topic unto itself. See 'Optimising your site for search engines', later in this chapter, for information.

✔ **Navigation** is the way that users move around a website to find and access information. Sites use menu bars, coloured or underlined text or icons to help users find and link to designated pages.

✔ **Search engine optimisation (SEO)** is the process of developing a website with the aim of achieving high visibility in search results, usually by employing tactics that make the site's design, menus, content, images and other elements visible or 'friendly' to search engines.

Incorporating attributes of a good site

Good sites have some common strengths:

✔ The visitor can tell who the company is and what it does.

✔ The site is organised so that visitors can easily find and access information.

✔ Visitors can quickly find out how to contact people at the company.

✔ The site loads on all computers and mobile devices quickly and reliably.

✔ The site is easy to read and use.

✔ The look of the site accurately conveys the company's image.

✔ The site doesn't crash or give error messages.

✔ Content is well written, clear and directed at visitors' wants and needs. Content is also tagged and categorised for easy indexing by search engines.

As you build your site, aim for the following three attributes:

✔ **Speed:** Most visitors only wait seconds for a page to load. Test your site or ask your site-hosting service to provide response-time measurements.

✔ **Graphics:** A picture's worth a thousand words only if it appears before the user tires of waiting. Save images at a low resolution of 72 dpi and in GIF or PNG format and use compression software to speed loading time.

✔ **Accessibility:** Hire someone who really knows computers to test your site, confirming that it works well with all the major web browsers and that all links get users where you want them to go.

Table 10-1 lays out points to consider as you design your website.

Table 10-1	Site Design Considerations
Dos	**Don'ts**
Do consider that your online customer may need personal assistance when you aren't available to offer it. Include contact information and promise a prompt reply.	Don't assume that customers who need personal assistance will be satisfied to wait until your business is open and someone is available to receive a phone call.
Do treat your website like all other marketing materials. Launch it when ready and not a second before.	Don't launch with site pages labelled 'Under Construction.'
Do protect ownership of your site. Add a copyright notice with the year at the bottom of your home page; for example, ©2012, Your Business Name.	Don't make assumptions about site ownership. If you use a website developer, be sure that you retain the copyright.
Do use small, fast-loading graphics and be sure that your site can load within five to seven seconds.	Don't overlook factors that slow loading time, including large graphics, unnecessary code and the speed of your hosting server.
Do follow current web advice at sites such as `http://searchenginewatch.com`, `http://searchengineland.com` and `http://smallbiztrends.com`.	Don't steal content from other sites. Seek permission from the site owner or author before using material you see online.
Do keep your site clear, clean, usable and easy to navigate.	Don't use your organisation chart as your navigation plan.
Do use keywords and code that optimise your site and make it findable by search engines.	Don't break search engine rules. Follow the Google Webmaster Guidelines at `http://support.google.com/webmasters/bin/answer.py?hl=en&answer=35769`.

Optimising your site for search engines

Improving your site's search position is a continuous process that starts the day that your site goes live. You don't need to submit your site to search engines to be included in search results. Search engine crawlers find your site on their own, by following links from other sites. You can, however, speed up the process by taking a few key steps:

✔ Avoid *splash pages,* which are entry pages that feature a graphic while the site loads. Search engines index content and keywords from the first page of a website, and splash pages usually contain little of either.

✔ Build a network of incoming links to your site from other high-quality, well-established sites. Search engines judge sites by the company they keep, so start by getting your site address listed in major directories and business association sites. Also, host a blog (see Chapter 12) that others can link to, publish guest posts and articles that include links back to your site, include your link in social media comments and conversations and develop shareable content that links back to your site.

✔ Make your site findable by building content around keywords customers are likely to use when seeking information like that offered on your site.

✔ If your site is large – say 50 pages or more – devote one page to a site map with links to all pages so they're easy for search engines to find and index.

✔ Present your site's navigation links using text with keywords rather than icons or buttons.

✔ Keep each individual page focused on a single topic. Build each page around keywords that define its focus so those searching for specific information are directed straight to the relevant page on your site.

Incorporate keywords into each page's content, code commands and photo or graphics labels and tags. But don't cram your content full of irrelevant keywords in an effort to manipulate your way to a higher search ranking. Google punishes what it terms *keyword stuffing*. It also warns against hidden text or links. And it blacklists for *cloaking,* which is presenting site content one way to search engines and another way to users.

When your site goes live, go to the submission pages at the major search engines and submit your URL, or site address. The submission pages are `http://google.com/webmasters/tools`, `http://bing.com/toolbox/webmaster` and `http://search.yahoo.com/info/submit.html`.

Additionally, register your site at Open Directory (`www.dmoz.org/add.html`), the human-powered directory that AOL, Google and others use in their searches. Submit your site for free, wait three weeks and if your site hasn't been picked up, resubmit it.

As you register your site with search engines, incorporate keywords into your description. You can test your keywords using the Google Keyword Tool at `www.googlekeywordtool.com`.

Evaluating the strength of your site

After your site is up and running, put it through HubSpot's free Marketing Grader test (`http://marketing.grader.com`) shown in Figure 10-2, and enter your website address to get a site analysis via email. You can also enter the addresses of competing websites for comparative purposes, if you'd like.

Check out 'The Best Damn Web Marketing Checklist, Period!' available online at `www.searchengineguide.com/stoney-degeyter/the-best-damn-web-marketing-checklist-pe.php`. This checklist is by the amazingly talented and generous Stoney deGeyter, president of Pole Position Marketing, a leading search engine optimisation and marketing firm.

Promoting your site

The launch of your website should begin an intensive effort to integrate your site address into all your other marketing materials. Start by including an invitation to your website on all communications that your business currently sends into the marketplace. Use this checklist:

- Your letterhead, order forms, invoices, fax cover sheets, envelopes and especially business cards.
- Your building sign and other promotional signs.
- The closing paragraph of news releases (see Chapter 17).
- The signature of your email messages.

Figure 10-2: Use the HubSpot grader tool for a free analysis of the marketing strength of your website.

> ✔ Your ads and brochures. If your marketing includes an emphasis on TV and radio advertising, try to choose a website address that's easy to hear, understand and remember.
>
> ✔ Your voicemail message.

Turn to Chapters 11 and 12 for advice on using social media, blogs and online link placements to achieve awareness and drive traffic to your site.

Advertising Online

Online advertising reached $100 billion in 2012, with most of the investment going toward search and banner ads but an ever-increasing flow of money going toward interactive and video ads.

Online advertising is a push-marketing vehicle in a pull-marketing world. (For definitions of those terms, flip back to the start of this chapter.) The danger for advertisers is that web users hate the intrusion of ads that interrupt their online activity. But – and here's the key to success – when an ad provides entertainment or information they embrace, it pays off doubly: once with a good impression and once with a click-through to your website.

Banner ads

Banner ads are the narrow image ads that run across third-party websites. When viewers click on the banner (called a *click-through*), they go directly to the advertiser's site. Interest in banner ads waned largely due to consumer resistance until a Google program allowing banner ads on sites that participate in the Google AdSense program re-inspired interest in the format. Here are a few factors that influence the effectiveness of a banner ad:

> ✔ **Creative design:** This includes questions that invite interaction, free offers and good use of colours.
>
> ✔ **Targeted placement:** Place ads on sites that your prospects are likely to visit.
>
> ✔ **Frequency:** Place a number of ads with similar messages. Try them out and then quickly – within a day or two – watch click-throughs to see what's working and yank all but the top performers.

A distant cousin to the banner ad is the *pop-up ad,* which appears in your browser window when you open some web pages. Pop-ups (and *pop-unders,* which hide beneath web pages) represent only a small percentage of online advertising, largely because consumers rank them among the least popular of all advertising approaches. Pop-up blocking software is in wide use, and Google, for one, doesn't allow pop-up ads on its site.

Pay-per-click (PPC) ads

Whenever a small ad appears in the margin of a search engine or social media page inviting you to click for more information, the advertiser pays only if you take the bait and click to reach the advertiser's site.

Search ads

Each time a search engine displays results of a search, it also displays a lineup of all-text ads focusing on the same keywords as those in the search. Google AdWords and Microsoft Bing Ads (representing both Bing and Yahoo!) are the leading search ad program providers. To participate, go to `www.google.com/adwords` or `https://secure.bingads.microsoft.com`. Follow the on-site instructions to choose the language for your ads, the geographic areas you want to target and the keywords you want your ad matched to. Then write a short ad, followed by the URL of the page you want respondents to land on.

A companion program to AdWords is the AdSense advertising program (`http://google.com/adsense`), which allows high-traffic information sites to earn revenue by displaying AdWords ads on their web pages.

Social media PPC ads

Social media ads work a lot like search ads, except they target specific people rather than topics. As the social media landscape is constantly changing, here are sites to visit for current advertising information and instructions:

- **Facebook:** Nearly a billion active users. Need I say more? Go to `www.facebook.com/business`.

- **YouTube:** The second-most popular search engine after Google. Direct advertising is through Google AdWords.

- **LinkedIn:** *The* network for business-to-business marketers. For information, go to `www.linkedin.com/ads/start`.

- **Twitter:** To promote tweets or place topics atop the Twitter trends list, go to `http://business.twitter.com`.

Almost every social media network has a way to let you place your ads before its members' eyes. Just enter the name of the network along with the word 'advertising' in a search engine to find the latest and necessary advice.

Chapter 11

Getting Interactive with Social Media

*B*y the end of 2012, Facebook had more than 1 billion active users. People on Twitter posted over half a billion tweets daily. Meanwhile YouTube reported that 72 hours of video were uploaded every minute. Wowza!

Social media is where the action is. By December 2012, the Pew Internet Project (www.pewinternet.org) reported that 67 per cent of online adults use social networking sites, yet marketers – especially small business marketers – still question whether social media is the right place for their messages. The answer is a resounding 'Yes, but'.

✔ **Yes:** Social media networks are where marketers need to be, because these networks are where the majority of all consumers are. Social medis is where *your* customers are – or, on the slim chance your customers aren't there, you can bet those who influence their decisions are.

✔ **But:** Social media can consume hours without a return on the investment if you don't have a good marketing objective and plan. And even then, marketing participation can backfire. You absolutely have to enter social media networks with an intent to build relationships and interact with consumers, not to hawk yourself or your wares through promotional messages that intrude, annoy and harm more than they help your business and brand.

This chapter helps you manage the balancing act.

Benefiting from Social Media Activity

Marketers used to have debates about whether to get involved with social media. Those days are gone.

Research by Social Media Examiner (www.socialmediaexaminer.com), the world's largest social media online magazine, shows that nine out of ten marketers now consider social media important for generating business exposure, and that more than two out of three marketers want to know more – particularly about Facebook and blogging. Here are a few other facts about social media to get you going:

- ✔ **It doesn't cost much.** Doing it well takes an effort, but most small businesses invest next to no money and handle social media interactions without additional staff or services.

- ✔ **It's not an all-or-nothing proposition.** You don't have to start everywhere. Figure out which networks the people you want to build relationships with use and start there. You can always expand to other networks down the road.

- ✔ **It addresses a longstanding marketing need.** For as long as people have sold goods and built reputations, they've sought ways to talk with those who can affect their success. This communication is what made rotary clubs, chambers of commerce, business lunch places and industry gatherings so popular. Those same motivations drive escalating interest in social media networks, which let you reach your customers where they are and when they want to receive messages.

Getting Started in Four Necessary Steps

To engage your business in social media, take the following four steps – if you haven't already done so – and then dive in. After that you need to commit to a managable set of ongoing activities. The result: Greater business exposure that leads to more website traffic, more qualified leads, and improved search engine rankings. Did you just hear the door slamming on your lingering doubts?

1. Define your objectives

In descending order, most small businesses say that their social media objectives are to connect with customers, enhance visibility and awareness, promote business offerings, share news quickly and stay on top of market and industry news and trends. What are your aims?

✔ Do you want your business to become known as a trusted thought leader in your field?

✔ Do you want to attract the attention of new customers or influencers by getting useful information in front of them?

✔ Do you want to broaden your network of contacts with others in your field?

✔ Do you want to spark more conversation with and receive more input from customers and prospective customers?

✔ Do you want to tap into consumer conversations to find out what people are saying about your business or business sector?

✔ Do you want to build relationships that lead to sales?

Out-and-out selling is repellent in almost any social situation, and doubly repellent on social media. No matter how you define a successful sale – whether you're aiming for cash register transactions, speaking engagements, press coverage, mailing list opt-ins or simply favorable impressions – don't push. Instead, take a social and roundabout route by delivering entertaining or educational messages of value with links that people want to follow to your website and point of purchase. Inspire their interest; don't require it. In social media, sales come as a result of achieving all your other objectives.

2. Choose the name that you want to use across all social media networks

If you've already reserved your business name as your website domain name, the logical next step is to simply use your domain name as your social media user name.

For example, *For Dummies* has the domain name fordummies.com, which it presents as @fordummies on Twitter and For Dummies on Facebook and LinkedIn.

Sometimes, though, using your domain name as your social media user name isn't possible because the name is too long (Twitter restricts names to 15 characters max) or because the name is already reserved by someone else on major social media networks. If that's the case, turn to Chapter 10 for advice on coming up with an alternate name for use on social media.

Sites such as `http://checkusernames.com`, `http://knowem.com` and `http://namechk.com` provide free, almost instantaneous services for checking to see whether user names are available across social media networks.

3. Develop your social media Bio

Everything you've heard about 'social media noise' is true. A whole lot of posting never gets through the online static. People tune out all messages except those that seem relevant to their wants and needs and those that come from sources they know and trust.

To work your way into your users' inner circle, introduce yourself in a way that causes people to take note and think, '*This* sounds interesting' or, '*This* is what I'm looking for'. Follow these tips:

✔ Create a Twitter Bio that conveys at a glance what your business does and for whom, along with what makes it trustworthy, distinct and likable (this is, after all, *social* media).

✔ Twitter limits Bios to 160 characters, and that's a good limit for descriptions on other networks as well.

✔ Include *keywords* – the words or terms that people use when searching for businesses like yours – so you show up in search results.

✔ With your Bio, deliver a sense of the kind of information people can count on you to deliver, as well as the tone – whether humorous, serious, controversial, authoritative, whatever – your messages will convey. Steer clear of self-aggrandising terms like *expert.* Convey *why* you're an expert instead, preferably in a way that makes people smile and want to find out more.

✔ If you're the primary player in your business, help people locate you by your personal *or* business name by incorporating both into your Bio. As proof it can be done, here are Twitter Bios for a couple of the marketing experts featured in sidebars throughout this book:

> **@ronjdub:** I do things like Knodes & Snapgoods.
> Doer | Thinker | Speaker. I use technology to create new possibilities and I'm a funraiser. Yes, fun.

> **@JeanneBliss:** Customer Crusader. President, CustomerBliss. Author, Chief Customer Officer and I Love You More Than My Dog.

Be sure that your social media Bio is an exact reflection of how you introduce your business and what customers encounter off-line as well. Consistency builds brands, and brands power success, whether with people entering your business through your front door or via your online pages. (If the term *brand* raises a question mark in your mind, Chapter 7 is for you.)

4. Set up an online home base

Social media isn't an end unto itself. Before getting involved in social media, establish the online home base to which you'll direct the interest your social media activity generates.

- ✔ If your business doesn't already have a website, flip to Chapter 10 for advice on building one.

- ✔ Turn to Chapter 17 for information about the online media centre your site should include, especially if your objective is to enhance credibility by becoming recognised as an authority in your arena.

- ✔ See Chapter 12 for information on creating a blog, which most social media powerhouses consider essential to social media success. A blog can double as your website or be a page of your website. Whichever you choose, it offers a source of continuously updated content and a place for all-important customer interaction.

Include the address for your website or blog in your social media descriptions and in content that you develop and offer through social media posts. By sharing your address, you help people reach your business online while also building relevant inbound links to your website, which help improve search engine results for your business name.

Diving into Social Media

If you've already taken the important step of reserving your user name across social media networks, then you know from looking at the hundreds of opportunities that being everywhere is impossible. (If you haven't reserved your user name, look back at Step 2 in the preceding section for tips.)

Narrow your options by taking one easy step: Talk with your customers and ask which networks they use. Where they are is where you need to be.

Beyond talking with customers, go to your competitors' websites and see which social media networks they use. Then visit their social media pages. See what kind of followings they've acquired and the nature of the information they share.

Then consider your own target audience and marketing objectives. If you're working to reach consumers, Facebook and Pinterest are strong choices. For business-to-business marketers, LinkedIn reigns. For general awareness development, Twitter and Pinterest are top contenders, while Facebook is great for building loyalty and customer service, and LinkedIn and Twitter help generate leads.

The most prominent social media networks fall into these categories:

✔ **The big dominant social media networks:** For networking, target audience interaction and Search Engine Optimisation (SEO), the three big players are Facebook, LinkedIn and Twitter. Google+ currently gets less user time and attention, but because it's indexed by Google and interwoven into other Google products like Gmail and YouTube, it should be included in your social media activities. For retailers and restaurants, Pinterest became a mega-player in 2012, and no doubt others will emerge as well, which is why following news from sites such as www. socialmediaexaminer.com is so important. It keeps you up to date in a constantly changing online world.

✔ **Location-based check-in sites:** If you find that your customers use mobile phone apps to check in and redeem purchase incentives at participating businesses, don't miss the chance to get in on the action. Use sites like foursquare to create valuable – and free – social media visibility for your business, prompting customer visits with your own check-in incentives and reward.

✔ **Review and rating sites:** TripAdvisor and industry-specific sites affect all businesses.

The following sections describe the lay of the social media land by summarising the major categories and sites. But what you see on these pages is just the tip of the social media iceberg. For video, you have YouTube. For photography, you have Flickr and Instagram. For books, you have Goodreads. For an updated list of social media networks, go to http://traffikd.com/ social-media-websites.

Facebook

First a distinction: A Facebook *page* is different from a Facebook *profile*. Profiles are for people and pages are for businesses. A page gives your business presence on Facebook. It provides a place Facebook users can go to access information, news and offers from your business. Plus, when users 'like' your page, your updates appear in their Facebook news feeds, where they can click to interact with your business.

Seeing why businesses use Facebook

Summarising from Facebook's own site, here are seven reasons 'why your small business needs a Facebook page'.

✔ More than half of users log in at least once a day, allowing you to maintain an interactive presence with them.

✔ By clicking 'like', customers can connect with your business and share their association with their Facebook friends.

✔ Facebook pages are public (unlike personal profiles). Businesses that update their pages with new content and posts are ranked highly by search engines and enjoy improved search results.

✔ When you post news, events, photos, or other content, your update shows in your fans' news feeds. If they comment or click to 'like' your post, their update shows in their friends' feeds. Then, if their friends also comment or click 'like', that's how viral sharing gets started.

✔ You can survey your page followers for free by using the easy Question or Poll tab.

✔ You can promote events for free. Click the Events tab on your page to announce events, invite customers, receive RSVPs and monitor anticipated attendance.

Creating and using a Facebook page

To create a Facebook page, log into your personal Facebook account or the Facebook account of the person who will serve as your Facebook-required 'page administrator'. At the bottom of the home screen, click Create a Page to get started, taking two precautions:

✔ Take care with the first page-creation step, which is to choose the classification and category for your business. This step is the one part of your page that you can't change later.

✔ When Facebook prompts you to share the fact that you've created a page, hold off. Wait until your page is complete before you announce it.

After your page has been created, you need to choose a *Vanity URL*. By default, your page address is a long string of impossible-to-remember characters. Go to www.facebook.com/username to register a name that features your company's social media user name. For example, the *For Dummies* page is www.facebook.com/ForDummies, as you can see in Figure 11-1.

After you're all set up, start using your page. If you don't do it yourself, assign someone to keep your page updated with interesting, relevant information that can engage your audience and prompt participation. And above all else, use Facebook to interact with your following. Send thank you messages to those who like your page, respond to messages and posts, survey followers and share the results and always follow up – promptly – on customer suggestions.

Twitter

Twitter is a messaging tool. In short posts of 140 characters or fewer, people tell what they're doing, what they're reading, who they're listening to and what they find interesting and important enough to share with others.

Go to Facebook.com to personalize your page address with your online name.

Feature your logo or icon for brand recognition.

Figure 11-1: Features of a Facebook business page.

Present a consistent business description off-line and online across media networks.

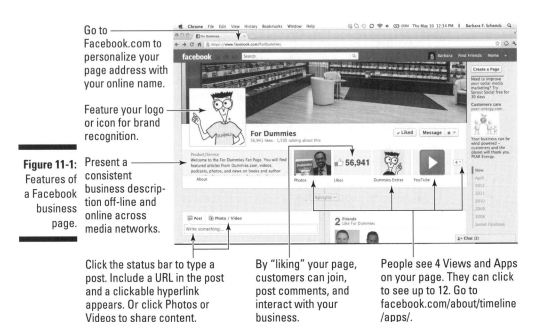

Click the status bar to type a post. Include a URL in the post and a clickable hyperlink appears. Or click Photos or Videos to share content.

By "liking" your page, customers can join, post comments, and interact with your business.

People see 4 Views and Apps on your page. They can click to see up to 12. Go to facebook.com/about/timeline /apps/.

Weighing the pros and cons of Twitter

The biggest criticism of Twitter is that 'no one cares what you had for lunch', but Twitter posts feature a whole lot more than trivial updates. Businesses use Twitter to share news, tips and useful information. They also use it to stay on top of news and opinions in their market areas. In the process, they acquire connections and stay in touch with local or far-flung audiences.

Just don't try to get opportunistic on Twitter (or any other social media network, for that matter). Start spewing sales pitches and people drop your feed faster than they can finish the cup of coffee you didn't want to read about. Instead, use your tweets to draw attention by sharing information and links to content that your followers will want to share and that – and this objective is your ultimate one – makes them think more highly of you as a valuable business resource.

For everything you could possibly want to know about why and how to use Twitter, read the Twitter Guide Book by Mashable.com, available at `http://mashable.com/guidebook/twitter/`. Mashable is the largest independent news source dedicated to covering digital culture, social media and technology. After your Twitter account is live, consider following @Mashable to stay on top of the latest news.

Creating and using a Twitter account

Just go to `http://twitter.com/signup`, register your user name, fill in the required information and you're ready to start posting messages, or *tweeting.* That's it. Then, anyone who wants to can follow and read your tweets – with no requests or acceptances required – and you can follow others just as easily.

To find Twitter users to follow, use the search function on your Twitter home page to locate friends, business associates, local and industry media outlets, customers, suppliers, businesses you use or admire, people of influence in your world and anyone who sounds interesting. When you find accounts full of interesting tweets, click Follow to add their posts to your Twitter feed.

Beyond following interesting people on Twitter, click on their accounts to see which accounts they follow. When you see an interesting account, click to follow it as well. After that, you need to get involved. Start reading what's called your *tweets timeline,* where posts from everyone you follow show up. Pay attention to how people word their messages. Click the links in their tweets to view the content they're tweeting. Check on the keyword or topic hashtags (words preceded by a #) they use to see conversations in areas that interest you.

As you start posting your own tweets, go to the 'Twitter Help Center' at `http://support.twitter.com` and click Twitter Basics for all kinds of useful information. Among the tips:

✔ **Make sure that you appear in Twitter Search by completing your description, including your user name, full name and bio, using key-words that you want associated with your account.**

✔ **Tweet, retweet, reply and mention others to keep active in search results.**

- To tweet, just type a message into the 'Compose new Tweet' box and hit return.

- To retweet, hover your mouse beneath a message and click Retweet. The post appears with the author's name and user name and is followed by a retweet icon alongside your user name. As an alternative, you can hover over the message, click Reply and then paste in the message you're retweeting. Consider adding *RT* at the beginning of the tweet to indicate a retweet. Also consider adding a few words of comment to add value to the message.

- To mention others, use their user names preceded by the @ sign. Mentions of others can help your message gain visibility, prompt conversations, get shared and gain replies – sometimes even from celebrities.

✔ **Keep tweets under the 140-character limit.** When you're composing a message, Twitter shows the character count, but don't take it to the limit. Keep posts under 120 characters because when people retweet, 'RT @yourusername' gets added to the tweet, eating up the characters you left unused.

✔ **Include links to useful content.** To shorten long links so they don't consume tweet characters, use an URL shortener such as bit.ly or let Twitter shorten the link for you. Just paste the link into your tweet and a message box pops up that reads, 'Link will appear shortened'. Then, in your message, give a good reason to click on the link; for instance, '3 great Twitter tips', or, 'Our newest customer survey results'.

✔ **Get familiar with Twitter third-party apps like HootSuite.** You can organise followers into groups, schedule messages and manage multiple Twitter profiles on the go from your mobile device without using a web interface.

✔ **Explore Twitter's advanced features.** After you're familiar with the basics, use the Twitter help area to explore how and why to tweet images and videos; connect Twitter to your blog, website or Facebook page; and develop your Twitter following and community.

LinkedIn

LinkedIn (`www.linkedin.com`) is the world's largest professional network with over 200 million users. If you use business cards, Rolodex files and networking opportunities, you'vea basic understanding of how LinkedIn works. It helps you exchange knowledge, ideas and opportunities with your contacts and those they're connected to.

You can set up a LinkedIn profile for free. What's more, LinkedIn profiles rise to the top of search results for your name, allowing you to control the information others see about you. To get started, go to `http://learn.linkedin.com`.

Viveka von Rosen knows how to use LinkedIn. Named one of Forbes's Top Ten Women in Social Media, she's not associated with LinkedIn but is a top trainer and consultant to those who leverage LinkedIn for personal and business success. You can benefit from her expertise by following the advice and using the checklist that appears in Tips for Becoming Successful on LinkedIn, which you can find at `www.dummies.com/extras/smallbusinessmarketing`.

Google+

Probably the most compelling benefit of a Google+ business account stems from its Google heritage. If your business is on Google+ and you develop an active Google+ community, your business is more likely to appear high in Google search results, and we all know what that means: website traffic.

Google makes joining Google+ super easy. Here's what to know:

- **Connections:** After you open a Google+ business page, you can put a +1 button anywhere you'd like, allowing your business to easily invite people to simply click to follow and recommend your business and products or services to friends and contacts across the web.

- **Target sharing:** As people follow your business, you can choose which Google+ circles to add them to based on their interests and their relationship with your business. Then, when you post content, you can make your posts public for all to see or you can make them visible only to followers in one or several circles.

- **Collaboration:** Through Google Hangouts, up to 10 people at a time can take part in a live video conference, which can be broadcast 'On Air' to anyone watching via your Google+ page or YouTube Channel.. On Air Hangouts are automatically posted onto your YouTube Channel where even more people can watch them and you can embed them in your website or blog or share on Facebook or Twitter.

- **Measurement:** Google's measurement tools show you what people are saying about your business, how many +1's your business receives and how your online activity affects your site traffic.

To create a page, go to `http://google.com/+/business`, follow the prompts and then customise your page with your logo, photos and other information that presents your image and offerings.

You have to tie your Google+ page to a specific Gmail account, which is difficult to change later. Consider setting up a specific account that you use only for your business activity on Google.

Pinterest

Think of a corkboard where you pin pictures of your wish list and favourite memories and you'vea good idea of what Pinterest is about. Except Pinterest goes further, letting you browse and re-pin images and videos from others as part of a global share-fest that, as of early 2012, was driving more online referral traffic than YouTube, Google+ and LinkedIn combined.

Businesses use Pinterest just like individuals do, creating boards on a range of topics that reflect the character of the brand and interests of customers, and then pinning business-generated content, re-pinning images from others and calling for and pinning content from followers. (For complete information, go to `http://pinterest.com/about/help`.)

To get your business started on Pinterest, follow these steps:

1. **Request an invitation from a Pinterest user or from** `http://pinterest.com`**.**

2. **Register, authenticating your business account using a Twitter account rather than a personal Facebook profile.**

3. **Go into Settings to complete a keyword-rich profile, designate your email settings and determine how you want Pinterest to interact with your other social media pages.**

4. **Start making boards – and here's where you have to get inventive.**

   Pinterest isn't your business photo album. Pinterest is about portraying the culture of your business and the interests of your customers. If you're a local retailer, what inspires your store offerings? Where do your customers dine, gather, exercise, holiday or otherwise spend their days and enjoy their interests? Feature those interests as you pin captivating photos, infographics, videos or other attention-stopping images on your boards.

   Create boards that cover a range of topic areas and use keywords as you give each a name. Use them to share bold graphics, videos and photos that people will want to re-pin. Post your content on your own website or blog first and then pin it on Pinterest. That way, the pinned image includes a link back to your site, driving traffic and search rankings.

Location-based and check-in sites

Over half of all mobile phone users carry smartphones in the UK, and more than half of those smartphones access location-based services such as maps, directions and location-based social networks like foursquare.

If you'vea walk-in location that serves customers, people may well be checking in as they enter your front door, whether you know it or not. The following services and networks are worth your consideration.

Google+ Local

The easiest way to lead people to your business is with a free Google+ Local page and Google map. To get going, all you need is a physical mailing address, a free Google account and a location in a country where Google Places is available. Go to www.google.com/places, click Get Started, follow the prompts and take these steps:

- ✔ If your business already appears on Google Maps but you didn't submit it, take advantage of the offer to claim your business with a Place page.

- ✔ Verify your listing and then enhance your Place listing by adding photos, videos, coupons and updates such as weekly specials. For help, see Chapter 7.

After you set up and manage your listing through Google Places, your customers can find your business through your Google+ Local page, where they also find information from other Google properties, including Search, Maps, Zagat scores and customer reviews and recommendations (see Chapter 6 for more).

foursquare

People using foursquare arrive at a business, check in and compete against others to become the 'Mayor' by racking up the most check-ins. What's in it for the business? Every check-in is free advertising within the customer's social media network. To get involved, take these steps:

- ✔ Go to http://foursquare.com/business to see whether your business is already listed as a venue. If so, click where it asks, 'Do you manage this venue?' If not, click, 'Add new venue to foursquare.'

- ✔ Provide the requested information, including the address of your business website's contact page or Google page.

- ✔ Wait 7 to 10 days for foursquare verification.

After that, start offering visitors rewards and incentives for foursquare check-ins, at no cost beyond whatever promotional offer you're extending.

New location-based and check-in networks

Social media is rapidly evolving, and probably no area of the field is undergoing more change than location-based networks.

To stay on top of the news and opportunities, read the world's largest online social media magazine, Social Media Examiner (www.socialmedia examiner.com). From the magazine's home page you can click to follow on Facebook, sign up for free email updates, add the site to your Google+ circles or follow @smexaminer on Twitter.

Rating and review sites

Probably the quickest way to grab the attention of small business owners is to mention the topic of bad online reviews. By taking some upfront and ongoing steps, you can improve the odds that good reviews outweigh and overshadow the occasional, usually inevitable one-star rating. Here's what you need to know and do.

Claiming your presence on review sites

If you aren't sure which rating and review sites are important, just ask your customers which sites they check out.

- Almost any business-to-consumer company can benefit by claiming its presence on Google Places (`www.google.com/places`).
- If you're in the travel business, your customers likely use TripAdvisor (`www.tripadvisor.com`).
- Restaurants get active on sites like TopTable (`www.toptable.co.uk`) and all kinds of local sites.
- Each business sector – legal, medical, consumer electronics and so on – has a set of review sites where customers weigh in and where smart businesses participate.

Encouraging reviews

The best way to get good reviews (and drown out the noise of bad reviews) is to offer amazing products and services. Around the corner from where I live is a foot spa, and here's how one review starts: 'I can't believe this salon has any reviews less than five stars. I wish that I could give it MORE than five stars.' If somewhere down the feed is a rant, the words from this totally satisfied customer more than silence the complaint.

To encourage reviews:

- Display review site logos in your business and on your website so people know where to go to post reviews.
- Directly invite your best customers to share their opinions. To make it easy, give customers cards featuring your review site URLs, possibly including a next-visit discount or offer – valid whether or not they post a review.

- Take care not to bias customer comments. Google offers the following precaution about soliciting customer reviews, which serves as good advice across all review sites:

✔ 'Reviews are only valuable when they are honest and unbiased. Even if well-intentioned, a conflict of interest can undermine the trust in a review. For instance, do not offer or accept money or product to write positive reviews about a business, or to write negative reviews about a competitor. Please also do not post reviews on behalf of others or misrepresent your identity or affiliation with the place you are reviewing.'

✔ Don't blitz your review pages with a deluge of reviews posted over a short period – a signal to review sites that some incentivising may be going on. Instead, cultivate a steady stream of reviews for the best results.

Keeping cool when a bad review shows up

Sooner or later, someone is likely to post a bad review of your business. When it happens, do the following:

✔ **Look for a shred of truth in the rant.** If the review points out even a tiny deficiency, fix whatever's wrong. Then use your blog, Facebook page, or direct contact with the reviewer (if you can reach the person, which isn't always possible) to describe the changes you've made. Research shows that disgruntled customers aren't just placated by businesses that resolve their issues – they actually become proponents, sharing the positive outcome of their experience with others.

✔ **Don't hit back.** The more attention you give a bad review, the more people notice it and the more you inspire the rage of an already disgruntled person. Instead, push the review out of sight by encouraging new, positive reviews. Remember that those who use online review sites take an occasional poor review with the grain of salt it deserves.

Announcing Your Social Media Debut

As soon as you create social media pages, launch your social media presence by getting the word out:

✔ Invite employees, suppliers, clients, friends and family to join and interact with your social media sites.

✔ Promote your profiles by including invitations to join you online in all your marketing communications.

✔ Cross-promote your profiles on each of your social media pages. For instance, add your Facebook and Twitter URLs to your LinkedIn profile, and add your Facebook URL to your Twitter Bio.

✔ Add 'Join us on' icons, to your website so people can simply click to join your social media networks. Just enter the word *widget* in the help search box.

✔ Include 'Join us on' signage at key points in your business.

✔ Include your Facebook and Twitter URLs in your email signature and on your business card, but only if you'vea plan to stay active and engaged in the networks. Nothing looks worse than a link to a page that hasn't been updated in months.

Keeping Your Social Media Efforts Active and Engaging

Participate with your social media networks through a combination of three activities:

✔ Sharing useful, relevant, interesting information, called *content,* created by your business.

✔ Sharing – basically re-gifting – useful, relevant, interesting content created and shared by others.

✔ Sharing your thanks, praise, expertise and input by adding your comments to others' posts.

Sharing content

Businesses that pull people to their pages online do so with useful, relevant, consistently presented information that takes time and discipline to create.

If you'vea blog this part gets easier, because maintaining a blog forces you to create useful information that you can then repurpose to feed into your Facebook and LinkedIn pages, feature on Twitter, pin on Pinterest and compile into newsletters and mailings. Chapter 12 is all about blogging and definitely worth checking out.

With or without a blog, however, take these steps:

✔ **Develop content that supports your social media objectives,** described earlier in this chapter.

  • **If you're seeking awareness and credibility,** share content that gains attention and establishes your business as a uniquely valuable resource. Examples include links to publicity, favourable reviews, research findings and white papers or blog posts with helpful and interesting content that people will want to read and share.

- **If you're seeking interaction with your target audience,** create and share surveys, host forums, or announce online or off-line events that prompt input, comments and conversations. LinkedIn Answers is a good place for this activity, as are Facebook Questions or Polls and Twitter Chats, which you can stay on top of by following @ChatSchedule.

- **If you're seeking customers,** create and share content that draws people to your business, perhaps by offering free samples or material, such as white papers, e-books or other useful, relevant information. Just be sure that you link the offer to your website home page or, better, to a landing page on your website that's cus-tomised to greet new visitors, fulfil their interest and invite them to join your mailing list or any customer-registration database.

✔ **Develop a reputation for content that supports your brand image.** For example, become known as the business that puts out a monthly list of top five tips in your business arena or that releases a quarterly opinion poll or annual best-practices white papers. The *For Dummies* brand is known for reader-friendly reference information. Other brands are known for their unique (and highly shareable) graphical presentations of information, known as *infographics.* By deciding on a type of content to share on an ongoing basis, you not only make content development easier but also create higher awareness, recognition and credibility.

✔ **Establish and stick to a posting schedule.** You can't achieve visibility or credibility with once-in-awhile social media involvement. Commit to a schedule that keeps your business visible without inundating your audi-ence. (The consensus seems to be that eight Twitter messages and four Facebook posts a day touches on the outer limit.)

✔ **Involve your employees** by sharing your social media objectives and approaches and assigning responsibilities that allow you to share the burden – and the enthusiasm.

✔ **Automate the process of posting** across multiple networks by using free tools like HootSuite (http://hootsuite.com), or Buffer (www.bufferapp.com).

The Checklist of Content-Generating Approaches, which you can find at www.dummies.com/extras/smallbusinessmarketing, features ideas to con-sider as you develop content for social media sharing and interaction.

Becoming a content conduit

If you share content from others, you benefit in a number of ways:

- ✔ You become known as a connected person who relays valuable information.
- ✔ You generate social media activity without having to generate content.
- ✔ You attract the attention of those whose content you share, likely leading them into your network and possibly gaining their interest in sharing your content as well.

To find interesting and shareable content, study your own social media feeds, read news sites that carry interesting information and scan industry blogs, sites and pages. Identify several sources worth watching carefully and use a RSS reader to receive alerts every time the sites are updated. When you see something that may interest your audience, don't just share it – let your audience know why you're sharing it and where it came from (for example, 'Great industry stats: Tip of the hat to @greatcontact').

On social media, sharing is the sincerest form of flattery.

Getting conversational

Use the social media networks that you establish to interact with customers, associates and followers online.

- ✔ Watch for comments posted to your content and respond, preferably within 24 hours. On Facebook, a simple 'like' may be enough. On Twitter, a retweet with a 'thx' may do. Best of all, a thoughtful response posted as a reply gives you a chance to say thanks and provide more information.
- ✔ Watch for any mentions of your business, products or people. Whenever appropriate, immediately retweet, repost, share or reply with thanks. You amplify your own presence and deepen connections all in a few keystrokes. The next section, on monitoring your social media mentions, helps with this step.

Keeping an Eye on How You're Doing

Monitor your social media programme in two ways:

- ✔ Watch to see who's talking about you and what they're saying.
- ✔ Observe how your comments and content are received and how your network is expanding as a result of your efforts.

Monitoring your social media mentions

Set up alerts so that you're notified when your personal name, business name, product name, business category, competitors' names and any other terms you want to monitor are mentioned online.

- ✔ Set the preferences on Facebook and Twitter so you're alerted by email when someone interacts with your posts.
- ✔ Use sites like `http://search.twitter.com` to search for posts about the names and terms that you're following.
- ✔ If you use Constant Contact, set up NutshellMail (`http://nutshellmail.com`) to email a summary of activity on the schedule you request.
- ✔ Set up online alerts through sites like Google Alerts (`www.google.com/alerts`), Bing Alerts (through your Windows Live ID account) and Social Mention (`http://socialmention.com`).

To make your life easy, direct all responses to a single RSS aggregator so you can open that one resource and see alerts for all your mentions in one place.

Measuring your social media effectiveness

Social media isn't just a popularity contest, although the number of friends, follows and likes you accumulate matters, especially if they come from members of your target audience or, even better, those who influence members of your target audience.

Most social media platforms feature areas where you can monitor your effectiveness.

- From your Facebook page, click Insights to view a summary of your activity and see which posts drew the most views and interaction.

- From your Twitter profile, click @Connect to monitor your interactions with and mentions by others, including which of your tweets was most shared.

- For location-based sites like foursquare, monitor redemption levels of exclusive promotional offers.

- Use Google Analytics to monitor your website traffic. Go to your account and open Traffic Sources to see which networks are driving traffic to your site.

- If your content and posts aim to generate leads, monitor which offers drive traffic and result in conversions.

The purpose of monitoring is simple: to help you do more of what works best.

Social media dos and don'ts

- Never ignore hard questions, whether on review sites, social networks or your own blog.

- Never participate online simply to sell or to place your URL.

- Always be open to advice and even criticism, which you should never delete.

- Always keep your communications helpful, useful and friendly.

- Always sound like a person and not a faceless corporation.

- Always be consistent in the way you present your business – and your brand.

Chapter 12

Packaging Your Message for Blogs and Other Online Channels

....

....

Ten years ago, advertising was the backbone of marketing communications. Whether you used print, radio, TV, flyers, sandwich boards or any other information-delivery mechanism, the whole push – and *push* describes it perfectly – was to elbow your way in front of prospective customers with messages that aimed to grab their awareness, gain their interest and stimulate their desire to buy whatever you were advertising.

Times have changed. *Push marketing* – which involves intruding on customers with outbound, one-way marketing messages – has been eclipsed by a preference for *pull marketing* that draws customers into interactive relationships with marketers. (Chapter 10 defines the differences between push and pull marketing in more depth.)

What drives pull marketing efforts is *content* in the form of valuable, relevant, entertaining, educational and conversational messages that people encounter online and act upon, whether by visiting the business in person or online, reposting or sharing, following up for more information or simply noticing and developing positive awareness.

The single easiest way to develop content is to start and commit to a blog that becomes the hub of an information-distribution strategy that flows blog posts through multiple online channels and, ultimately, into search results that help optimise the page rank of your website. So blog. Repurpose blog content. Share information from others. Comment on third-party blog posts. Interact with your readers. Leverage your posts through multiple online channels. Repeat. Blogging is today's marketing key and is the topic of this chapter.

Joining the 200-Million Blog Contingent

Blogs, short for *web logs,* are online chronicles of news, ideas, facts and opinions. They're part editorial, part journal and a good part dialogue between the blogger and the blog's readers.

The number of blogs published worldwide is a moving target, but the ticker along the top of microblogging site Tumblr showed over 108 million blogs in May 2013. The WordPress site ticker in July 2013 showed over 68 million sites. That's 176 million blogs right there. Add in self-hosted sites and sites on other platforms and estimates of 250 million blogs are well within the realm of reason.

What's more, people are actually reading all that blog content. A tracking study by NM Incite, a Nielsen/McKinsey company, showed that three of the ten largest social networks – Blogger, WordPress and Tumblr – drew a combined 80 million unique visits during a single month in 2011, accounting for one in four active online users in the United States.

Who blogs?

Technorati (http://technorati.com), the first blog search engine and host of the Internet's leading blog directory, compiles statistics on who blogs and why. Technorati reports that bloggers fall into these categories:

- Hobbyists who blog for fun (61%)
- Professional full- or part-time bloggers who consider blogging their jobs (18 per cent)
- Corporate bloggers who blog for the companies or organisations they work for (8 per cent)
- Entrepreneurs or individuals who blog for their own businesses (13 per cent)

These stats tell you that bloggers defy the dated and probably never-accurate stereotype of pyjama-clad sofa loafers. Out of every 100 bloggers, 13 are people a lot like you, taking a few hours every week to blog for their businesses.

Why blog?

Small business leaders blog to share their expertise and experiences, become more involved in areas they're passionate about, meet and connect with like-minded people, and gain professional recognition. They use their blogs to announce business developments, answer frequently asked questions, provide educational information, share product news and knowledge, announce specials and promotions, build brand awareness, establish themselves as thought leaders in their fields and draw prospective customers to their blogs and businesses.

To that list, you can add this bonus: improved search engine rankings for your website. When you revolve your posts around high-interest, low-competition keywords (for help, use the Google's Keyword Planner at `http://adwords.google.com/keywordplanner`), focus your blog topics, blog consistently, and build interest and trust within your target audience, then higher search engine rankings – an objective of all online marketers – naturally follows.

Here are a few examples of small business blogs that consistently show up on best-blog lists:

- ✔ The Small Business Blog: `www.sme-blog.com`
- ✔ Enterprise Nation Blog: `www.enterprisenation.com/blog`
- ✔ Small Business Blog: `www.smallbusiness.co.uk/blog`
- ✔ Sage UK Blog: `www.sage.co.uk/blog`

Launching a Blog

Blogging allows you to create linkable messages – *content* – that your target audience can view and share. Each time a reader shares a post, it carries your name, your message and a link back to your site to new contacts for your business.

Good blogs share common elements:

- ✔ They're graphically simple.
- ✔ They're full of short entries, or *posts,* that you update frequently and present chronologically, with the newest posts listed first and most prominently.
- ✔ They advance a distinct point of view and focus on a particular interest area.
- ✔ They use RSS (Really Simple Syndication) or other file formats that allow one blog to distribute and share posts with others so third-party websites can repost or excerpt posts with a link back to the originating site.

Getting started

The great news is that you don't have to start from scratch to begin blogging. Instead, you simply choose a blogging platform – most are free – and, with practically no tech knowledge, you can begin blogging within minutes.

By most accounts, the top platforms include

- ✔ **WordPress:** According to a study by Technorati, WordPress is the most popular blog-hosting service, used by over half of respondents. You can create a free hosted blog through `http://wordpress.com` (featured in Figure 12-1) or a self-hosted blog through `http://wordpress.org`. See the sidebar 'To host or not to host your blog' for a glance at the differences involved.

- ✔ **Blogger:** The platform at `www.blogger.com`, which is owned and managed by Google, is free and quick and easy to use. The only downside is that Blogger doesn't offer a self-hosting option that allows customisation of your site.

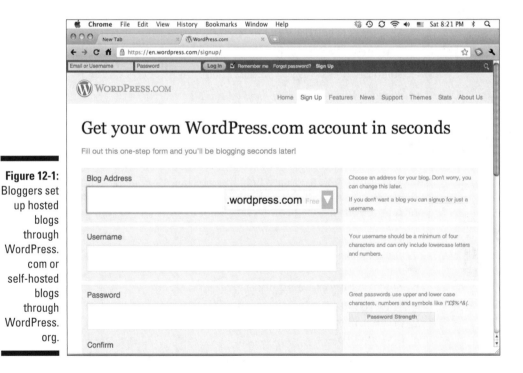

Figure 12-1: Bloggers set up hosted blogs through WordPress. com or self-hosted blogs through WordPress. org.

✔ **Tumblr:** This platform is known as a microblog site. A Tumblr account is free and gives you access to 'the easiest way to blog,' quoting from the Tumblr website (www.tumblr.com). From your computer or a mobile app, Tumblr lets you create short posts that others can 'favourite' or 'reblog'. What you can't do is easily archive your posts. In many ways, Tumblr resembles Twitter but with an emphasis on photos. Tumblr reports that average users post 14 posts a month, half of which contain photos, with the rest split among text, links, quotes, music or video.

Committing to a blog

If you're going to blog, you have to start with a few commitments. First, commit to a topic area for your blog. You can't just blog about whatever happens to be on your mind from one day to the next (unless what's on your mind is so interesting and well-written that people want to follow you just for your random observations).

Focus your blog on a subject of high interest to the target audience you want to engage and of equally high interest to you and those in your business, because you'll be posting about that subject several times a week for years into the future. Aim for a blog topic that

✔ Those you want to reach want to know about and talk about. Your aim is to provide interesting, informative posts that draw responses from readers.

✔ You're able to research, because good blog posts include news and information that others don't already know.

✔ Revolves around keywords that those in your target audience are likely to use in their web searches but that don't already have high levels of competition in search engines. Use Google's Keyword Planner at http://adwords.google.com/keywordplanner as you search for good topic terms.

Then, after committing to a blog topic, commit to the blogging process:

✔ Post regularly with valuable, interesting content, ideally following a weekly schedule that your readers can get used to and count on.

✔ Keep your posts relevant to your topic area.

✔ Join the blog community, posting content that other bloggers will want to repost, commenting on other blogs, welcoming guest blog posts and interacting with those who comment on your blog.

You know that you've committed to a blog concept when you can comfortably introduce your blog in a single sentence that describes its topic, its target and its unique point of view. See the nearby sidebar, 'Hello world. Meet my blog.'

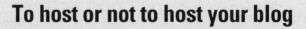

To host or not to host your blog

A hosted blog is a blog that's hosted on the blog platform site and a self-hosted blog is a blog you host on your own website. Here are a couple of the differences:

✔ Choosing a hosted solution through sites like WordPress or Blogger makes sense if your blog is your first website because you can simply open an account, log in and start posting with little expertise and no cash. Your blog is limited to the design themes and plug-ins or features the blog platform provides for free, and it will have a name like yourname.wordpress.com unless you pay extra to include your domain name in your blog address. But it also comes with the support of the blog host, including data

protection, program updates, fast server response, unlimited bandwidth and more.

✔ If you host your blog by embedding it in your own website, you need to devote a little (but not a whole lot) more time, technical expertise and money. You upload and install the blog platform software and pay your own domain and site-hosting fees. In return, you've complete control over your site. You can customise your blog theme or design, accept advertising and add features such as a shopping cart, a membership form or other blog extensions. Another plus: You get greater search optimisation benefits because your blog address includes your domain name.

Crafting your blog-post approach

Good blogging follows a blogger-designed posting schedule and an established blog-post format.

Establishing an editorial calendar

To plan your blog posts, take these steps:

1. **Divide your blog into categories that address various aspects of the topic you plan to blog about.**

   By establishing categories, you improve your blog in two ways: You can save posts by categories, which makes them easily findable by those searching your blog archive, and your categories become a planning tool as you plan monthly posts.

   For example, John Jantsch uses the following categories on his widely cited Small Business Marketing Blog (www.ducttapemarketing.com/blog/): Duct Tape Marketing, DTM Favs, Marketing Plans, Marketing Strategy, Referral Marketing, Social Media and Web Marketing.

2. **Plan your posts on a monthly basis.**

   Every month, use your blog categories to guide your editorial decisions. Look through your category list and decide on blog posts that allow you to address a wide range of category titles. Need ideas? Look for questions you're asked repeatedly by clients and others, address them in a blog post and then share the link the next time the question arises.

You don't have to post everything all by yourself or even with your staff. Consider placing a standing invitation for guest posts on your blog, along with your topic and word-count requirements and your interest in blog exchanges. Also reach out directly to bloggers or business associates for guest posts. Or find other blogs on your topic and feature information from a few posts, along with links back to the authors.

Breaking down a blog post

Every blog post needs to do two things: convey information of interest to the target audience and inspire the target audience to take a desired action, whether by clicking to reach your website or by clicking to share the post – or both. Here's what you need to include in your posts in order to achieve these goals:

- ✔ **A blog post title or headline:** This title needs to grab attention and interest, not unlike an ad headline. Include keywords that describe the post so it can be found by people when they're seeking similar information in web searches.

- ✔ **Subheadings:** Subheadings should feature keywords and give those who skim and skip around your post a good idea of what the text contains.

- ✔ **A post description:** If your blog platform allows you to enter a *meta-description,* do so, writing a keyword-rich summary of your post that appears as a snippet in search results. Otherwise, search engines simply grab the first 160 characters they see on your page, so be sure that the introduction to your post summarises the post, incorporates keywords and stands well on its own in search results.

- ✔ **Accurate information:** Present your information in good old-fashioned journalistic fashion, with the most important info first and supporting info in the following paragraphs.

- ✔ **In-text links:** These links lead blog readers to landing pages where they can access the information or take the action mentioned in the post. (See Chapter 15 for information on landing pages.) Limit links to one for every 100 words of text. More than that looks a little spammy.

- ✔ **Calls for engagement:** These calls come in the form of newsletter sign-ups, RSS subscriptions, social sharing buttons, comment requests, invitations to participate in polls or answer questions, or any other simple request that prompts the interaction you seek.

- ✔ **Credit where credit is due:** If you've quoted someone or included shared content, cite your source, along with your thanks.

- ✔ **A blog post author byline:** Whether written by you or someone else, end the post with the author's name, title and contact information.

'Hello world. Meet my blog.'

Put 'Dan Schawbel Personal Branding Blog' into a search engine and you won't have time to view all the results. The blog Schawbel founded is, to use the coveted term, *highly optimised*. Dan's blog has been named the number one job blog by CareerBuilder and an *Advertising Age* top-30 marketing blog, and is syndicated by Reuters, Forbes, Fox Business and other major networks.

Here's an introduction from the blog's 'About' page:

> The *Personal Branding Blog* (www.personalbrandingblog.com) is

your #1 resource for personal branding online. It was founded on March 14, 2007, by Dan Schawbel, a world renowned personal branding expert. This blog teaches you how to create your career and command your future, using the personal branding process, as outlined in *Me 2.0.*

In 50 words, the introduction tells you who started the blog and when, why it exists, what it focuses on and how it benefits its clearly defined target audience. Come up with a similarly clear introduction and you're well on your way to growing your blog's subscriber base.

When you're done, proofread and proofread again. And finally, double-check that search engines are likely to find your post, which means using plenty of text, references to experts, outbound hyperlinks to respected sites and your physical location.

Measuring blog ROI

Blogging can be fun and personally gratifying, but it only works for your business if it delivers a *return on investment* (ROI) by developing leads, prospective customers and, ultimately, customer relationships.

To make blogging effective, start with a clear idea of what each post is to accomplish. After reading the post, what do you want people to do? If you want them to click to a landing page on your site, you can measure page traffic. If you want them to fill out a form and download an e-book or white paper, you can measure registrations and downloads. If you want them to share, easy enough – you can measure social media shares.

Know what you want blog post readers to do. Present a clear call to action. Then measure success by counting site visitors, completed lead forms, inbound links, e-newsletter or blog subscribers, social media shares or any other next step you invited readers to take.

Using blog posts as the backbone of your online content-distribution strategy

After your blog post is live on your site, repurpose and republish it to place it in front of more readers and to give people additional chances to see the information, because a good deal of content gets overlooked during a single post.

Automated plug-ins like `http://twitterfeed.com` automatically post your new content to Twitter. Here are some ways to repurpose your blog posts for subsequent sharing:

✔ Send out links to your blog post through your social networks, each accompanied by a short message that summarises an aspect of the content and why that content is interesting and relevant.

✔ Use Twitter to send out key points, subheads or interesting sentences, along with the post link, leaving plenty of space so others can add a short comment when retweeting. Take this step when the blog post is fresh, but also take this step weeks or months after the content posted on your blog to give it new life and to draw new visitors to your blog.

✔ Offer your post as a guest post on another blog. When approaching other bloggers, for guest posts or to generate publicity for your business, follow the advice in the nearby sidebar, 'How to approach other bloggers'.

To republish your blog posts, consider these ideas:

✔ Update and retitle content from old blog posts to give them new relevance, and then repost them on your site. By revising and republishing with a new angle, example or advice, old content becomes new, even to past readers. It also becomes valuable to those who may have missed the original post, which studies prove to be remarkably high numbers of blog subscribers. Just be sure that the update is significant enough that Google doesn't see it as a duplicate post, which works against you as you try to build search authority on key terms.

✔ Publish past blog posts in an e-book that you offer as an incentive for subscribing to your blog or newsletter. Make the book shareable and include a link back to your blog and the effort both amplifies the message of your posts and drives new traffic to your blog.

How to approach other bloggers

Bloggers are always on the lookout for good content that brings subscribers and readers to their sites, but they've no time – and even less tolerance – for marketers who request link exchanges, mentions or publicity without even bothering to get to know the blogger, the blog topic or the blogger's point of view in advance. The following is some advice for when you want to approach other bloggers:

✔ Read a good many posts on the blog you're targeting. Read the *About* page. Read the *Contact* section so you know that you're approaching the right person in the right way and following the requested steps.

✔ Make your message short, personal and tailored to the blogger you're approaching. If you cut and paste material and send it to a list of bloggers, you're on the wrong track.

✔ Introduce yourself, tell them why you're writing and present your request in a way that delivers value to the blog. Keep it brief and interesting. Say who you are and what you do, and provide links to your blog and website, both of which should be ready to make a great impression on your behalf. Don't include attachments.

✔ Make no assumptions. Don't assume the blogger is interested, and don't assume the blogger knows your business or product. If you're hoping to place a guest post, offer to submit a copy of the post for the blogger's consideration. (And make sure that what you submit fits the topic and tone of the blog and that it provides a point of view and expertise the blogger couldn't create without you.) If you're hoping to have information about your product included in a future post by the blogger, offer to send a sample of your product or even a number of products that the blogger may use in contests to build blog readership.

✔ Don't close your email with a signature that defines you as an SEO (search engine optimisation) or online marketer. Bloggers like to hear from bloggers, writers or other experts. And be sure to include a link to your blog.

✔ If you don't hear back, follow up with some kind of update and second request. The blogger may be swamped. The blogger may not have been interested when your email arrived. Your message may have ended up in a spam file. Be persistent. Be personable. Be positive. Be valuable.

Adding video to blog posts

Adding video to your blog does more than make your site more interesting. Doing so also gives you content to post on YouTube (www.youtube.com) – now the world's second-largest search engine – which helps you further boost your search rankings.

Here are a few ideas for videos:

✔ A Q&A or announcement from your CEO

✔ An interview with or testimonial from a customer

✔ A talk with an industry expert or leader

✔ A speech or presentation that people who couldn't attend may want to watch

✔ An interesting aspect of your operation

✔ A demonstration of your product in use or a new piece of equipment

✔ A how-to segment

✔ Introductions of new staff members

To prepare your video for online posting, keep these points in mind:

✔ Edit the video down to no more than a couple of minutes in length. Viewer completion rate for 30-second videos is extremely high, but after that point it plummets. Fewer than half of all viewers watch for longer than two minutes, so if your video features a call to action, be sure that it appears long before the point where most viewers click away. If you don't know what to cut and what to keep, slice out anything that's vague or trite and leave in anything that's surprising, unusual, humorous or new and different.

✔ Give the video a title that includes the keywords of your blog and of the video segment.

✔ Add a description that summarises the content.

✔ Add the video to your YouTube channel. If you don't yet have a channel, go to `www.youtube.com`, click 'Upload', and you reach a screen with instructions on steps to take.

Cross-Promoting Off-line and Online Content

When you or someone in your business makes a major presentation or generates news coverage, use your blog as the hub of a digital distribution service that amplifies and leverages the news.

Turning news into content

Each time you distribute a news release, rewrite the information in blog style using a conversational tone; incorporate links to any relevant photos, video or supporting resources; and post it on your blog. From there, you can push it out via social media, following the information in the earlier section on using blog posts as the backbone of your content-distribution strategy.

Don't know what to blog about? Make a list

On 4 January 1936, *Billboard* published the first Hit Parade. Decades later, vinyl records are antiques and the stars on the initial list are history, but Billboard still makes news with its roundups of chart-topping songs, albums, movies and now even ringtones. In other words, people like lists. If you can't think of what to blog about, offer your wisdom in the form of a list. Here's why lists work better today than ever before:

✔ **Lists make a clear promise.** In an over-communicated world, lists specify exactly what they offer: *The top five trends in blogging. Three reasons for inviting guest blog posts.* They tell journalists and consumers exactly what they're going to get, and they assure readers that the information is concise, organised and authoritative.

✔ **Lists get talked about, retweeted and reposted.** According to viral content experts, lists get retweeted at triple the rate of other posts. Plus, the words *top* and *ten* are among the most retweeted words. Need more incentive? Many people retweet without ever opening the link they're sharing, which makes the promise of a list head-line even more valuable.

✔ **Online users search for lists.** You've done it yourself if you've entered *top* into a search engine. Example: Top home-pricing tips.

✔ **Lists establish you as an authority.** When you blog about *top trends this year* or *five ways buyer preferences are changing,* you post unique, highly shareable information, and you establish yourself as a thought leader in the process.

When your news release results in media coverage, repost the information on your own site, in full or by breaking the piece into small segments that you precede with a summary introduction and end with a link to the originally posted content. Use the same approach to extend the reach of articles or blog posts you publish on other sites.

Giving long life to presentations

When someone in your company gives a major presentation, turn the event into content you can share online in any of the following ways:

✔ Turn the speech into a blog post that you feed out through social media and your e-newsletter, place as an e-article or offer as a guest post.

✔ Post a recap of the event, along with a list of questions people asked.

✔ If you presented slides, post it on SlideShare (`www.slideshare.net`), the world's largest community for sharing presentations. Simply click 'Signup' to establish a free account and then upload your presentation slides, video or documents for public or private sharing. Then post the link to the presentation in social media status updates.

✔ Embed your presentation on your website and blog, along with a keyword-rich title and description, so your visitors can view it without leaving your site and you can post social media announcements that feature the presentation link.

✔ If your presentation did an interview, post the audio or video on your site and then announce it via social media.

Be sure to add a call to action, inviting viewers to join your mailing list or to subscribe to your newsletter or blog to receive information on upcoming events. And always include 'share' buttons. Who knows, your presentation could go viral.

Part IV

Getting the Word Out with Ads, Mailers, Promotions and Publicity

Tell when news can be released

For Immediate Release

Start with place and date of release

For more information contact:
Barbara Findlay Schenck
BFSchenck@gmail.c

Provide name and contact information

...ZENS OF EXPERTS AND INTERACTIVE RESOURCES
...ATURE IN NEW EDITION OF BEST-SELLING SMALL
...USINESS MARKETING BOOK

Use a benefit-oriented headline

PORTLAND, OR, August 15, 2012 – After dozens of years and tens of thousands of copies sold, a third edition of *Small Business Marketing For Dummies*, now titled *Small Business Marketing Kit For Dummies*, is available in print and digital versions. The new edition features a CD-ROM, interactive elements, and advice from a ro... on everything from product innovation to social media to customer segment...

Lead with the major news points

Still directed exclusively at businesses with small budgets and cramped schedules, *Small Business Marketing Kit For Dummies*, 3rd Edition, features expanded advice on business and personal branding, all-new chapters on social media and blogging, and completely revamped instructions for generating publicity and customer interaction in today's screen-connected, linked, and blogged world.

For Dummies can help you get started with a huge range of subjects. Visit www. dummies.com/extras/smallbusinessmarketing for free bonus content, including forms designed to help your marketing efforts.

In this part . . .

✔ Load up with info on traditional marketing tactics.

✔ Get the inside track on new technology, new approaches and new marketing examples.

✔ Learn how to plan and buy ad space and time.

✔ Find out about direct mail – electronic or postal – as well as the value of brochures, promotions and trade shows.

✔ Discover how to place stories and manage news about your business to achieve mentions and visibility in online and traditional media outlets.

Chapter 13

Creating and Placing Print and Outdoor Ads

. . . .

In This Chapter

▶ Writing copy and choosing strong visual elements for your print ad

▶ Understanding print media terms and rates

▶ Running your ad in newspapers and magazines

▶ Advertising on billboards, signs, posters and sandwich boards

▶ Getting found in print and online directories

. . . .

*W*hen was the last time you opened the Yellow Pages?

If your answer is typical, it tells just how much directory advertising has changed over a few years. The year 2011 was a tipping point, when more people got their information from the Internet than from newspapers and when online advertising got most of the ad revenue as well.

Yet even though the numbers are declining, a YouGov survey in March 2013 revealed that 84 per cent of the UK population had read a printed daily newspaper in the past year, with readership highest in London (93 per cent) and the lowest in the Midlands (79 per cent) – free newspapers and magazines available at bus, tube and metro stations seem to make up much of this figure. However, almost a third (29 per cent) of young people aged 18 to 24 years old claim to have not read one at all, preferring online news instead. So, you better know your customers before you abandon traditional advertising altogether (turn to Chapter 2 for help in defining your customers). If you're advertising to an older age group, putting ink on newspaper is still an essential way to get your word out.

If your target audience is younger – especially the 18 to 24 age group – you may want to consider ruling out traditional newspapers in favour of messages delivered via web-connected devices and TV. Even then, plenty in this chapter is for you because the younger audience is a primary target for out-of-home ads (covered at the end of this chapter) and ads in highly targeted publications where your message can catch them while they're flicking through one of the thousands of special-interest magazines.

Writing and Designing Your Ads

In the best print ads, the headline, copy and graphics work together to capture attention, inspire the target market, promote the product's benefits, prompt the desired consumer action *and* advance the brand of the business that placed the ad. (For more about brands, turn to Chapter 7.)

Whether you create ads yourself with help from someone experienced in the fields of copywriting, design and ad production or you turn to pros who create ads for a living, use this section to understand the key steps in the print ad production process. From writing headlines and copy to making design decisions to preparing materials for reproduction by print media outlets, the upcoming pages highlight what you need to know.

Packing power into headlines

A *headline* is a print ad's major introductory statement. This statement is the large-type sentence or question that aims to stop readers in their tracks, target the right prospects and pull them inside the ad to read more.

Four out of every five people who see your ad read only the headline. Here's where the rest of the readers go:

- One reader sees your headline and moves on because he doesn't have time to study the details at the moment.

- A second reader sees the headline and rules herself out as a prospective customer because she doesn't want or need your product or service or because she can't afford what you're offering at this time.

- A third one finds your headline all that's needed to reinforce an existing (hopefully positive) opinion.

- A fourth one (should you be so lucky) finds the headline powerful enough to trigger the desired consumer action.

- A fifth one is stopped by your headline and inspired to dive into the ad copy to find out more. Oh lucky day!

Knowing the attributes of a good headline

Your headline has to pack marketing power. The headline is your only chance to communicate with 80 per cent of your prospects, and your hook for baiting the other 20 per cent into your ad. If a headline doesn't grab and inspire, your body copy doesn't stand a chance. Here's what your headline needs to do:

✔ Flag your prospect's attention by saying, in essence, 'Stop! This message concerns you.'

✔ Appeal to your target prospect individually and immediately.

✔ Promote an answer or solution to a problem.

✔ Convey a meaningful benefit.

✔ Advance your brand image.

As if the preceding weren't already a heavy load, the headline has to accomplish those things in words that people can read and grasp in five seconds. But even within that limitation, you've a little creative elbow room:

✔ Headlines can be short or long, as long as they're irresistibly compelling.

✔ They can sit at the top, in the middle, or along the bottom of the page.

✔ They can be a single word, a phrase, a complete sentence or a question.

Crafting your headline

Whether you write your headlines yourself or call on the talents of a professional copywriter or advertising agency, follow these tips:

✔ **Lead with your most powerful point.** Too many ads use a clever come-on for a headline and then divulge the benefit somewhere toward the end of the copy, where few people see it. Reverse the sequence. Create a headline that conveys a benefit or asks a question that can stop people in their tracks. Then use your copy to fulfil the interest you pique.

✔ **Turn features into benefits.** If you say that your product works at double the speed of competing products, you've stated a feature. If you say that the consumer can save the equivalent of two days annual leave, you've stated a benefit. If you add that the consumer gets an extra free bonus with every purchase, you've fuel-injected the message.

✔ **Make your headline easy to read at a glance.** Choose very legible typeface and think twice before using all capital letters, which are harder to read and, as a result, easier to overlook.

- **Don't end your headline with a full stop.** The last thing you want is to encourage the reader to stop at the end of the headline.

- **Be believable.** An old line about advertising goes, *If it sounds too good to be true, it probably is.* Beyond that, media ad departments screen ads and reject ones that advance deceptive messages.

Adding power to your headline language

As you take a critical look at the language you use to develop your headlines, consider the following advice:

- **Positive statements carry power.** Figure out the pain your customers want to eliminate and use your headline to promote a solution. For example, if your customers want to save time, tell them how your product allows them to work less. Offer an answer to their nagging problems.

- **Use compelling language.** After you settle on a headline, see whether you can push more impact into the words. For example, if your headline says *stomach,* ask yourself whether *guts* would pack more punch.

- **Find words that prompt mental images.** Instead of saying *reduce fear,* paint a picture by saying something like *eliminate white knuckles.*

- **Replace technical terms with words that most people understand.** Keep your headline simple, clear and free of jargon.

- **Use the word *you.*** *You* is the most magnetic word in advertising. Every time you get ready to write *we,* turn the spotlight to the consumer by using *you.*

- **Tell *how.*** People are attracted to the feeling of interaction conveyed by the word *how.* Write a headline that includes *how to . . .* or *how you . . .* to draw prospects into your ad copy.

- **Use power words.** A widely cited study by the psychology department at Yale University found that the most powerful English words include *you, results, health, guarantee, discover, love, proven, safety, save* and *new.*

Writing convincing copy

Copy is the term for the words that fill the body of an ad. Good copy talks directly to the reader. Its point is to connect and persuade. Instead of following the standard rules of grammar, copy is usually written to sound like how people talk. Copy is conversational yet crisp and, above all, convincing.

The first sentence of your ad copy only has to do one thing: Make the reader want to continue to the second sentence. The second sentence needs to lure the prospect on to the third sentence. And so good ad copy goes, carrying consumers through your ad, building credibility and trust and convincing readers of the merit of your message until, finally, the ad makes an irresistible offer and tells the prospect exactly how to respond.

As you lead prospects through your ad, aim to accomplish the following points:

- ✔ **Tell your basic story.** Provide enough information to convey what you're offering, the benefits that a buyer can count on and information that backs your claim.

- ✔ **Sweeten your offer.** Add a guarantee, special financing terms, trade-in opportunities, a promotional price or package, special options, a free or limited-time trial, or other incentives to increase consumer responsiveness.

- ✔ **Convey urgency.** Consider limited-time offers, promotions that reward only the first 100 respondents, or statements such as *while stocks last.*

- ✔ **Explain what to do next.** Don't assume that prospects know how to reach you or how to find your business, whether in person or online. Explain when and how to respond.

As you review your copy, imagine that your prospect is saying, 'Well, let me think about it; right now I'm just shopping.' Then add statements of value, action inducements, or other ideas to overcome prospect hesitation. But for each statement you add, look for one to delete. The cleaner you can keep your ad, the better. Flick through a magazine or newspaper to see for yourself. Does your eye linger on the ads crammed full of text or those with strong headlines, bold graphics and short blocks of copy?

If your ad includes prices, see Chapter 3 for advice on how to convey costs while inspiring readers.

Making design decisions

Advertisers, ad agencies and media outlets have spent enormous amounts of time and money to determine what does and doesn't work in the design of print advertisements. No pat formula exists – life in the marketing world isn't quite that easy – but when readers are asked which ads they remember positively, the following design traits emerge.

Adding visual appeal

Whenever you can, include an attention-getting visual element in your ads, following these tips:

- ✔ **Use art.** Ads with stopping power nearly always have a photograph, an illustration (a drawing, cartoon or other art) or both. The art may present the product, show the product in use or relate to the product by reflecting its characteristics through what's known as *borrowed interest,* delivered by art that serves as a metaphor for the product.

  For example, a restaurant ad may feature art of the entryway (the product), a photo of diners (the product in use), or an illustration of a sprig of rosemary or a bundle of herbs (borrowed interest reflecting the natural elegance of the restaurant and its recipes).

- ✔ **Let your visual *show* what your ad is about.** You don't have to be literal. An ad for housekeeping services could feature a mop, broom and vacuum cleaner. The ad may be more effective, however, if it communicates the benefit of more free time by showing a person in a bubble bath, feet propped up on the rim, open magazine in hand, in an immaculately clean setting.

Commissioning original photos or artwork ensures that your ads feature one-of-a-kind images. Another option that's often more affordable though usually non-exclusive is to purchase rights to use what are called *stock images,* which you can locate through an online search for 'stock photos and images'.

As you invest in artwork, consider buying rights to feature the image not only in ads but also in direct mail, on your website and in other venues that together leverage the image into a campaign symbol for your business.

Keeping it simple

Streamline your design to help readers focus on your ad's important points. Here are two ways to keep your ad design uncluttered:

- ✔ **Frame the ad with open space.** Isolate your ad from those around it while providing the visual relief toward which the reader's eye naturally gravitates.

- ✔ **Make the ad easy to follow.** If you imagine a big letter 'Z' placed over your ad space, you get a good idea of the path of most readers' eyes as they view ads. Design your ad accordingly, so readers grasp your message and see your name and logo before exiting your ad space. If your ad lacks an obvious focal point, or if two design elements compete for dominance, the reader is likely to pass over the ad altogether.

You see ads that break these basic rules, but unless your ad is in the hands of an accomplished designer, you're wise to keep its design clean and simple.

Knowing your type

Choosing the right type is an art that makes a tremendous difference in how your ad looks and, more important, how easy your message is to read. As you work on ad designs, you may find the following terminology helpful.

A *typeface* is a particular design for a set of letters and characters. For example, Garamond is a typeface. Helvetica is a typeface. Times New Roman is a typeface.

A *type family* is the full range of weights and styles available in a typeface. For example, you can stay within the Helvetica family and select bold, italic and light versions in a great number of sizes. Helvetica, **Helvetica bold** and *Helvetica italic* are all part of the Helvetica type family.

A *font* is the term used for a full set of characters (letters, numbers and symbols) in a particular typeface and size. For example, This font is 10-point Garamond. **This is 10-point Garamond bold.** *This is 10-point Garamond italic.*

Limit the number of typefaces and sizes that you use in an ad, unless you're intentionally trying to achieve a jam-packed or cluttered look (which may be the aim of a carnival promoter or a retailer announcing a giant warehouse clearance event). Additionally, follow this advice:

✔ **Headlines** need to be attention-grabbing, so designers usually choose typefaces that are capable of standing out while also communicating clearly. Choose *sans serif* typefaces, which have no decorative lines at the ends of the straight strokes in the characters. Probably the most popular sans serif typeface is clean-cut Helvetica.

✔ **Body copy** needs to be easy to read, so designers often opt for *serif* typefaces such as Garamond, Century Schoolbook, or Times New Roman because they have flourishes (serifs) that serve as connectors to lead the eye easily from one letter to the next. Avoid any font that's overly stylish or hard to read, avoid combining more than two type fonts in an ad and definitely avoid using type in sizes too small for ageing eyes.

Designing every ad to advance your brand

Small businesses have small budgets. Don't reduce your investment's impact by changing the look of your ads from season to season or, worse, from week to week. Here are a few ways to advance your brand:

✔ **Find an ad look and stick with it.** Settle on a recognisable format that readers can link to your name and brand. A consistent ad design gains you marketplace awareness and impact and also saves you time and money by eliminating the need to redesign every new ad.

✔ **Prominently present your name.** Huge advertisers can get away with postage stamp-sized presentations of their logos because their products and ad looks are so familiar. Small business budgets don't allow for that level of awareness, so make your name apparent in every ad.

✔ **When in doubt, leave it out.** This adage is good advice for do-it-yourself ad designers (and all other designers, too). As you consider tossing in an additional type font, different type size, ornamental border or any other design element, remind yourself that good design is usually the result of subtraction – not addition.

Translating ad production terminology

Even if you pay the pros to produce your ads, it helps to know the language of print ad design and production:

  ✔ **Ad proof:** This copy of your ad is the last thing you see before the presses run. When you review ad proofs, look closely at type set in all capital letters, which is where many typos slip through. Read your phone number twice and double-check your address. See that mandatory information (copyright lines, trademarks, photo credits and so on) is in place. Then hand the proof to the best proofreader in your organisation for a second review before you initial your approval.

  ✔ **Display advertising:** Print ads that combine a headline, copy, art elements and the advertiser's logo in a unique design are called *display* ads. All-word ads are called *classified* or *directory* ads.

  ✔ **Four-colour:** This term is the one traditionally used to describe full-colour printing, because (flash back to junior school art class) you can create all colours from the primary colours of blue, red and yellow (or, in printer terms, cyan, magenta and yellow). Before digital production, full-colour printing involved separating a photo into these three colours and then reproducing it by laying one ink over the next until the image matches the original. Black (the fourth 'colour') is used for type and other details

  ✔ **Spot colour:** Colour used to highlight an otherwise black-and-white ad.

Making Sense of Print Media Rates

Publications that accept print ads have a *rate card* that specifies pricing, deadlines and production requirements. Here are definitions of key terms:

  ✔ **Bulk or volume rate:** A reduced rate offered to businesses that commit to placing a certain amount of advertising over a contract period. Increased volume results in decreased rates.

  ✔ **Cash discount:** A discount for prompt payment. Reduce the cost of your media charges by up to 2 per cent by settling your bills quickly.

  ✔ **Closing date or deadline:** The date by which you must submit ad material to a publication if your ad is to appear in a certain issue.

✔ **Column inch:** A column inch is 1 column wide by 1 inch high. Most newspapers measure ad space in column inches, though once in a while you see ad rates quoted in *agate lines,* which equal ¹⁄₁₄ of an inch. Just multiply by 14 to arrive at the price per column inch.

✔ **Combination rate:** A discounted rate offered to advertisers who buy space in two or more publications owned by the same publisher or by affiliates in a syndication or publishing group.

✔ **Cost per thousand (CPM):** The cost of using a particular medium to reach a thousand households or individuals. (The 'M' stands for the Roman numeral designation for one thousand.) CPM also allows you to compare the relative cost of various media options.

The CPM formula: Media rate ÷ circulation or audience × 1,000 = CPM.

If a full-page newspaper ad costs $2,200 and the circulation is 18,000, the CPM is $122.22 ($2,200 ÷ 18,000 × 1,000 = $122.22).

✔ **Earned rate:** The rate that you pay after all discounts are applied.

✔ **Flat rate:** The cost of advertising with no discounts.

✔ **Frequency discount:** A reduced rate offered to advertisers that run an ad a number of times within a given period.

✔ **Local or retail rate:** A reduced newspaper ad rate offered to local or retail businesses. If you place ads in an out-of-town paper but sell your product through or in connection with a local business, see whether the business can place your ad or whether you can receive the local rate by mentioning the local business in your ad.

✔ **Make-good:** A no-charge repeat of your ad, which you can request if your ad ran with a publisher error or omission.

✔ **Open rate:** The highest price you pay for placing a particular ad one time with no discounts. Also called the *one-time rate* and the *basic rate.*

✔ **Pick-up rate:** A discounted price that many newspapers offer for ads that are rerun with no changes within a five- or seven-day period.

✔ **Short rate:** The amount you owe to the publisher if you don't earn the rate for which you contracted. If you sign a contract to run a certain amount of advertising but over the contract period you run less advertising than anticipated, you owe the publisher the difference between the contract rate and the rate you actually earned.

Placing Newspaper Ads

More opinions exist about what works in newspaper advertising than there are newspapers, and that adds up to a lot of differing ideas. Some advisers tell you to avoid the Sunday edition and the day that the supermarket store ads appear because those papers are crammed with ads and your ad can get lost in the chaos. Others counter with the fact that those big and busy issues are crammed with ads because they're the best-read papers of the week. Some people tell you to place clever, small-space ads with high frequency, and others advocate dominating the paper with big-format ads, even if you can afford to run them only on a few carefully chosen dates.

Most of the advice you hear is absolutely right – but only some of the time. So how do you proceed?

- ✔ **Know your target prospect** so that you can make an educated guess about which days and sections of the paper that person is likely to read.

- ✔ **Know your objectives** (see Chapter 8) so that you can select and time your ad placements accordingly.

- ✔ **Know how newspaper advertising works** so that you can prepare a schedule that takes advantage of media discounts. That's what the upcoming sections are about.

Scheduling your placements

Myths are rampant about which days get the most newspaper readership. The fact is, from Monday to Friday, the number of people who open their papers varies only a few percentage points, with Tuesday's paper outpulling the others because in most markets it carries the food ads. If you want your ad to generate results, heed these tips:

- ✔ **Place your ad on the day that makes sense for your market and message.** Here are a few examples:

  - • If your target prospect is an avid price shopper, don't miss the issues full of supermarket ads.

  - • If your target is a sports fanatic, advertise in Monday's sports section, where your prospect is reading the weekend recaps.

  - • If you're promoting weekend dining or entertainment, advertise in the Thursday and Friday papers and in entertainment sections – unless you're trying to influence prospects in out-of-town markets, in which case you'd better run your ad Tuesday and Wednesday to allow time to make weekend travel plans.

  - • If your ad features an immediate call to action (*Call now for a free estimate*), don't choose the weekend papers if you're not open to handle the responses.

- ✔ **Advertising in the Sunday paper usually costs more – and delivers more.** The number of single-copy sales is 10 to 40 per cent higher on Sundays than on weekdays. What's more, readers spend up to three times as long with the Sunday paper as they do with weekday papers, and Sunday's paper tends to have a longer shelf life. Even if your newspaper charges a premium for Sunday ad placements, calculate the cost per thousand and you're likely to find that the cost of reaching readers is cheaper on Sunday than on any other day.

Using small-budget, small-size ads

Even though more readers note full-page ads than half-page ads, and more note half-page ads than quarter-page ads, small-budget, small-size ads still pull their weight. They're the only way to go if you don't have the budget to run larger ads multiple times, because a one-time ad is incapable of building the awareness or recognition you need your marketing efforts to achieve.

Though partial-page ads pull fewer readers, the number of readers doesn't drop as fast as the cost of the space. For example, though a full-page ad pulls about 40 per cent more readers than a quarter-page ad, the quarter-page ad costs roughly a quarter of the price. As you work out a small-budget ad plan with your advertising salesperson, here's some general advice to follow:

- ✔ **If you have to choose, opt for placement frequency over ad size.** Plan the largest ad that you can afford to run multiple times and don't worry if the most you can afford is only a partial page.

- ✔ **Match your ad size to your message.** If you're opening a major new location, go for the biggest ad you can afford. But if you're promoting a £5.99 product, a big, splashy ad is likely overkill.

- ✔ **Aim to dominate the page.** Even partial-page ads can have a page-dominating effect. Span the width of the page with a ⅓-page horizontal ad. Or run a half-page vertical ad, which echoes the shape of a full-page ad and dominates the page as a result. Long, skinny, one-column ads that run all the way down the page also draw attention, especially if they're placed along the paper's outer edge.

- ✔ **If you're not the biggest, be the most consistent.** Ask your newspaper representative about a top-of-mind awareness (TOMA) programme that offers outrageous discounts in return for running your ad – however tiny – several times a week, 52 weeks a year.

Requesting your ad placement

Right-hand page, as far forward as possible is repeated like a mantra by print advertisers. But you won't find any solid proof that an ad on the right page of an open publication does any better than one on the left page, and the same can be said for other hallowed rules about ad placement. In fact, research shows that newspaper ads placed above the fold pull no more readers than those placed below the fold, and ads next to editorial content pull the same as those next to other ads. An ad's success depends on its content, not on its placement.

Create a strong ad, *then* decide whether you'll reach your prospects if your ad runs anywhere in the paper (called a *run of paper* or *ROP* placement) or whether you need to request – and possibly pay extra for – a *preferred position*. The following advice helps you make your placement decisions:

- ✔ **Make an 'if possible' request with your ROP ad placement.** Most papers do their best to honour reasonable placement requests that accompany ROP orders, at no extra charge but on a space-available basis. Ask for placement in the front section, sports section, business section or any other preference. But be willing to settle for what you paid for, which is placement anywhere in the paper. Most readers flick through nearly all the paper on a daily basis, and that's why most advertisers are confident rolling the dice with ROP ads.

- ✔ **Ask about special rates** for display ads placed in the property and classified sections, as well as in special interest supplements that target your specific market.

- ✔ **If your ad has a voucher, tell your ad representative in advance.** Request placement on an outer edge of the page for easy cutting out and in a position that isn't up against a coupon on the reverse side of the page.

- ✔ **Leverage your budget.** Work with your newspaper to arrive at a contract rate based on the nature of your business and your advertising volume. Ask about a contract addendum assuring that a certain percentage of your ROP placements is in a preferred placement.

Finding value in the classified section

The classified section is the bargain basement of the newspaper, and it just keeps getting smaller as more and more marketers move their classified ads online. (See the sidebar, 'The great ad flight to Craigslist and other online classified sites.') Still, if your market isn't Internet-savvy, classified ads can still pay off. Here's what to know:

- ✔ **Small-print classified ads** are typeset by the newspaper and arranged into interest categories.

- ✔ **Classified display ads** feature headlines, illustrations, special typestyles and advertiser logos. They're available in sizes smaller than those accepted in the rest of the paper, and they stand out on the otherwise all-type pages of the classified section.

The great ad flight to Craigslist and other online classified ad sites

Craigslist.org launched in 1995 and is now not only the largest classified site but also one of the most popular websites in the United States. Serving more than 700 local sites in 70 countries, Craigslist gets more than a billion page views annually. The offerings of Craigslist – and other online-ad sites, such as Monster.co.uk – have desiccated much of the income stream of newspaper classified departments, not intentionally but by the benefits they offer anyone selling anything to tech-savvy buyers.

On Craigslist, posting ads is free, except for job posts in select market areas, brokered apartment rentals in New York, and therapeutic services throughout the United States. Plus, posting ads is immediate, user-friendly, and customisable, with the option of including photos and messages that link to your website, which boosts the search ranking of the page your ad points to while also providing ad readers the information they need to self-qualify their interest before contacting your business directly. One more benefit: Online ads remain active until you take them down, unlike print classifieds, which often expire too soon or continue to run even after the product has sold or the job has been filled.

Classified ads follow many of the same guidelines as other print ads:

- ✔ Use a short headline set in boldface capital letters to draw readers in.

- ✔ Write your ad to talk directly and personally to a single target prospect.

- ✔ Avoid abbreviations unless you're certain that most people are going to understand them.

- ✔ Place your ad in a number of classified categories if it appeals to more than one interest area.

- ✔ Include your contact info and give the reader a reason to call – to request an estimate, find out the price, view the product, schedule an appointment or take some other action.

Placing Magazine Ads

When a full-page colour ad in a major national magazine costs hundreds of thousands of pounds, you may wonder why your small business should even bother considering magazine advertising. The reason is that thousands of special-interest, small-circulation (and vastly more affordable) magazines exist, as well as local, regional or even city newspapers and magazines in which you can place an ad for a fraction of the full-edition price.

Selecting magazines

The only magazine worth your ad investment is one that's consistently read by people in the target audience you aim to reach. Find out which publications your customers, prospective customers and those who influence your customers subscribe to or read regularly.

Beyond conducting customer research, also look into which magazines serve your industry or those in your target audience. Try searching the online databases available in your local or city library, especially the British Library Business and IP Centre in London and regional centres in Birmingham, Leeds, Liverpool, Manchester, Newcastle and Sheffield.

Scheduling placements

As you schedule magazine ads, consider the following:

- **Frequency matters.** Be sure that your budget is big enough to place your ad in the same magazine at least three times over a three-to-six-month period. Or, if you want to advertise during a single month, choose three magazines with similar readership profiles and run your ad in each one, building frequency for your message through *crossover readership* among publications. One way or the other, you need to reach your target audience multiple times to make an adequately strong impression.

- **Magazines have long lead and response times.** For example, if you're trying to inspire summer holiday business, you need to run your magazine ads well in advance of July and August in order to allow prospects time to read your ad, request information and make plans. Unlike newspaper and broadcast ads, response to magazine ads builds slowly and continues for months and even years.

- **Full-page ads dominate, but partial-page ads compete well.** Partial-page ads frequently share the page with other ads and end up toward the back of the magazine, but they also share the page with editorial content, which means that readers often spend more time on the page than they do with a full-page ad.

- **Concept and design make or break your ad.** If you're advertising in a high-quality magazine, *definitely* invest in professional copywriting, design and production to create an ad that represents you well in the highly competitive ad environment.

- **Success stories are built on frequent placements of small, well-designed, black-and-white ads.** If you can't afford the production and placement of a full-colour ad, run a small black-and-white or classified ad instead. Use the space to invite readers to *Request our colour catalogue, Visit our website,* or other invitations that lead readers of your small-space ad to a larger presentation of your business.

QR codes: Let customers point and shoot to reach your business online

Known as two-dimensional bar codes because they can be scanned side-to-side or top-to-bottom, *QR codes* (for Quick Response) are read by smartphone apps to decode and interpret a website address and use the phone's network to reach the corresponding page. Using QR codes is free for all involved. To get a QR code, just enter your site address into a QR code generator like `http://qrcode.kaywa.com` or `www.qrstuff.com`. To read QR codes, download one of the many QR scanning apps (or use the in-built scanner on your smartphone). To see how QR codes work, scan the code in this box with your smartphone and you'll go straight to my author page on Amazon. When using QR codes in your advertising, be sure that you send people to a mobile-friendly version of your site (see Chapter 10 for advice).

✔ **Work with magazine ad reps.** Explain your business, your desire to reach the magazine's circulation and your budget realities. If you have an ad that's produced and ready to go, ask to be contacted when *remnant space* (last-minute, unsold ad space) is available – usually at a fraction of the regular cost. Also enquire about regional editions or any other means of placing your ad at a reduced rate.

✔ **Take advantage of merchandising aids available to advertisers.** The magazine may have a *bingo card* that invites readers to circle numbers for additional information from advertisers. All you have to do is offer a brochure or other free item. You receive labels for all respondents – a great way to gather enquiries and build your database.

Also, ask for *tear sheets* mounted on boards reading *As Seen in XYZ Magazine* for display in your business.

✔ **Reprint colour ads for use as posters or direct mailers.** Maximize the cost and leverage the credibility of being a major magazine advertiser by turning the ad into promotional material.

✔ **Consider including a QR code.** Turn print media into an interactive tool that allows readers to scan and click to reach your website home page, landing page, online video, or other content referenced in your ad. See the nearby sidebar, 'QR codes: Let customers point and shoot to reach your business online'.

Considering Yellow Pages, Directories and Their Digital Alternatives

If your customers are the kind that lug the phone books that hit their doorsteps through the front door (and not straight to the recycling bin), then traditional Yellow Pages listings are important to your business. If your customers have moved their directory searches online, you should, too. The decision is really that easy. When it comes to Yellow Pages and other directory ads, go where your customers go.

But one way or another, be sure that your business shows up in whatever directories your customers use, online or offline. Otherwise, they won't find you at the very time they're most ready to buy.

Research conducted in 2011 by the Local Search Association found that

- ✔ Search engines are the top choice for consumers seeking local information, but Yellow Pages – in print or online – are most trusted.
- ✔ Consumers under the age of 34 are more likely to use online searches, while those over age 55 use print Yellow Pages and other traditional sources, such as newspapers, for local information.
- ✔ Rural residents and those with lower incomes tend to use print Yellow Pages more than suburban and urban consumers.

Most experts conclude that future usage will continue to slant even further toward online directories over print directories. And all agree that, regardless of how consumers seek information, being found in searches is absolutely essential, because after looking up a business, the majority of consumers make a business contact, and after contact, eight of ten make a purchase.

Creating and placing print directory ads

Before buying ads in the printed Yellow Pages or any of the independent directories pitching for your business, take two steps:

1. **Find out which books your customers use – if any.**

   Simply ask callers how they found your number. Admit that you're seeking their input as you determine which directories customers prefer.

2. **Ask the directory salespeople for proof of how their books are distributed and then do your own research to confirm that the books are reaching and being used by consumers.**

If you know owners of companies with ads in the directory, call to ask how well the directory worked. Or get old copies of the directory and compare ads in your category. If your competitors were in the book a few years ago and are out of it this year or in with reduced-size ads, the ads probably pulled less-than-impressive results.

If you decide to place ads, you've a few decisions to make:

- ✔ **Choose the right classifications.** Each category you add costs more money, so limit entries to sections your prospects are most likely to check.

- ✔ **Select the right size.** If you don't have many local competitors, you hardly need a large ad to stand out in your field. Also consider the nature of your competitive arena. In some business categories, the most established and respected firms run the smallest and most subdued ads.

- ✔ **Decide whether to add colour.** Study the section where your ad will run to see whether colour is necessary to compete on the pages. If you opt for colour, read the rate card carefully because colour charges vary from one directory to another but always mount up quickly.

- ✔ **Write the right ad.** Research shows that directory readers look for two things: a solution and a business they can trust. They also appreciate information, business hours and directions to listings of products or brands and professional endorsements and affiliations. But in a tight space, what you really need to present is your business name, an easy-to-read phone number and web address, and how to reach your street location. If your customers are tech-savvy, a QR code can lead them to additional information.

- ✔ **Keep your ad simple.** Then use a border to set it apart.

Don't accept the first directory ad price you're given. Directory ad prices are based on size, ad placement history and whether the ad you're placing is larger than in previous years. Tell the rep that you need to compare rates with other directory offers, and chances are good that your comments will be met by a better price. After you agree to a price, be sure to get it in writing, and *always* insist on a proof of your ad before the directory prints.

Getting found in online directories

To place free (and sometimes paid) ads with some of the big-name directory sites, start with the following websites:

- ✔ `www.google.com/local` (see Chapter 6 for help in establishing a free local business listing on Google Places)

- ✔ `www.yell.com`

✔ www.freeindex.co.uk

✔ www.thomsonlocal.com

✔ www.hotfrog.co.uk

Using Billboards and Out-of-Home Ads

Out-of-home ads include billboards, roadside signs, waiting room signs, wall murals, building or facility signs, vehicle signs, cinema ads, bus, metro or tube ads, digital kiosk ads and even flyover signs. Wherever prospective customers are likely to be standing, sitting, or waiting, you'll probably see an advertising opportunity, usually accompanied by the name of the company to contact for advertising information.

In the UK, a small number of companies (including CBS Outdoor, Clear Channel and JCDecaux) manage most of the outdoor ads you see in towns and cities, on the side of roads, bus shelters and inside metro, tube and train stations. Contact them to find out about available locations, costs and contracts. Or, when you see a billboard in a desirable location, look along the bottom of the sign for the owner's name and then call for availability and cost information.

In scheduling outdoor ads, a few key terms apply:

✔ **Circulation** is measured by the number of people who have a reasonable opportunity to see your ad or sign message.

✔ **A full showing** or *#100 showing* describes the number of boards necessary to reach 100 per cent of the mobile population in a market at least once during a 30-day period. A *half showing* (or *#50 showing*) reaches 50 per cent of the mobile population. Anything less than a *#25 showing* isn't considered adequate for an advertising campaign, although the placement of one or two boards may be useful as directional signage.

In placing and creating billboards, two truths prevail:

✔ **Location is everything.** Before buying an outdoor ad, drive by the ad site to be sure that the location is in an area that reaches your prospects and enhances your image and that the sign is lit for night-time visibility. Then, after your ad is posted, drive by it occasionally to confirm that lights are working, the installation is correct and that the ad is free of graffiti.

✔ **Ads must pass the at-a-glance test.** Most viewers look at an ad for five seconds, read seven words and take away two ideas – your name and the reason to buy your product. Use large, legible type with adequate spacing between letters, words and lines; strong colour contrasts; and graphics that people can see and understand in a flash.

For more affordable outdoor ads, look into tourist-oriented directional (TOD) signs (available through the local highways authority on local roads and Highways Agency if you want to place them on motorways or national trunk roads), vehicle signage (including magnetic door placards) and posters, which are becoming more and more affordable to produce. Just search for 'digital poster printing' to reach links to resources.

Finally, a walk down any high street confirms that sandwich boards and street signs are making a comeback. If you choose to go this route, be sure that you're in compliance with local authority guidance and follow this advice:

- ✔ Create a sign that reflects the brand and quality of your business image.

- ✔ Use colourful graphics, with highly contrasting colours to pull attention.

- ✔ Put a border around the sign so it doesn't merge into its surroundings.

- ✔ Highlight a special or a promotional offer to invite people inside.

Chapter 14

Broadcasting Your Message on Radio, TV and Online

*W*ith an estimated 26.8 million private domestic households (approximately 97 per cent) in the UK owning televisions, your customers are unquestionably tuned in to the broadcast world. Whether they're tuned in to TV ads or not is another question. Nearly all TV viewers skip the ads at least some of the time.

Still, research confirms that TV ads are the most memorable form of advertising. And few advertising channels can beat radio for delivering an immediate message to a targeted and often captive audience.

The drawback is that low-budget broadcast ads – especially TV ads – air alongside ads by mega-marketers who spend millions on slick productions that make locally produced ads look as cheap as, in comparison, they are. Furthermore, even the most frugal TV ad and schedule can break a small business marketing budget, and for that reason many small businesses rightfully cross TV advertising off the list of possible marketing channels.

Yet others – especially restaurants, retailers, campaign and event organisers, and those seeking to reach local audiences in small, relatively affordable market areas – consider broadcast advertising essential to success. If broadcast advertising is important to your small business, this chapter helps translate the lingo, guide production and placement decisions and leverage broadcast investments through website and social media placements.

A Guide to Buying Airtime

If you're placing ads on local radio or TV, you may be able to handle the task on your own but if your marketing is nationwide or if you're spending more than £10,000 on your media schedule, use a planner or media buyer to wheel, deal, apply clout and bring the kind of muscle that comes from experience in the field. (See Chapter 9 for help choosing and hiring professionals.) You pay a consultancy fee or a percentage of your overall buy, but you save time and confusion, and you almost certainly obtain a better schedule and price. If you use an advertising agency to create your ad, media planning and buying is usually part of the service.

If you're doing it yourself, begin by requesting a media kit from each station you believe will reach your target market. The media kit should contain the following:

- ✔ Audited research data, including statistical profiles of the age, gender and consumer-buying patterns of their audience
- ✔ Summaries of advertising success stories
- ✔ Sample advertising packages
- ✔ Rate cards

Use the media kit to confirm that the station reaches your target audience and also as a cost guideline. In broadcast, prices can vary depending on airtime availability, what times of day and year you air an ad and the size schedule you buy. To win advertiser commitments, some stations throw in added-value enhancements and bonus schedules. Ask and you just may receive.

Knowing some station and ad-buying terminology

Get acquainted with the following terms before talking with broadcast media representatives:

- ✔ **Area of dominant influence (ADI):** The area that a station's broadcast signal covers.
- ✔ **Availability:** Often referred to as an *avail,* an advertising time slot that's open for reservation.
- ✔ **Dayparts:** Segments of the broadcast day.

Radio time is generally segmented into the *morning drive time* (6 to 10 a.m.), *midday* (10 a.m. to 3 p.m.), *afternoon drive time* (3 to 7 p.m.), *evening* (7 p.m. to midnight) and *late night* (midnight to 6 a.m.). Drive times draw the most listeners and command the highest ad rates.

TV time is broken down into *breakfast time* (6 to 8.59 a.m.), *coffee time* (9 to 11.59 a.m.), *day time* (12 to 5.29 p.m.), *early peak* 5.30 to 7.59 p.m.), *late peak* (8 to 10.59 p.m.), *post peak* (11 p.m. to 12.29 a.m.) and *late night* (12.30 a.m. to 5.59 a.m.).

✔ **Flight:** A schedule of broadcast ads concentrated within a short time period. Ad flights create a level of awareness that generates a *carryover effect,* causing prospects to think that they just heard an ad even if that ad's been off-air for weeks.

✔ **Increments:** Stations sell ads in lengths – *increments* – of 10 seconds (written as *:10s* and called *tens*), 15 seconds (:15s), 30 seconds (:30s) and 60 seconds (:60s). The majority of all TV ads are :30s.

When buying radio time, :60s are usually only slightly more expensive – and sometimes no different in price – than :30s. If you opt for the longer ad, though, be sure that you can create an interesting, entertaining ad capable of holding listener attention for a full minute. The rule in radio is to use only as much time as you need to say what needs to be said. If your offer is easy to explain, a :30s may be all you need. Shorter ads (:10s and :15s) are used as reinforcements, rotating into a schedule to build frequency through short reminder messages.

✔ **Sponsorship:** Underwriting a programme in return for on-air announcements (called *billboards*) that tell the sponsor's name and tag line or brief message.

On commercial stations, advertisers can sponsor reports, such as the traffic update or the weather forecast, or they can sponsor public service announcements: 'This traffic report is brought to you by TomTom.'

On public broadcast stations, sponsorships are the major vehicle available to marketers. Financial planners, medical and legal professionals and others use programme sponsorships to gain awareness without looking promotional. When you hear, 'This programme is brought to you with the generous support of . . .', you're listening to a sponsorship billboard.

✔ **Spot:** The term *spot* has several meanings:

- The time slot in which an ad runs: 'We're going to run 30 spots a week in prime time.'

- The ad itself: 'We're going to produce three spots to rotate over a month-long schedule.'

- TV time purchased on specific regions rather than on an entire network: 'We can't afford a national spot on ITV for X Factor costing £1 million pounds but we can afford one in the much smaller Tyne Tees region for £2,500.'

✔ **Total Audience Plan (TAP):** A radio package with a specified number of ads spread throughout each of the dayparts. The station decides on the schedule, playing the agreed-upon number of your ads in each time period. Ads that run as part of TAPs are called *rotators*.

TAP programmes are usually the most affordable packages that stations offer. Still, negotiate the deal. Ask about weighting the schedule toward the dayparts when your prospects are most likely to be listening, or see whether the station will throw in additional spots to enhance the schedule. It's okay to beg – just don't get greedy!

Achieving broadcast reach, frequency and rating points

Reach is the number of people who hear your ad or, in the case of TV, the number of households that are tuned in when your ad airs. *Frequency* is the number of times that an average prospect is exposed to your ad.

The accepted rule is that a broadcast ad needs to reach a prospect three to five times before it triggers action, which usually requires a schedule of 27 to 30 ad broadcasts. Chapter 8 has more information about how reach and frequency work together in advertising schedules to put your message in front of enough prospects enough times to make a marketing difference.

If you have to choose, opt for frequency over reach. Instead of airing ads on ten stations (wide reach), choose two of the stations and talk to the same people repeatedly (high frequency).

Reach achieves awareness, but *frequency* changes minds.

How much is enough?

The age-old question among broadcast advertisers is how much and how often ads need to air. This is where rating points come to the rescue. A *rating point* measures the percentage of the potential audience that a broadcast ad reaches. If an ad airs during a time that's calculated to reach 10 per cent of the potential audience, then it earns 10 rating points.

Rating points are based on actual market performance, measured through surveys conducted by firms such as BARB (Broadcasters Audience Research Board) Nielson. The findings have a margin of error, but they remain the best way to compare broadcast audiences within a market area. Stations subscribe to the findings and share the numbers with advertisers as part of their sales efforts.

Gross versus target rating points

Gross rating points (GRPs) are the total number of rating points delivered by an ad schedule, usually over a one-week period. If you air 30 ads in a week, each reaching an average of 5 per cent of the total potential audience, your schedule achieves 150 GRPs.

Target rating points (TRPs) are measured exactly like GRPs, except that they count only your target audience. If your target market consists only of men age 35-plus, then your TRPs are measured as a percentage of the men aged 35-plus who hear or see your ad.

GRPs measure your *total* reach; TRPs measure your *effective* reach.

Most media planners agree on the following scheduling advice:

- ✔ **The rock-bottom minimum for GRPs is 150 per month.** If your budget can't cover a schedule with 150 GRPs over a month-long period, the effort likely won't be worth the investment.

- ✔ **To build awareness, schedule at least 150 GRPs for three months in a row.** You can divide your schedule into 50 GRPs every week or 75 GRPs every other week, but commit to a multi-month schedule if you expect broadcast advertising to result in awareness for your business.

- ✔ **Buy up to 500 GRPs per month to blitz the market.** For grand openings and major promotions, you need the kind of impact that only high-frequency broadcast buys can deliver.

You can make a broadcast buy without ever mentioning rating points, but you shouldn't. When a station rep offers to schedule, for example, 'Thirty spots at an average of £25 each', what are you really getting for your money? Follow up with a request: 'Would you calculate how many gross rating points that schedule delivers? Also, what percentage of the audience fits our target profile of (for example) men age 35-plus?'

Bartering for airtime

Barter is the exchange of merchandise or services instead of monetary payment for advertising time. For example, a restaurant may trade for ad time by catering a station's Christmas party, or a hotel may swap weekend spa break packages that the station can use in on-air competitions. Here are a couple of ways to barter for airtime:

✔ Trade a product or service that the station wants or needs – for its own use or for use in on-air promotions.

✔ Trade your product to a third-party business that then trades a like value of time or product to the station. For example, you trade £1,000 of plumbing services to a contractor, who then trades £1,000 of contracting services to a station's remodelling project. The station gives the contractor £1,000 of airtime, which you get as your end of the deal.

Unless you're making a direct trade with a station, bartering takes time and expertise. For assistance, search for barter services online or in the Yellow Pages or enquire with your media planner about making barter contacts.

When bartering, proceed with exactly the same care you'd exercise if you were making cash purchases of media time:

✔ See that the schedule delivers adequate reach and frequency.

✔ Verify that the station reaches your target audience.

✔ Be sure that the timing matches your marketing plan.

✔ Include an expiration date on product certificates you provide as part of your agreement. You don't want to end up paying for this year's advertising out of ad budgets in years to come.

✔ Try to leverage your budget. You may be able to trade for airtime at up to two times your product value, but even a pound-for-pound trade saves money over a cash buy because your product price includes profit.

✔ Be careful that on-air promotions involving your products are consistent with your business image and contribute to your brand's strength.

Broadcast Ad Guidelines

Whether you're producing a TV or radio ad, some general broadcast advertising guidelines apply. Later in this chapter, I outline best practices and advice for producing radio and TV ads specifically.

Establishing your own broadcast identity

Over time, you want listeners or viewers to recognise your business before they even hear your name. Consider the following identity-building techniques:

✔ **Voice-over:** Have one announcer voice all your ads.

✔ **Style:** Establish a broadcast ad style – for example, an ongoing dialogue between two people or ads that always advance a certain kind of message. (Want an example? Think of the 'I'm a Mac, I'm a PC' ads featuring David Mitchell and Robert Webb).

✔ **Music/jingles:** If you use music or sound effects, use the same notable background in all your ads. As for jingles, some people love them, some hate them and sooner or later, almost everyone tires of them. Before investing in a jingle, first be sure that you'll air enough ads to achieve an association between the jingle and your name. Second, the jingle must be appropriate to your brand image. Any station or studio can direct you to jingle producers.

Writing your ad

Don't write your own ad. Instead, put into words what you want your ad to accomplish, and then bring in professional help to develop your concept and write your script. Follow these tips:

✔ **Write a *creative brief* (see Chapter 8) that summarises whom you want the ad to talk to, what you want it to accomplish and what consumer action you want it to inspire.**

✔ **Develop an ad concept capable of grabbing and holding audience attention without distracting from your ad message.** This is where professional writers really earn their fees.

✔ **Grab audience attention in the first three seconds, before your audience heads to the refrigerator or another station.**

✔ **Tell a story.** In a 30-second ad, you've about 20 seconds to inform, entice and entertain – and even less if you cede time to a jingle or other sound or visual effects. The other seconds get divided between an attention-getting opening, your ad identification and a call to action. Be sure to do the following in your ad:

- Feature your name (or product name) at least three times.

- Feature your call to action, preferably twice.

- If you include an address, provide an easy locator (for example, 'Just across from the train station').

- If you want calls or website visits, present an easy-to-recall number or site address.

Turning your script over to the producers

When you need to begin production, radio and TV stations usually offer their services. Whether you take them up on the offer (and if you want a unique ad, you may not want to) or use an independent producer, follow these steps:

1. **Review the producer's work samples.**

   As you watch and listen to samples, ask yourself whether an ad enhances or diminishes your impression of the advertiser and the advertiser's commitment to quality. If you like what you see and hear, enquire about pricing, which, at station-based studios, is likely to be free or close to it.

2. **Obtain a budget.**

   Request detailed allocations for studio time, tape and materials, music fees, talent, editing time, ad duplication and other costs. Particularly, review the costs and usage restrictions for music, sound effects and talent, following these tips:

   • **Music and sound effects:** Studios have access to libraries of royalty-free or nominally priced music and sound effects, but always confirm costs and usage rights. Some rights are *outright* (you can air the ad wherever and whenever you want at no additional fee), whereas others cover only designated exposure and are *renewable* (meaning that you pay again) for further use.

   Never make the mistake of pulling favourite music from your personal collection for commercial use because whoever owns the rights can sue you for copyright infringement.

   • **Talent:** Your ad may involve an announcer and possibly actors as well. For locally aired ads, you'll probably use talent that the studio provides. If you use members of a union, such as Equity or The Actors' Guild of Great Britain, be prepared for higher rates, paperwork *and* more experienced talent.

   When using non-station talent or recording outside the studio, obtain talent releases. You should check with your production company and your solicitor or legal team to be sure that you're requesting appropriate releases for your project.

3. **Meet with the talent.**

   Before rolling tape or cameras, ask the talent to perform a dry run of the ad. Take time to correct the pronunciations of your name and products if necessary. Also, alter sentences that contain tongue twisters, and trim time-gobbling extra words. Then request another read to be sure that the ad sounds right and fits within the allocated time frame.

If you don't like what you see or hear, speak up. Announcers can adjust their voices to sound younger, older, happier, sadder – or as if they're talking to children rather than adults or to an individual rather than a group. A good director can handle the talent direction for you, representing your thoughts while adding professional expertise.

4. **Attend the editing session.**

   Editing is where money burns quickly. Make and approve decisions on the spot to avoid the need for a repeat session.

5. **Produce your ad and provide all stations with duplicate copies, called *dubs*.**

   Unless you intentionally create a series of ads targeting various audiences, don't allow each station to air its own version of your ad. Frequency works only when people hear the same ad repeatedly.

Review your ad outside of the studio with its perfect sound system and lack of interruptions. Sit in your car, preferably in traffic, or in your living room with all its distractions. Turn on your ad while others are around to see whether they stop to tune in. Turn it on halfway through to see whether it still presents a coherent message. Then review it a dozen more times to see whether it holds your interest without driving you to distraction.

Producing Radio Ads

In 30 or 60 seconds, a good radio ad grabs attention, involves the listener, sounds believable, creates a mental picture, spins a story, calls for action and manages to keep the product on centre stage and the customer in the spotlight – all without sounding pushy, obnoxious or boring.

Done perfectly, a radio ad is a one-on-one conversation with a single target prospect, written and produced so well that the prospect hears the introduction and says, in essence, 'Shh, be quiet everyone, I need to hear this. It's talking to me.'

Great writers *write out loud* when creating radio ads. Here's how:

- ✔ **Use language that's written exactly the way people talk.**
- ✔ **Write to the pace that people talk, not to the pace at which they read.**
- ✔ **Include pauses that give people time to think and the announcers time to breathe.**

- ✔ **Cut extra verbiage.** You wouldn't say 'indeed', 'thus', 'moreover', or 'therefore' if you were explaining something exciting to a friend. Don't do it in your radio ad, either.

- ✔ **Rewrite elaborately constructed sentences full of phrases linked together with *who, which* and *whereas*.** For example, instead of, 'The new fashions, which just came off the Paris runways, where they made international news, are due to arrive in London tomorrow at noon', go with, 'The newest Paris runway fashions arrive in London tomorrow at noon. You're invited to a premiere of the world's leading looks.'

- ✔ **Tell listeners what to do next.** Prepare them to take down your phone number ('Have a pen handy?') or repeat your number for them. Most important, help them remember your name so they can look you up later.

Don't waste radio time telling people to 'Look us up in the Yellow Pages'. Chances are good they don't use the Yellow Pages, and if they do, they'll probably find your competitors there, too.

Producing TV Ads

'I saw it on TV' has become a mark of having made it into the advertising major leagues. To get there, though, be prepared to make a financial commitment. Successful TV advertisers have two things in common: They earmark adequate ad production budgets and they fund media schedules that span at least a multi-month period. If you can do both those things – produce a quality ad and fund an adequate schedule – TV advertising can deliver awareness and credibility for your business.

You can reduce costs by airing ads on satellite channels at a fraction of the price of major station ad rates, but look long and hard to be sure that the stations you choose reach adequate numbers of the audience you're targeting. Also, remember that while the media cost of satellite TV is relatively low, your ad's production value still needs to be high enough to meet viewer expectations and to show well in this competitive advertising arena.

Do not create your own TV ad or marketing video. Bring in the pros, share your objectives, leave room for creativity and then evaluate their ad concepts and recommendations against the aims you seek to accomplish.

Why the insistence? Consider this: Your ad will play to an audience that has been trained to expect feature-film quality. To compete on a small business budget, you need a strong, simple ad concept and clean, well-edited visuals.

The first step toward making a good impression is to get help from those who deal in video productions daily.

Hiring professionals

As you select a creative partner for your ad production, refer to the advice in Chapter 9 and consider the following resources:

- ✔ **Advertising agencies:** If you want to receive major attention for a fairly small-budget project, interview small rather than large ad agencies.

- ✔ **Video production services:** Search online for 'video production services' and look for a studio that offers the full range of creative services, including scriptwriting, production and editing.

Airing pre-produced manufacturer ads

High-quality, ready-to-air ads may be available to you through your manufacturers or dealers. The ads feature the manufacturer's products, but they include time to add a tag line directing viewers to your local business. If you go this route, consider the following:

- ✔ Run manufacturer ads only if your business is the exclusive distributor or regional representative.

- ✔ Look into the possibility of obtaining the manufacturer's cooperative support in the form of shared media costs.

Considering Infomercials

Infomercials are programme-style ads that you come across when you're channel-surfing because you can't sleep. They promote housewares, financial and business opportunities, exercise and beauty items, self-help offerings, sports and workout equipment and such aptitude development products as memory enhancement and reading programmes. Oh, and psychic services.

Infomercials solicit viewer action in two ways:

- ✔ **Sales-generating infomercials** invite viewers to call free to place debit or credit card orders.

- ✔ **Lead-generating infomercials** ask viewers to call for free catalogues, brochures or other offers.

With a success rate as low as one out of four, infomercials are high risk.

Still, the topic of infomercials comes up among small business marketers in part because of the direct and measurable results that infomercials generate and in part because the ads look fairly straightforward and easy to produce. Looks can deceive, though. As with all other broadcast ads, viewers have been trained to expect a certain calibre of production value.

Products featured in infomercials have mark ups high enough to absorb the significant cost of creating and airing the infomercial. For example, if an infomercial product sells for £19.95, it probably cost only £4 to £6 to manufacture. The average national infomercial production budget is more than £150,000, though you can find video production houses that can create your infomercial for a tenth of that amount – or less.

Big budget or small budget, all infomercials promote products with broad appeal that aren't available through retail channels and that most viewers can afford to buy without great deliberation.

If infomercials are in your marketing plan, keep these success factors in mind:

- ✔ Make your product the star of the show. Describe its unique benefits, show how it solves a viewer problem and explain why people should believe in it. Never fake product demonstrations. It's illegal. Enough said.

- ✔ Use short sentences, short words and short segments, broken at least three times during the programme by your call to action.

- ✔ Use unscripted testimonials that allow past buyers to ad lib as they share their praise.

- ✔ Focus on selling, not on entertaining. Before airing the infomercial, be sure that you're ready with a call centre, a credit card merchant account, a shipping solution and a website that can handle the anticipated traffic.

Most viewers respond, if they're going to, after watching the infomercial only once, so evaluate the ad's effectiveness immediately after the first showing. If it draws a good response, re-air it to reach yet more buyers. If it doesn't, head straight back to the editing booth. Start with the first three-minute segment, which is the portion that grabs or loses most viewers.

Logging In to Webinars

Sometimes called *web seminars* or *webcasts,* a *webinar* is an event that a business or an individual hosts to address an audience that can be located anywhere that has access to online connections and phone lines.

In the context of advertising, webinars provide your customers or prospective customers valuable information through online presentations that help you achieve visibility in your field and a stronger reputation as a thought leader. They also help forge and deepen customer relationships.

To attend a webinar, participants log in via a web browser or web conferencing tool to view presentation visuals and to hear the webinar's audio portion, which can also be reached via a phone connection.

Some webinars simply share expertise. More often, though, they generate leads from those who listen in, like what they hear and follow up by joining mailing lists, requesting meetings or proposals, registering to download e-books or other content or taking other steps toward client relationships.

If you're thinking about hosting a webinar, consider these points:

- ✔ **Upside:** When you host a webinar, you can speak from anywhere, using a web conferencing tool or Internet browser to share audio and visuals, usually in the form of PowerPoint slides, with people who can log on from anywhere.

- ✔ **Downside:** The fact that almost no one likes the sound of the name *webinar* hasn't slowed webinars from becoming the content-delivery means of choice for those who want to establish themselves as experts and thought leaders. As a result, among invitees, webinars have acquired a ten-a-penny reputation. As proof, just go to a site like `www.webex.com/webinars` to see the number of free and fee-based webinars in dozens of categories.

- ✔ **Takeaway:** Expect your webinar to face strong competition for attendee attention. To succeed, you must

  - Know the audience you want to reach, including what problems they face and want addressed.

  - Decide on a topic that addresses a real problem that hasn't been addressed a million or a dozen times already.

  - Select a presenter who is great in terms of reputation, expertise and engaging style.

- Be prepared to announce and promote your event because no one is sitting around waiting for a webinar invitation.

- Host a terrific event by getting familiar with webinar-hosting tools like WebEX, GoToMeeting, GoToWebinar and AnyMeeting. As a cool new alternative you could also try a Google+ Hangout, which can be broadcast live and shared via YouTube.

- Record your presentation for post-presentation sharing and download, making up for what may be meagre attendance with what can be terrific leveraging of webinar content after the event.

Webinars require three implementation steps: planning, announcing and hosting your event. Turn to Chapter 18 for help preparing the webinar presentation and PowerPoint slides.

Chapter 15

Snail-Mailing and Emailing Your Customers Directly

In This Chapter

▶ Defining one-to-one marketing terms

▶ Setting up for direct sales

▶ Using direct mailers to market your product or service

▶ Creating and sending your mailers by surface mail

▶ Marketing through email

*T*elevision ads win awards and build awareness. Social media wins buzz and launches relationships. Direct mail wins customers and return-on-investment contests.

Direct mail is called *one-to-one communication* because it delivers your marketing message to carefully selected prospects and customers one at a time. One-to-one communication is the exact opposite of mass media advertising, which uses the shotgun approach – that is, you create an ad and use newspapers, magazines and broadcast media to spread the message far and wide. One-to-one communication aims your message only at specific and well-defined individuals.

Most marketers believe that the two approaches work best in a tag-team arrangement: You use mass media advertising to build awareness, desire and perceived value for your products, and then you use one-to-one marketing to call for the order.

If you can only afford to do one or the other, however, consider placing your bets on the one-to-one marketing approach, aiming each pound you spend straight at qualified prospects rather than scattering your budget through mass media to reach prospects and non-prospects alike.

Using One-to-One Marketing

When you employ one-to-one marketing, you bypass mass media vehicles and take your ad straight to the letter boxes, telephones and computer screens of individuals who are prime prospects for your product or service. You may hear the terms *direct marketing, direct mail, direct-response advertising* and *database marketing* used interchangeably in discussions about one-to-one marketing, but they each represent different aspects of the direct marketing arena. For the record, here are definitions of those terms and others:

✔ **Direct marketing** involves a direct exchange between a seller and a buyer, without the involvement of retailers, agents or other intermediaries.

✔ **Direct mail** is the primary means of direct marketing communication. It involves sending promotional announcements in the form of letters, postcards, packages or emails directly to targeted prospects.

✔ **Direct-response advertising** announces a promotional offer and invites consumers to respond directly to your business – by phone, in person or by clicking a QR code to reach a landing page on your website – to make a purchase or obtain additional information.

✔ **Database marketing** entails compiling detailed information about customers and prospects and then using the data to match and send specialised offerings to consumers in different *customer segments,* based on the demography, interests and values of customers in each group.

✔ **Direct sales** are purchase transactions that occur directly between a buyer and seller. Mail order and e-commerce are the primary vehicles for direct sales. (See Chapter 10 for information on e-commerce.)

✔ **Telemarketing** involves communicating with prospects and customers over the telephone –by *inbound calls* made by consumers to telephone numbers that they see in ads, sales materials or online, or by *outbound calls* made by a business to the homes or offices of target prospects.

Be aware that most people hate outbound telemarketing calls so much that almost 19 million phone numbers are registered on the Telephone Preference Service (TPS) – a central list of UK consumers who have opted out of receiving marketing calls. Companies are legally required to screen their outbound marketing lists against the TPS before making cold calls (see www.tpsonline.org.uk).

Direct Sales: Do-It-Yourself Distribution

The name says it all: Marketers who employ *direct sales* strategies sell to consumers directly, without involving middlemen, retailers, agents or other representatives. Instead, they use direct response ads, direct mailers, catalogues and e-commerce (see Chapter 10) to communicate one on one with prospective buyers.

Below are a few examples of how direct marketing tools can generate direct sales for small businesses:

- **Direct response advertising:** A jewellery maker advertises his wares by placing small, black and white magazine ads. But instead of aiming to build general awareness, the ads invite readers to call a free-phone number to purchase the featured item or to visit the jeweller's website to view and order from his complete line. Either way, the instructions in the ad lead straight back to the jewellery maker and not to any retailer or other intermediary.

- **Direct mail:** The self-publisher of a book featuring lists and ratings for summer youth camps promotes the book by sending direct mailers to a subscriber list rented from a major parenting magazine. She also works with bloggers and uses social media and online ads to build a network of inbound links to the page of her website featuring the book for sale.

- **Catalogue distribution:** A kitchen accessories company generates direct sales by mailing its catalogue to the households of current and past customers, ad respondents and subscribers of gourmet magazines.

The Direct Marketing Association warns against two big direct sales land mines: non-delivery of merchandise and misrepresentation of offers. Every year a few direct marketers hurt the reputation of all by implementing programmes that fail to communicate honestly or to deliver the products as promised. If you sell directly, protect your own reputation and the reputation of all who participate in direct marketing by following this advice:

- **Be clear, honest and complete in your communications.** Your ad *is* the shopping experience for direct buyers, so make it thorough and consistent with what the customer sees when the order arrives. Make sure that your ad accurately describes your product and represents your price, payment terms and extra charges. Don't make outlandish claims and don't make promises that defy belief or that you can't live up to.

- **Describe the commitment involved in placing an order.** Decide how to handle returns and communicate your policy in your marketing materials.

Be aware that laws exist that enforce honesty in direct mail marketing. If you promise 'satisfaction guaranteed' (or if you make a money-back guarantee), regulations mandate that you give a full refund without question and for any reason. If you offer a risk-free trial, you can't charge the customer until the customer receives and is satisfied with the product. If you don't plan to refund a customer's money under any circumstances, your marketing materials must state, 'All sales are final'.

✔ **State the estimated time lag between order receipt and product delivery.** If the average order takes four weeks for delivery, avoid complaints and concerns by informing customers of the delivery time frame in your marketing materials and when they place their orders.

✔ **Get good customer data.** Your success relies on clear customer input. Whether online or in printed direct sales materials, provide detailed instructions on how to submit customer and payment information.

✔ **Describe payment options.** Cash, debit or credit card? (Research shows that credit card privileges increase response rates, so plan your policies accordingly.)

✔ **Keep track of consumer questions and complaints.** If, in spite of your best efforts, your ads result in misunderstandings, pull and revise them.

Marketing with Direct Mailers

All direct mailers, regardless of look, message or purpose, are alike in one way: They go straight to your prospects' letter boxes or inboxes rather than reaching them through mass-media broadcast and print ads.

Setting up for success with direct mail

Direct mail is among the easiest of all marketing communications to monitor for success. With each mailing, you know exactly how many pieces you're sending and therefore how many prospects you're reaching. And because direct mailers almost always request an easy-to-track direct response (in the form of a sale, an enquiry, a visit to your business, a click or some other prospect action), within days (for email) or weeks (for surface mail), you can count the responses to determine the effectiveness of your direct mail effort.

Most successful direct mailers incorporate these factors:

✔ **A targeted list:** To be great, a direct mail list must reach genuine prospects for your product or service. (See Chapter 2 for help in creating a prospect profile.)

✔ **A compelling offer:** The *offer* is the deal – the catalyst to which the consumer reacts.

✔ **An attention-getting format:** Some mailers involve nothing more than a regular or oversized (*jumbo*) postcard. Others involve only a good sales message in a white envelope or an email message. Some are elaborate packages that contain samples and other enclosures (including brochures, CDs or product samples). Just be sure that your approach is consistent with your company's brand image (see Chapter 7) and capable of conveying your message and meeting your marketing objectives (see Chapter 8).

Deciding between email and 'going postal'

Email tends to dominate conversations about direct mail, largely because email is so immediate and inexpensive. But don't write off the benefits of direct mail sent by surface post, primarily because you can send what's now called *snail mail* to new prospective customers, while email to strangers falls into the dreaded (and illegal) category of spam.

For a look at the differences between using surface mail or email to send direct mail, see Table 15-1.

Table 15-1	Differences between Sending Direct Mail by Surface Mail and Email
Surface Mail	**Email**
Is often considered junk mail	Is often considered and blocked as spam
Arrives in a letter box with less mail than in previous years	Arrives in an increasingly crowded inbox
Can be sent to all prospective target prospects	Can be sent only to those who have opted in or had previous contact with your business
Typical response rates are 3 to 4 per cent when mailings go to those on your house list of customers and prospects, and lower when sent to rented lists of people who match the profile of your target audience	'House lists', which can include only established customers or those who have opted in to your mailings, result in open rates of around 20 per cent and conversion rates just under 2 per cent

(continued)

Table 15-1 *(continued)*

Surface Mail	Email
Can be used for reaching new prospects	Can be used for making offers to established contacts who have opted in to your list
Great for presenting photos, visuals or samples	Great for conveying messages that prompt recipients to click for more information
Great for sending material with a 'keeper' quality	Great for immediate response offers such as 'register now' or 'download now'
Costs time and money to produce and send	Can be produced and sent immediately and with little expense, and can be used to test and quickly alter headlines or offers

Making your offer

Good mailers make great offers that relate to – and build credibility in – your product or service. They're also unique, valuable and attractive.

Don't use your existing promotional materials or items emblazoned with your company name or logo as your offer. People get promotional material for free daily, and they certainly don't want to take the time to respond and ask for it unless the material is extremely unique or exclusive.

A good offer contains the following elements:

- ✔ **A great deal:** This deal may be a free sample or gift, a trial offer, a special price, an event invitation or special payment terms, depending on the objective of your mailer and the nature of your product. In crafting your offer, be aware that the word *free* pulls more responses than discounts or other price offers.

- ✔ **A guarantee:** To improve results, offer an assurance that working with your business is risk-free and reliable. For example, extend a money-back guarantee, a delivery guarantee or a service guarantee. And keep your promise – for good business purposes and for legal reasons.

- ✔ **A time limit:** This limit increases interest and response, even if the deadline is only implied (such as 'Please reply by December 15').

Table 15-2 shows how a public relations agency that's seeking to build relationships with CEOs might weigh offers as bad, better and improved.

Table 15-2	Examples of Direct Mail Offers	
Bad Example	*Better Example*	*Improved Example*
Invite the CEO to request a free brochure featuring case histories of agency success stories.	Invite the CEO to request a free guide featuring advice on 'How to Write News Releases and Manage Media Interviews'.	Invite the CEO to specify how many free copies of 'How to Write News Releases and Manage Media Interviews' she would like you to deliver.
Why?	*Why?*	*Why?*
A brochure is a promotional piece, and this 'offer' asks the CEO to take time to request the kind of thing that other companies send out on a routine basis.	This free resource delivers a benefit to the recipient. It contains advice that public relations professionals usually sell by the hour. It also addresses the CEO's needs.	The CEO has a good reason to respond to this offer. It promises a valuable and unique item. Because only the CEO knows how many copies her company can use, the response request has meaning.

Don't go overboard with your offer. Remember that your goal is to receive *quality* responses. If your offer is *too* great, it will generate responses from people who simply want the deal.

Personalising your mailer

The best mailers are, above all, personal. (The opposite of a personalised mailing is one addressed to *The Occupier* or *Resident*.) You can personalise your mailer in a number of ways:

✔ On envelopes you can use what look like handwritten addresses. (Computers and mail-house technology automate this seemingly arduous task.)

✔ On printed letters you can personalise the salutation line, and on email messages you can personalise the subject line, so long as you're absolutely certain that you know you're using the recipient's name correctly. If you're not sure, don't guess and don't worry; the jury is still out on whether personalised subject lines lead to higher open rates.

✔ In letters and email messages, you can boost response rates by customising your message to indicate awareness of the recipient's location, past purchases or past interactions with your business. For example, a vet can send patients reminders about a pet's history, or an estate agent can include information on homes in the recipient's local area.

No matter what, don't make your mail look like bulk mail by using an awful catch-all greeting such as *Dear Friend* or, worse, *Dear Valued Customer.* If your mailing is too extensive to allow for personalised greetings, replace the salutation with a headline.

Putting Surface Direct Mail to Work

With all other forms of advertising, you send messages through media channels matched to your market profile in general, but with direct mail, you aim your marketing investment precisely at those prospects who possess the exact characteristics that make them likely to buy from your business.

Developing a great list

Most surface direct mail programmes involve one of the following types of lists:

- **Demographic lists:** These lists include addresses for people who match the age, profession, household income and other lifestyle aspects of those most likely to purchase your products.

- **Geographic lists:** These lists include addresses for people who live in the cities or postcode areas that match your market area.

- **Geodemographic lists:** These lists include addresses of individuals in your targeted geographic market area who also match the demographic attributes of your prospect profile. For example, a geodemographic list might target prospects in a specific postcode area who live in homes assessed at £300,000 or more.

You can create your own list, called a *house list,* by using your customer contacts as well as the names and addresses of prospects that you collect from other sources. Or you can choose to invest in *outside lists* from mailing service businesses and organisations, professional associations, magazines or other list owners.

Creating your own house list

If you market in a local or clearly defined market area, you probably want to create your own list. As you go about assembling the names for your list, follow these steps:

1. **Include your established customer and prospect base.**

   Begin with the names of current customers, obtained from sales records, requests at the time of purchase or loyalty programme enrolment, or through competition entries and other forms. Then add the names of those who have expressed interest by responding to your ads or in other ways sharing their names with your business.

2. **Turn to local business and community directories.**

   For example, a golf club that's seeking to build its membership numbers might create a mailing list that includes golfers in the target market area who have golfed as guests or in tournaments at the club, along with the names of all target market business CEOs. It may also form strategic partnerships with a local hotel to acquire names through a joint promotion.

3. **Enter the names into a database.**

   For this task, you can use database software, use the mail or data merge programme in your word processor or employ the resources of a professional database manager to keep your mailing list organised. (See the sidebar 'Using mail specialists' later in this chapter.)

4. **Segment names according to geographic location, demographic profile, past purchasing patterns or lifestyle interests.**

   By segmenting your list, you can send tailored messages that match the interests of people in portions of your overall list.

Finding and renting good outside lists

Mailing services, printers and list brokerage businesses can assist with list development or list rental. Define your target audience by stating where your most likely customers reside and who they are in terms of age, income, family size, education and other lifestyle factors (see Chapter 2). Then turn to the following resources for lists that suit your needs.

For publication subscriber lists, contact ad representatives at publications that serve your industry or market area to find out about list availability, prices and terms. Ask each publication if it breaks down its subscriber list into interest or geographic segments. If so, you can rent a portion of the list to reach only those subscribers who are most likely to respond to your offer.

Suppose you're marketing a new travel bag. You can start by contacting a travel magazine to enquire about buying access to its subscriber list. But if your bag won't appeal to *all* subscribers, you can ask about ways the list can be *segmented.* You may be able to target your mailer geographically by obtaining names only for subscribers in, say, the South West. Or maybe you can send your mailer only to subscribers who list home addresses. (This eliminates the names of travel agents and others who receive the magazine in their offices.) Furthermore, you may be able to purchase a list segmented by subscriber income level or even by the type of travel the person prefers. You're on your way to a list tailored to your prospect profile!

Using mail specialists

Mailing services go by many names: *direct response specialists, bulk mailers, database managers, mail processors* and *list managers*. They provide professional assistance in the following areas:

- Merging, updating and maintaining databases, including deleting duplicate addresses, standardising addresses and inserting postcodes, carrier routes and delivery-point bar code information

- Pre-sorting your list by computer to qualify for the lowest possible postal rate

- Addressing envelopes with inkjet technology; label printing and affixing

- Folding, inserting and sealing direct mail packages

- Packaging, sacking and delivering mailings to the post office

- Generating postal reports and certification reports

For the names of direct mail specialists, search online for *Mailing Lists* and *Mailing Services UK.*

If you decide to obtain lists through mailing services and list brokers, search the Internet for *mailing list brokers uk* to reach the sites of businesses that provide pre-assembled or customised lists for use in direct mail programmes.

When renting a list, note the following:

- You pay from £50 to several hundred pounds for one-time use of 1,000 names – and more for targeted industry and business lists.

- You need to rent a minimum number of names (list owners usually require minimum orders well into the thousands).

- You're required to conduct your mailing following the list owner's specifications. Most owners insist on handling the mailing from within their own operations or through a recognised, bonded mailing service to protect their list's value and to ensure against multiple use or resale of names.

- Let list owners review and approve your mailer before you send it to the names on their list.

To improve the quality of your list, consider renting two lists that reflect your prospect profile and then combine them (called a *merge/purge* operation). Names that appear on both lists are your best prospects. A golf resort may obtain the names of golfers age 35 and over living in a targeted metropolitan area *and* the names of homeowners of target market properties assessed at £500,000 or more. After merging and purging the lists, the resort has a better chance of reaching people with the interests *and* the financial abilities to match the resort's customer profile.

When you purchase labels from a list owner, you're *renting,* not buying, the names. Don't try to use the list beyond the scope of your agreement or to duplicate the labels for additional mailings. The list usually includes 'plants' that tip off the list owner to misuse. After you conduct your mailing, however, individuals from the rented list may respond to your company for more information. From that point on, you may market to these respondents.

Creating your mailer

The best mailers feature the following materials and information:

- ✔ **A clear offer:** Feature the offer on the envelope, the letter, the letter's postscript and any additional enclosures.

- ✔ **A free response mechanism:** Allow the customer to respond at no expense, whether through your website, a free telephone number or a pre-paid envelope or postcard. Be sure to collect complete customer data, including an email address, allowing you to later invite the person to opt in for future digital communications.

- ✔ **A reply card:** Some people prefer to mail in their responses, even if you also invite a response through a toll-free number or web address. On your reply card, give people a chance to say yes or no. Doing so may seem counterintuitive, but giving them the chance to decline your offer increases the chance of them accepting it. To save money, contact your post office or a mailing service for help obtaining a business reply mail permit. That way you pay only for the responses you receive rather than paying to place a stamp on every reply card you enclose.

- ✔ **A letter:** People may tell you that no one reads the letter or that the letter just gets in the way of other enclosures, but they're wrong. Unless your mailer takes the form of a postcard or self-mailer, the letter is an essential ingredient of direct mail.

Sending your mailer

The Royal Mail website at www.royalmail.com/marketing-services-occasional offers a range of tips and advice on planning, designing and delivering your direct mail through their network.

The following are tips for sending mailers:

- ✔ For a small mailing, you'll probably find it easier to skip pre-sorting and simply stamp and send your mailers.

- ✔ For larger mailings, a mail service provider can help you select postal services and handle many of the details and much of the legwork.

✔ To handle your own large mailing and to qualify for commercial pricing, be prepared to do your own pre-sorting, meet postal regulations, apply for postal permits, complete all required documentation and follow all the instructions for labelling, packing and preparing your mailing.

Meeting postal regulations

Mailers must match precise dimensions in order for post office equipment to process them. Before printing your mailer, visit your post office or check online to make sure that your mailer conforms with regulations.

Take particular care when it comes to your mailer's address panel. Postal equipment reads addresses using high-tech, postal character-recognition equipment. If your recipient address doesn't appear in the correct place on the envelope or if other design elements intrude on the space, your mailer may take longer or cost more to process.

Specifying postal instructions

When you send bulk mail, you can include instructions, or *endorsements,* that tell the post office what to do with mail that's undeliverable as addressed. Without an endorsement, returned items are thrown away.

An endorsement reading *Return Service Requested* instructs the post office to return the piece with the corrected address or the reason the mail was undeliverable. The item isn't forwarded, but you have the information you need to update your list. You can also instruct the post office to discard the piece but notify you of the new address (*Change Service Requested*) or to forward the piece (*Forwarding Service Requested*).

Each endorsement results in an additional charge, so base your instructions on the price you're willing to pay for the service, your confidence in the accuracy of your list and your mailer's value. If you're sending a valuable gift in each mailer, you probably want to request return service.

Following up

Half of all responses arrive within two weeks of the date that people receive a direct mailing in their mailbox, but keep your expectations in check. A 1 to 3 per cent response rate is considered a success with a purchased or outside list. If you use internal lists that are full of highly qualified names, you can hope for a higher return.

Responding quickly

Don't wait even one week to get back to your direct mail respondents. If you don't think that you can handle the volume of responses in a timely manner, send your mailers out in *flights* – groups of several hundred every three or four days. Doing so ensures that the responses are staggered as well. Do the following in your response:

✔ **Thank the respondent for the enquiry.** Many people forget that they sent in a card, so refresh their memories.

✔ **Provide the item that you promised in your initial mailing, along with a description that highlights its value.**

✔ **Introduce your business in terms of benefits that matter to the consumer.** See Chapter 8 for advice on how features and customer benefits are different.

✔ **Offer the next step in the buying process.** Include an introductory offer, invitation, discount voucher or some other means to heighten interest in an effort to convert the prospect into a customer.

Creating a database of respondents

After fulfilling the request, enter the respondent's name into a database for timely future contacts. Within eight weeks, contact prospects a second time by mail, phone or – if they've invited you to do so – an email newsletter or update. (See the later section 'Email Marketing' for reasons *not* to send unauthorised email messages.)

As you enter names into your database, include

✔ The source of the lead

✔ The date of the first and each subsequent contact

✔ The respondent's name, mailing address and email address

✔ Information that can help you customise future contacts (such as the answers to questions that you asked on your reply card)

✔ Additional space in which you can log follow-up activity

If your business has a limited number of prospects, you can maintain this database manually. But if you're managing a larger number of leads, consider using a Customer Relationship Management (CRM) software or a database management company.

Sending a second mailing to non-respondents

Within 30 days of your first mailing, contact recipients who haven't yet responded. (If you're using an outside list, rent the list for two-time usage and obtain a duplicate set of labels for this purpose.)

Research proves that following up with non-respondents increases your overall response rate dramatically. Doing so also gives you much more value for the cost of the list rental because the second-time usage is usually a fraction of the cost of the initial usage. You can also make the second-round contact via email or phone. With any approach, your objective is to build on the first contact and move the prospect closer to buying action.

Keeping your list current

Surface mail address lists become outdated at a rate of almost 2 per cent a month. To keep your list current, follow these steps:

✔ Request address correction information from the Royal Mail. Make the request by including an endorsement on your mailer (see 'Specifying postal instructions' earlier in the chapter).

✔ When renting mailing lists or using mailing services, ask whether the lists have been updated against the National Change of Address (NCOA) database that is managed by the Royal Mail.

✔ Confirm the interest levels of those on your list. Every 12 or 18 months, give prospects in your database a chance to opt out of their relationship with you. It may sound crass, but disinterested prospects aren't prospects at all – they're simply a marketing expense.

When adding an opt-out option on your reply cards, consider these examples:

• 'Yes, send me whatever great offer you're making in this mailing.'

• 'I'm not interested at the moment, but please keep my name on your list for future invitations.'

• 'No, I'm not interested right now. Please remove my name from your list with the promise that you'll welcome me back in the future if my needs change.'

Knowing the difference between direct mail and junk mail

Direct mail becomes junk mail when consumers feel that the offer isn't personal. For example, a high-rise apartment resident who gets a mailing for landscaping services automatically determines that the mailing is junk mail. Timely and targeted messages that communicate information and offer good value, however, aren't considered junk mail. As a direct mail marketer, your job is to toe the line.

Email Marketing

It's only partly coincidental that the preceding section on junk mail is followed by this section on email marketing. The sequence isn't meant to imply that email mass mailings *are* junk mail, but a good many of them belong in the junk mail category, and for legal and marketing reasons, you want to be sure that yours don't.

You also want to be sure that your email messages get opened trigger clicks, not just to your website but to a landing page where you're ready to capture contact information and fulfil interest with no additional navigation required. This section outlines best practices to follow.

Spam: Is it or isn't it?

For the one in millions who may not know, *spam* is the term for electronic junk mail that's sent to a large number of email addresses. None of the addressees requested the information, and most of them feel invaded when they find the messages in their inboxes. Spam is the opposite of opt-in mailings and something to avoid at all costs.

What's more, it's illegal. In the UK (and EU) two main anti-spam laws exist – the Data Protection Act UK and the Privacy & Electronic Communications Regulations (PECR). In a nutshell, these laws make it illegal to send an unsolicited marketing message electronically to an individual unless their contact information was acquired in the course of a sale or 'the negotiations for a sale'.

Furthermore, you must always include the option to opt-out of future marketing messages at the bottom of each email and it must be easy to do so. For further information on spam, take a look at the Information Commissioner's Office (ICO) website at www.ico.org.uk.

Keeping your email legal and welcome

The unanimous advice from reputable online marketers regarding unsolicited email is this: *When in doubt, don't.* Instead, commit to an opt-in policy and limit your email marketing messages to the following recipients:

- ✔ Those who have opted in by providing their email addresses and asking for more information. In fact, many email marketers now use a double opt-in system that allows a person who opts in to confirm (or deny) the decision by responding to a first email.

- ✔ Friends, colleagues, suppliers, customers or prospects who have requested similar information in the past.

- ✔ Those who were referred to you by a colleague or by a group related to your business with the assurance that they'd appreciate receiving your information.

Don't publish lists of your carefully collected email addresses on your site. You've probably seen company sites that include customer lists, event sites that post participant lists, or athletic event sites that post finish results, including names and email addresses. Opportunistic mailers cruise the Net looking to cherry-pick from lists like these.

Also protect your customers by hiding their addresses when you send the same email to a list of recipients. To maintain the privacy of each recipient, enter your own address in the 'To' line of your email and enter all recipient addresses as *blind carbon copies* by using the *BCC* address option.

Many Internet service providers won't allow you to email more than 50 people at a time, and breaking a large list into groups can be far too time-consuming. Instead, search online or in your market area for email marketing services. Providers such as Constant Contact and MailChimp are among many that offer safe, simple solutions, mailing advice and analysis of mailing results.

Rating your email marketing

Email marketing efforts are evaluated based on the following terms, each involving the word *rate:*

- ✔ **Bounce rate:** The percentage of undeliverable addresses that bounce back to the sender because the address doesn't exist (a hard bounce) or the person's inbox is too full or otherwise unavailable (a soft bounce).

- ✔ **Delivery rate:** The percentage of mailers that actually make it through to recipients' inboxes.

✔ **Click-through rate (CTR):** The percentage of recipients who click at least one link in the mailer, indicating their interest in the message.

✔ **Sharing or forward rate:** The percentage of recipients who click to forward or share the email with others – the next to highest indicator of a successful mailer.

✔ **Conversion rate:** The percentage of recipients who take the recommended action by filling out a form, subscribing to a newsletter, downloading a publication or purchasing your product – the ultimate direct mail success indicator.

✔ **Unsubscribe rate:** The percentage of recipients who ask to unsubscribe to your mailer. Honour unsubscribe requests quickly, and watch which mailings trigger the most unsubscribe requests, indicating a lack of interest in your message. At the same time, however, also watch which mailers have the lowest open rates, because many disinterested recipients don't even bother to unsubscribe – they just hit 'delete,' pushing your open rates downward.

Sending email that gets read and gets results

Few marketing environments are less tolerant of intrusion than the email inbox. When you're confident that your email is welcome in recipient inboxes, use these tips – to make each mailing effective:

✔ **Extend a meaningful offer** that you announce in your subject line, explain in your message and extend through your call to action.

✔ **Send your email from a real person or from your business instead of** an anonymous sender like info@ourcompany.

✔ **Use a short subject line** (five to seven words) that headlines your mailer, draws attention and builds recipient interest. Remember:

• Use your subject line to alert recipients that the message is aimed specifically at them. For example, 'Calling All Mac Users in Headingley' is far more targeted than 'Sale Computer Prices'.

• Keep the presentation of your subject line simple, with upper-lower case type, widely understood words and absolutely no asterisks, symbols, exclamation marks or the use of £, all of which trigger recipient suspicion – if your message makes it past spam filters.

✔ **Personalise your mailings** by using the recipient's name or indicating knowledge of the recipient's location, past purchases or other distinctions that flag the mailing as a directed message and the opposite of spam.

✔ **Keep your message simple and easy to read at a glance.** Use up to ten lines of plain text broken into multiple paragraphs or bulleted lists, with few or no images, because most decision makers view email on mobile devices, which don't load images well. If images are important, consider including a link to an HTML web version of the message.

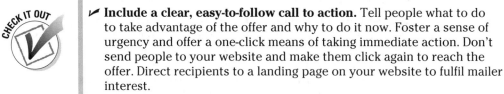

✔ **Include a clear, easy-to-follow call to action.** Tell people what to do to take advantage of the offer and why to do it now. Foster a sense of urgency and offer a one-click means of taking immediate action. Don't send people to your website and make them click again to reach the offer. Direct recipients to a landing page on your website to fulfil mailer interest.

✔ **Include an email signature** at the end of every message to present your business information, physical address and phone number, website address, email confidentiality statement and promotional information such as a newsletter subscription invitation.

✔ **Include a 'share this' button** so recipients can post your offer on social networks, along with a 'forward to a friend' button to let friends invite friends to take advantage of your offer.

Chapter 16

Brochures, Promotions, Trade Shows and More

- -

In This Chapter

▶ Producing and distributing brochures and sales literature

▶ Writing and circulating newsletters

▶ Getting creative with other marketing opportunities

▶ Exhibiting at trade shows

▶ Hosting promotions that work

- -

Mass media advertising and direct mailings are the most obvious ways to promote your business, but the communications toolbox includes a long list of other effective communication vehicles. Brochures and flyers, free giveaway items known as *advertising specialties,* product promotions and trade show appearances are all means of bypassing traditional advertising as you carry your message into the marketplace.

Most of these alternatives come with low price tags, so many small businesses use them with a nothing-ventured-nothing-gained-or-lost attitude. But even though large sums of money are rarely at risk when you print a stack of flyers or order pens imprinted with your name, your reputation is still on the line. This chapter offers advice so that every marketing investment you make – however large or small – works to your advantage while contributing to a favourable image of your business.

Publishing Brochures

People who aren't professional marketers hear the word *collateral* and think of the assets you have to pledge when you're trying to get a bank loan. To marketers, though, collateral means brochures, flyers, fact sheets, sales folders, posters and all the other forms of printed material that carry your logo, message and reputation into the marketplace.

Of all forms of collateral, you hear the most talk about brochures. It used to be that every business had a brochure. Even today, when most people turn to websites for business information (if you don't have one, see Chapter 10 pronto), most marketers feel naked without a printed piece that they can hand out. Few, though, can say *why* they need a brochure – and many don't.

You need a brochure if

- ✔ You don't use the web.

- ✔ Your business would benefit from a printed piece that you can send ahead of sales presentations to pave the way for your visit or that you can leave afterwards to help the person you met with share key points about your business with others who may influence the purchase decision.

- ✔ You're trying to communicate with individuals who aren't easily or affordably reached by mass media but who are likely to pick up literature at information kiosks or other distribution points.

- ✔ Your service or product is complicated and involves details that your prospects need to study in order to make informed decisions.

- ✔ The price of your product and the emotional involvement demanded by its purchase are high enough that prospects will consult with advisors, associates or spouses before making the decision, in which case they benefit from a brochure that conveys your message in your absence.

Before you decide to produce a brochure or any other form of sales literature, see that you can answer yes to these questions:

- ✔ **Do you have an adequate budget?** Can you allocate enough money to create a publication that makes a favourable impression of your business?

- ✔ **Will the publication strengthen your image?** Can you commit to designing, writing and printing a quality, image-enhancing piece?

- ✔ **Do you have a distribution plan?** Do you know how you're going to use the publication? Sales material does no good sitting in a cupboard or the boot of your car.

Differentiating types of brochures

Sales literature can range from elaborate folders filled with sets of matching fact sheets to flyers and laser-printed cards that sit on counters or in racks. This section helps you sort through the opportunities.

✔ **Capabilities brochure:** This 'about our business' piece tells your story, conveys your business personality and differentiates your offerings from those of your competitors. If you're marketing a professional service business (such as a law firm, accounting firm, financial services firm or some other consulting business) or a business that offers high-emotion products (such as a home builder or a car company), this type of brochure is a marketing necessity. It gives prospects and customers a tangible piece to review as they deliberate their decision or, post-purchase, reinforce their positive thoughts about your company.

Capability brochures are among the most expensive kinds of brochures to produce, so give yours a 'keeper' quality. A financial planner may include a net worth asset worksheet; a home builder may include a checklist for how to get the most value out of a new build or renovation budget. The goal is to give prospects a reason to hold onto and refer back to the piece.

✔ **Product brochure:** This piece describes a specific offering of your business. This kind of brochure is important when marketing products that require more than spur-of-the-moment consideration, such as those with high prices, those purchased with input from more than one person and those that involve cost and technical comparisons before a buying decision takes place.

✔ **Modular literature:** This involves a number of sheets or brochures that all use a complementary design. This format allows you to assemble a package of easily updated individual pieces that you can mix and match inside a presentation folder or hand out individually, depending on the interests of your prospect and the impression you want to make.

A modular format is a great approach if your business offers a range of products that you can represent on separate marketing pages, if your price lists or other information change frequently or if your prospects have widely differing interests or needs. Just be sure that all pieces look like a matched set when they're viewed together but that each one is capable of serving as a stand-alone piece when presented separately.

✔ **Rack cards:** These cards get their name from the fact that they fit into standard brochure racks that hold 4-9-inch literature. Some rack cards involve nothing more than a 4-9-inch card printed on one or both sides. Others take the form of a single, folded sheet that opens up to a multi-panel brochure. Still others include a number of pages folded and stapled down the middle (called *saddle-stitched*). Many businesses create inexpensive rack cards by printing the same image three times on an 8½-x-11-inch sheet of paper (*3-up* is the printing term), which they then cut into three cards of 3⅔ x 8½ inches.

The most important thing to remember about rack cards is that only the top few inches are immediately visible to the consumer. The rest is hidden under the brochure that sits right in front of yours in the rack. So be sure that your name and a message announcing your customer benefit appear in that small, visible top space.

✔ **Flyers:** The least expensive promotional piece you can print is a flyer, which usually takes the form of an 8½-x-11-inch sheet of paper printed on one side or both to announce a sale, open house or limited-time event. In producing a flyer, write copy that people can understand at a glance (remember, a flyer is a throw-away piece, so don't expect people to hang on every word). Design it following the advice for creating a print ad in Chapter 13.

On a good printer or at a quick-print shop, you can run off a thousand copies for little money. For the investment, flyers usually look like what they are – low-cost handouts. The calibre of design and copy, the quality of paper and printing and the way you get your flyers into circulation, however, can enhance the image they make.

Copywriting

The best brochures talk directly to your target audience, anticipating questions and providing answers before the reader even thinks to ask. Good brochures win your prospects' attention and interest and move those people a step closer to a buying decision.

Put differently, your brochure isn't about what you want to say; your brochure is about what your prospective readers want and need to know in order to take the action you want them to take.

Your brochure text, called *copy,* needs to cover the following:

✔ **A headline and subheadlines** that convey at a glance what your business is, what it does and how it provides unique benefits that address the interests of your target readers.

✔ **Copy that talks directly to customers** by using widely understood language that's similar to the way you would talk with them directly if you could – by answering their questions and addressing their solutions as if you were meeting face to face. For example, 'Tired of the rising cost to heat your home? We can help. Here's how.'

✔ **Statements that convey the competitive advantages of your business.** Don't present these advantages as boastful statements but rather as facts that customers can count on and benefit from, including important licenses, registrations, patents, processes, awards and achievements.

✔ **Client lists and testimonials that allow satisfied customers to speak on your behalf.** Feature only statements that are believable (nothing is worse than testimonials that seem scripted) and for which you've obtained permission in writing to use the quotes with attribution.

✔ **A clear call to action.** A brochure is a marketing tool. It needs to compel prospects to take the next step in the purchase process, whether you're aiming to prompt reservations, appointments, phone calls, business visits, website visits or requests for additional information. Use your brochure copy to lead the consumer to the desired decision and then support your request with all the necessary information.

For example, if you're asking for phone calls, include your phone number on every page. If you're encouraging website visits, give a reason to visit and prominently display your site address (and social media details), possibly with a QR code that readers can scan to reach your site quickly (see Chapter 13 for the lowdown on QR codes). If you want visits to your office, shop or showroom, including your hours of operation, a street address, a map and directions is a no-brainer.

Arrange your copy to address customer interests in this order: first, identify the customer's problem; second, describe specifically how you can help; and third (and never first), talk about you.

After you write your copy, don't send it off to print until it's been proofed multiple times. Proof it yourself and have the best writer on your staff proof it. Have a great friend or best customer read it. Proof it for typos, of course, but also for credibility and persuasiveness.

Even if your brochure is intended for new customers, be sure that it rings true to those who know your business well. Brochures are read most carefully by people who are ready to finalise or who have just completed a purchase. By writing your brochure with committed consumers in mind, you minimise the tendency to oversell and instead focus on the benefits and promises that customers believe they can count on from your business.

Designing and printing brochures

Only a few years ago, design decisions revolved completely around budgets. You could afford professional printing or you couldn't. The same either-or option held true for printing brochures in full colour over black and white and for using photos rather than easier-to-reproduce illustrations.

Today, between your own colour printer and an ever-growing list of online brochure-production resources, design decisions centre less on what you can afford and more on what image you want your brochure to convey. Effective brochures contribute to a positive image of your company by presenting a design and message consistent with the reputation and brand of your business (see Chapter 7 for more information on developing your brand).

For top-quality printing of highly customised brochures, local printers are still the top choice. But for producing standard-sized brochures on tight budgets, online resources are increasingly the way to go.

Open a search engine and type in 'brochure printing online uk' to find sites that allow you to use brochure templates or to upload your own customised brochure design file. You choose the quantity, pay the surprisingly affordable price and receive your order within days.

For a quick comparison of using local printers versus online services, see Table 16-1.

Table 16-1	Local Printers versus Online Printing Sites
Local Printers	*Online Printing Sites*
Customised printing of your original design	Printing from your uploaded brochure design file or from your choice of a range of templates, not only for brochures but for all forms of printed sales material
Convenient location close to your business	Online service with lower pricing due to the lack of bricks and mortar overhead
Personal service from people familiar with you and your business	Convenient access online whenever and from wherever you wish, sometimes but not always backed by personal assistance
Your choice of paper and design features, including unusual sizes, folds, cuts and special effects	A range of templates, sizes and papers from which to choose
The option of extremely quick turnaround, for a price	Quick turnaround plus shipping time
Assurance of a completely original piece	Templates can result in brochures that lack originality or reflection of your business and brand image

In the design and printing phases of creating your brochures, consider the following:

✔ Match the quality of paper, printing and design to your brand image, your marketing message and your brochure purpose.

✔ Be sure that your business name and contact information are prominent on the brochure back. For rack brochures, be sure that your name is visible along the upper portion of the front cover. For multipage brochures, include contact information on every single page or two-page spread.

If you don't have design skills within your company, don't risk trying to create your own brochure. Even customising a template involves an eye for design and a level of production skill. Invest in the talents of a graphic artist or choose a print shop that provides design assistance so you end up with a unique piece that reflects your business and message.

Getting brochures into the marketplace

Great brochures can't address customer questions or strengthen your company's image if they're sitting in a storage room, so don't hoard them.

Printing the first brochure is the most expensive. After that, you're paying only for ink and paper, so print enough brochures to ensure that you won't feel a need to protect your supply. Then follow the steps below to get them into circulation:

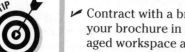

✔ Send copies to customer, media and industry contacts.

✔ Send a copy in advance of face-to-face meetings so that your prospect gets a sense of you before meeting you.

✔ Contract with a brochure distribution service to maintain supplies of your brochure in brochure racks such as those in visitor centres, managed workspace and anywhere that potential customers may be.

✔ Use your brochure as a step in your sales process, sending a copy, along with a customised letter, as a follow-up to in-person meetings and as a way of staying in touch with pending prospects.

Making the Most of Newsletters

Unlike brochures, which deliver marketing messages to target audiences, newsletters are informal, friend-to-friend communications. They reach customers and those who've indicated an interest in your business with newsworthy information, useful updates, reminders of what your business does and interesting, helpful ideas.

Newsletters can accomplish the following for your business:

✔ Build credibility and reputation

✔ Provide a means of frequent communication

✔ Deliver news from your company and your industry

✔ Answer questions, usually through a question-and-answer column

✔ Offer tips that enhance your company's credibility while also building customer confidence and loyalty

✔ Share profiles of employees, customers and success stories

✔ Convey industry information (with permission, of course)

Planning your newsletters

Newsletters work only when they're distributed on a consistent basis, which means that you have to commit to the long haul before you produce the first issue. As you make your decision, consider the following:

✔ **Define the purpose of your newsletter.** Who is it for? What does your target audience need and want to know? What kind of information will you share? Know what you expect from your newsletter before you design or write the first issue.

✔ **Establish how often you'll produce and send your newsletter.** How often are you and your staff able to get a newsletter assembled and distributed? How often is your customer interested in hearing from you?

✔ **Determine your initial mailing list.** You may start with a list that includes customers, prospects, suppliers and other business friends. Then grow your list by featuring a free newsletter subscription invitation on your website and in direct mailers and other marketing pieces.

✔ **Decide how you'll deliver your newsletter.** How many will you send, and how often? Are you going to handle the task in-house or hire assistance from writing, design and mail service pros? Will you print and send the newsletters by surface mail or produce digital newsletters to send by email? Work out the costs and be sure that you can afford to commit to the project for at least a full year.

Packing newsletters with useful content

Here's great news for small budget marketers: The most effective newsletters look inexpensive, newsy and current, which translates to the fact that newsletters are among the most economical of marketing materials.

Whether you're creating printed or digital newsletters, consider the following points:

✔ **Stick with a simple format issue after issue.** The more your newsletter looks like a highly designed marketing piece, the less it looks newsy.

✔ **Feature many short items rather than a few long ones.**

✔ **Include invitations that require reader response to deepen customer relationships and to help you gauge the effectiveness of your newsletter.** For instance, if you announce a new product, offer to provide trial samples on request.

✔ **Include valid dates when presenting time-specific offers.** Prospects may read printed newsletters – in particular – well into the future, long after your offer has expired.

✔ **Use your newsletter to promote reasons to visit your business or website.** For example, a holiday resort mayinclude this item:

Our new online reservation service is off to a great start. More than half of our visitors click to view room photos and floor plans, and 38 per cent of those who view our property online make a reservation request. If you haven't visited our site lately, go to www.ourhotel.com. Be sure to enter our online prize draw for a free weekend stay. Also, if you'd rather receive our newsletter electronically than by post, just click the e-newsletter request icon and we'll transfer your mailing information to our confidential electronic file. Either way, we look forward to sending you quarterly updates, special packages and resort news.

✔ **Combine sales messages with news updates so that readers view your newsletter as more than a promotional mailing.** For example:

Short break holidays to Newcastle and Gateshead continue to rise in popularity, based on the number of telephone, email and website enquiries received by the Newcastle Gateshead team in 2012, which were up 22 per cent on the previous year. For advice on where to stay and to get the best offers visit www.newcastlegateshead.com.

✔ **Prominently feature your business identification and contact information.** On printed newsletters, include your logo, phone number, mailing address, email address and website address on every page of every issue to encourage communications. On digital newsletters, include your street address and phone number so people can follow up in person.

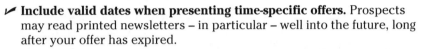

Microsoft Office features a library of free, downloadable templates you can use when producing printed newsletters. Go to http://office. microsoft.com/en-us/templates/results.aspx?qu=newsletters.

For help producing digital newsletters, see the advice from widely recognised e-newsletter expert Michael Katz in the sidebar, 'Tips from a gargantuan, elephantine fan of e-newsletters'.

Tips from a gargantuan, elephantine fan of e-newsletters

Michael Katz, the founder of Blue Penguin Development, is the guy executives at Constant Contact, one of the biggest names in email marketing, refer to as an e-newsletter legend. Others refer to him as an e-marketing genius. He calls himself a gargantuan, elephantine fan of e-newsletters, for good reason. His Solo Professional E-Newsletter has 6,500 subscribers in more than 40 countries. Here's his advice for e-newsletter success.

Why e-newsletters work: They keep you in front of clients, prospects and colleagues and give you a platform for sharing your focus and perspective. Plus, they're easily forwarded, easily archived, interactive and cost almost nothing.

What makes an e-newsletter work:

1. Content matters most. Publishing is easy. Sending content that makes people want to stop what they're doing is more challenging – and the only way to gain permission to stay in the inbox.

2. Stay focused. Don't try to cover lots of topics and involve lots of voices. Keep your focus narrow and write to a specific target audience.

3. Newsletters only work if you keep sending them. Establish a monthly schedule and commit to a year of publishing so you don't give into the 'four-month itch' – the point at which enthusiasm wanes just before newsletter results start to show.

Mistakes to avoid:

1. Don't write a 'Me-Newsletter' full of items about what you're doing, who you're working with and why you're so wonderful. Give readers useful information, not promotion.

2. Don't strip away personality in an attempt to sound professional – and dry and boring. Drop the jargon. Write in the first person. Use a casual voice and tone to talk about things you really believe in.

Information to include: Don't worry about selling to readers. Instead, teach them. Include valuable information, and when there's a need you can fill, your phone will ring.

Coming up with content: If you know enough to run a business in a given industry, you've a lifetime of content. Those who buy your products and services will always be novices, so use that gap between your expertise and their interest in finding out more to guide your content development.

Bottom line: E-newsletters work only if the recipients want to hear what you have to say. Develop a reputation as a source of useful, interesting, unbiased information within your area of expertise and you expand readership and your customer base, too.

For more information, visit `http://michaelkatz.com` to sign up for a free bi-weekly newsletter, access site resources and explore a number of e-newsletter assistance programme options.

Producing and circulating e-newsletters

People subscribe to online newsletters because they want

- ✔ Work-related news from their employer or business organisation, or news pertaining to their personal interests and hobbies
- ✔ News about prices, sales and special offers
- ✔ Advance notice of upcoming events

The key word is *news*. Keep your newsletter current, informative, relevant and to the point. Also keep the language casual – as if you're talking one on one – and easy to skim through in a matter of seconds.

Formatting your e-newsletter

The first rule of newsletter production is to know the purpose and frequency of your newsletter and stick to what you promise to provide. The second rule is to create a newsletter that's easy to open and read on the greatest number of screens, including mobile devices, where most executives and others now get their email.

Using plain text in your newsletter makes it easy to assemble and easy to open on all devices. Using HTML is more complicated, but it allows you to present colours, fonts and graphic images and to track the rate at which recipients open your mail or click through to links. HTML comes with some cautions, however. For one thing, spam filters sometimes block all-HTML email messages or HTML messages with a heavy images-to-text ratio.

If you opt for an HTML format, consider these tips:

- ✔ Make life easy by typing your newsletter into a pre-formatted template, available through email services or findable through an online search for 'free email templates'.
- ✔ Consult a web designer to set up at least your first issue.
- ✔ Contract with an email marketing service such as Constant Contact, which offers information and a trial offer at `www.constantcontact.com`.
- ✔ Send your newsletter in both HTML and plain-text formats so people can read it one way or the other. As an alternative, set up your newsletter opt-in form so that people can choose the format they want to receive at the time they subscribe.

Companies such as Constant Contact and MailChimp provide attractive, customisable templates on their websites that you can format without a working knowledge of HTML.

Following opt-in rules when sending e-newsletters

Don't send unsolicited newsletters, ever. Instead, take the time to inform people about your newsletter and invite them to become free subscribers. Follow these guidelines as you build your electronic mailing list:

- ✔ Make it easy to sign up by simply clicking to open a subscription form on your website's home or landing page.

- ✔ Reply to each subscription request by welcoming the subscriber, describing the newsletter's purpose and frequency and providing an easy way for the recipient to confirm interest or unsubscribe.

- ✔ Don't reveal the names on your distribution list. Your software should allow you to send bulk emails so that recipients can't see who else is on the same list.

- ✔ Test your newsletter by emailing it to a few email accounts before sending the full distribution. Use the test to check the formatting and to be sure that the links all work.

- ✔ Send the newsletter in batches if your distribution list is large. By sending a portion of the list each day instead of, say, a weeklong period, you can better manage the responding emails and phone calls.

- ✔ Include an opt-out function and promptly honour unsubscribe requests. Otherwise, you're in violation of anti-spam regulations, which you can read about in Chapter 15.

Finding Marketing Opportunities throughout Your Business

For all the money that small businesses spend on marketing, they often look right past free opportunities to add marketing messages to their own products, vehicles and more. With the right moves, you can amplify your marketing message with practically no investment at all.

Turning your packages into ad vehicles

Every time you package a product for a customer, you're creating a vehicle that can give your marketing message a free ride. You incur practically no cost when you add an in-pack advertising message that's certain to reach a valid prospect because the recipient has already made a purchase.

Manufacturers can affix or print ads straight onto product cartons or enclose materials in the box to invite the purchase of accessories, warranties, service programs or other offers. Repair businesses can affix service labels that remind owners who to call for future needs.

Retailers can drop into each shopping bag an invitation to join a frequent customer club, to request automatic delivery of future orders or to redeem a special offer on a future purchase (called a *bounce-back offer* because it aims to bounce a customer back into your business). For example, a pool or hot tub chemical supply company can enclose a flyer offering a monthly service programme, automatic twice-a-year chemical delivery or an annual maintenance visit.

Building business with gift certificates

You'd be astonished at how many small businesses make a gift certificate request seem like an inconvenience, when actually this kind of request is the sincerest form of customer compliment. If someone wants to give your business offerings as a gift, roll out the red carpet. Here's how:

- ✔ **Create a gift certificate form.** This form can convey the gift's details while also enhancing the gift's perceived value simply by its creative presentation. Use quality paper, a professional design that matches your company image and a look that's appropriate to the nature of your business offering.

- ✔ **Package the certificate in an envelope or a gift box.** The gift certificate buyer is a current customer making an effort to bring a new person into your business. Reward the effort with a package that flatters both the gift giver and your business.

- ✔ **When the gift is redeemed, get in touch with both parties.** Reinforce your relationship with the gift buyer by sharing that the certificate was redeemed and that you and your staff were flattered by the gift choice. Send a separate mailing to the gift recipient, welcoming the person to your business and enclosing an offer such as a free subscription to your newsletter, a special new-customer invitation, a frequent-shopper club membership or some other reason for the person to become a loyal customer of your business.

- ✔ **If the deadline is nearing on an unredeemed certificate, contact the gift recipient.** Offer a short extension or invite a phone or online order to build goodwill rather than let the certificate lapse.

Getting good use out of business cards

Even as talk of business-card obsolescence rages, people are ordering more cards today than ever before. That's because business cards are still the tools that break the ice, make good impressions and ease follow-up contact for you and your business.

Even the highest-quality business cards cost only a few pence each, and the price keeps going down with each new card-printing service that opens online. You'll be hard-pressed to find a more economical way to get your name and brand image into your marketplace.

To create a business card that makes a strong statement, use a professional design, a typestyle and ink selection that match the graphic image of your brand (see Chapter 7), quality paper, good printing and a straight cut (nothing looks cheaper than a card with a crooked cut). Follow this advice:

- ✔ **Invest a few hours with a graphic designer to achieve a distinctive, professional design that enhances your company image.** Unless you're certain of their design talents, don't ask staff members or quick-print shop designers to create your card.

 For online production, take a look at the fantastic range of business cards available at www.moo.com.

- ✔ **Be sure that your card features your business name and logo, your phone number and your contact information in a type size that people can easily read.** Also include a slogan or tagline or a short description of your business offerings.

- ✔ **Keep your card design simple.** Use a standard size that's convenient for recipients to file, and present contact information in a typeface that scanning software can read.

- ✔ **Print cards for each employee.** Everyone having their own card is great for staff morale, and when employees use their cards to introduce your business to their friends and business contacts, you recoup the cost of the cards many times over.

 If you print the back of your card with simple directions or other information, keep your logo, name, title and contact information on the front. Many people scan business cards or keep them in files in which only the front side is visible.

Making the most of advertising specialties

Advertising specialties are ubiquitous and inexpensive mind-joggers for your business. They include giveaways such as pens, pencils, fridge magnets, mouse pads, matchbooks, notepads, paperweights, calendars, calculators, t-shirts, golf umbrellas and a long list of other items that can be printed, engraved, embossed or emblazoned with a business logo.

Most specialty advertising items are cheap – and they often look it. When investing in an advertising specialty, follow this advice:

✔ Select items that relate to your business and that advance a reminder of the benefits you offer.

✔ Choose items that your customers want or need and things that they'll notice, pick up and keep for at least a short time.

✔ Opt only for items that add to your business image, not detract from it.

✔ Decide how to feature your name on the item. If the item is targeted for prospects or clients who value quality and exclusivity, make your name subtle and scaled to the item rather than in a gaudy design that monopolises the item and assures its quick trip to the rubbish can.

✔ Know how you'll distribute the items before you place an order for advertising specialties.

For information on the unbelievably wide range of specialties available, search online for 'ad specialties and promotional items uk'.

Choosing and Using Trade Shows

Trade shows bring together businesses, suppliers, customers and media representatives for a day-long or multi-day extravaganza of selling, socialising, entertaining, product previewing and competitive sleuthing.

Attending trade shows is a great way to maintain customer contacts, introduce suppliers and customers to your business, develop and maintain media relations and stay on top of industry and competitive developments. The drawback – a big one – is that regardless of your industry, you've a long list of trade shows from which to choose.

Because attendance at even one show costs a significant amount of time, money and energy, choose cautiously, using these guidelines:

✔ Study shows carefully. Track the number of presenters and attendees over recent years (if the number is going up, it probably indicates a well-regarded show). Also see whether leading media outlets are among the sponsors, another indication of the show's reputation.

✔ Decide whether you need to invest in a booth or whether you can achieve visibility by buying an ad in the show guide, making a presentation, hosting a fringe event or simply working the floor.

✔ If you host a booth, know whom you want to attract to your booth, what you want to communicate and what action you want to inspire.

✔ Know how to capture trade show visitor information and how to follow up with your trade show contacts.

Table 16-2 presents advice to follow and actions to avoid.

Table 16-2	Dos and Don'ts for Trade Show Attendance
Dos	*Don'ts*
Do prospect before the show, using letters, direct mailers, phone calls and email to encourage prospects to visit your booth.	Don't count on prospects to seek you out or find you on their own. Most shows simply have too many distractions.
Do arrive at the show with preset appointments for meetings with your top-choice media reps, journalists, customer prospects and vendors.	Don't count on spontaneous encounters with key contacts at the show. Take the time in advance to introduce yourself and schedule appointments.
Do use your staff well. Be sure that they wear business identification or, better yet, logo shirts or uniforms. Present with your best presenters and use other team members loose to meet with suppliers and do competitive research.	Don't let your whole team hang out in your show booth, which gives the impression of a dull spot. Instead, have ongoing client or media meetings underway, a greeter meeting passers-by in the entry area and other staff members out working the show.
Do have moderately priced handouts and logo items for distribution, along with a means for collecting prospect names for follow-up. After the show, send a thoughtful letter and gift to prospects who were serious enough to complete a short form to qualify their interest.	Don't set up for 'trick-or-treaters.' You don't have to give something to every visitor, and you shouldn't waste money (or weigh down your prospects) by giving out expensive or heavy literature or catalogues. Prospects appreciate follow-up packages delivered upon their return from the show.

Dos	Don'ts
Do invest in a professionally designed booth that reflects your business image and current marketing message.	Don't try to do it on a tight budget by using a self-designed booth and do-it-yourself graphics.
Do use lights, banners, moving displays, bright colours, floor carpeting and seating areas to break your booth into parts, along with other devices that draw attention and make your booth look like a hub of activity.	Don't be bland and don't expect a banner with your logo to double as a booth design. You need ad enlargements, graphics and huge, colourful photos to draw attention to your booth.
Do gather competitive intelligence. Visit other booths to get brochures and listen in on presentations. Beyond that, position your staff at buffets, in areas where people are making calls and other locations where show attendees are talking about their businesses.	Don't be vulnerable to eavesdroppers. Reserve private rooms, hospitality suites or other places to make presentations to clients or to gather your staff to share trade show intelligence. When you're done, take all your notes with you so they aren't available for others to see.

Building Sales through Promotions

The purpose of a promotion is to create a desired consumer action over a short period. Businesses stage promotions to attract new customers, to win back lapsed customers, to alter customer buying patterns (for example, by prompting larger or more frequent purchases), to develop business during slow seasons or hours or – increasingly – to attract customers into social media networks for easy and ongoing interaction.

Regardless of the promotion purpose, the objective is accomplished by offering one of the following types of action incentives:

✔ **Price savings:** Incentives include percentage discounts, two-for-one deals and other appealing reductions. The bigger the incentive, the more attractive it is to the consumer, of course. But be careful to come up with an offer that can inspire customers without giving away too much or attracting interest only from those who want the deal, with no interest in a long-term relationship.

✔ **Samples:** Businesses introducing new products or trying to win over competitors' customers offer samples or free trials to prove their advantage and get their products into circulation. First, be sure that your product shows well in comparative tests. Second, accompany the sample with a bounce-back offer that prompts the customer to make an after-sample purchase or to take a follow-up action (for example, subscribing to your newsletter) to cement the new relationship.

✔ **Events and experiences:** Events draw crowds, spurring increased sales and sometimes even attracting media coverage. Use product launches, VIP visits, new inventory arrivals, business milestones, holidays and other occasions as reasons to invite customers and prospects into your business. (See Chapter 17 for advice on getting your business information to the media.)

✔ **Voucher and rebates:** A *voucher* provides an offer that a customer can redeem at the time of purchase. A *rebate* provides an offer that a customer can redeem following the purchase, usually by completing and sending in a form. Less than 2 per cent of vouchers in circulation are redeemed, yet vouchers remain a popular promotion staple. They catch reader attention when placed in ads, and they provide a measurable way to reward customers with price reductions. When using vouchers, protect your profitability through small-print advisories that state expiration dates and that the coupon *is not valid with other special offers*.

Before staging a promotion, be clear about each of the following points:

✔ The objective you're working to achieve.

✔ How you'll measure success.

✔ The target audience that you intend to influence with the promotion.

✔ The incentive to offer and why you're confident that this incentive is capable of motivating your target audience.

✔ How to inform and train your staff to handle promotion response. Nothing is worse for a consumer than to respond to a promotion or to arrive at what's billed as a promotional event only to discover that no one at the host business seems to know anything about it.

Keep the promotion description simple. If you can't explain the promotion and incentive in a single sentence, the description is too complicated for the quick response you want to generate, and, as a result, the idea almost certainly won't fly.

Chapter 17

Public Relations and Publicity

. . . .

In This Chapter

▶ Understanding the different types of public relations

▶ Generating publicity for your business with the media

▶ Writing and disseminating news releases and preparing for media interviews

▶ Managing bad publicity

. . . .

*L*et's smash two notions right up front:

Public relations is not simply whitewashing.

Publicity is not free advertising.

There! With those two misconceptions out of the way, count on this chapter to confirm what public relations is, what publicity is and how you can use each of them to increase your company's visibility, supplement and reinforce your advertising and enhance your reputation in your market and industry.

If you wait until you face an image problem to launch a public relations campaign, you have waited too long. Use public relations and publicity to *enhance* your image, not just to right a wrong or fix an image disaster.

The Relationship between Public Relations and Publicity

The same people who think that *marketing* is a dressed-up word for *sales* will tell you that public relations is a way to get publicity and that publicity is a way to get free media coverage. That's like saying fashion is about hem lengths. There's a shard of truth in there, but that shard is hardly the full story.

Taking a wide-angle view of public relations

The Chartered Institute of Public Relations (CIPR) say 'Public relations is about reputation – the result of what you do, what you say and what others say about you . . . Public relations practice is the discipline that looks after reputation with the aim of earning understanding and support and influencing opinion and behaviour.' Other professionals say that public relations involves activities that aim to establish, maintain and improve a favourable relationship with the public upon which an organisation's success depends.

In the *Small Business Marketing For Dummies* arena, public relations means doing the right thing and then talking about it – using publicity and other non-paid communication opportunities to inform those whose positive opinions favourably affect your business.

Here's a list of the different areas of public relations and what each one does:

- **Media relations:** Establish editorial contacts, distribute news releases and story ideas and become a reliable and trustworthy news source by providing guest posts and editorials and participating in media interviews, forums and events. Publicity is part of media relations, and media relations is part of – but not all of – public relations.

- **Employee or member relations:** Use newsletters, meetings and events to interact with internal audiences and to demonstrate that your company's interest in doing the right thing starts at home.

- **Community relations:** Build ties to your local market area by joining groups, serving on boards, spearheading charitable endeavours and donating time, products, services or funds to causes and projects that benefit your community. As you undertake community relations efforts, do so first because you believe in the cause and second for the visibility you receive as a good community member.

- **Industry relations:** Join industry associations, participate in industry events and serve as a board member in groups that represent your business arena. A strong industry role keeps your business in the forefront and establishes your credibility with colleagues, consumers and editorial contacts.

- **Government relations:** Build relationships with elected officials. Acquaint them with your company so they've a favourable impression should they be asked to comment on your business or should you need their help in the future. (Just as with bankers, you're wise to make friends with politicians long before you need their help.)

✔ **Issue- and crisis-management:** Sometimes, news about your business is confusing and, once in a while, it may even threaten your image. One function of public relations is to explain and build support for complex issues and to manage crises when they arise.

Focusing on publicity

When you get mentioned in the media, that's *publicity*. It sounds so simple, but a surprising amount of planning and effort goes on behind the scenes before a company gets a 'free' mention in a newspaper or magazine, on a blog or social media page, in a TV or radio story or even in another company's newsletter.

Those who spend much time generating publicity will tell you that the results of their efforts are *valuable* but hardly *free*. It takes both time and money to develop news stories, make and maintain media contacts, stage events and implement programmes worthy of editorial coverage.

But each time you succeed in generating positive publicity, you score a triple victory. First, you win valuable editorial mentions in mass-media vehicles. Second, you win consumer confidence, as people tend to believe the editorial content of mass media more than they do paid advertising messages. And third, you generate third-party mentions and features that you can share in social networks and newsletters and reprint to distribute via direct mailings, sales presentations and press kits.

Becoming a News Source

To generate publicity, you have to start with a news item of interest, and that takes knowing the differences between promotional messages. If there's even a chance that editors, reporters or bloggers – or their audiences – are going to say 'so what?' about the story you're advancing, it'll never see the light of day.

But even beyond a news story, to achieve publicity you need a media kit in both hard-copy and digital form that reporters, editors and others can access for more information. And of course you need a list of media contacts and a strategy for maintaining media relationships and responding to media interest.

Creating a media kit and online media centre

If you want to be cited in media outlets, called on by meeting planners or contacted by local organisations seeking a lunchtime speaker, you need to be ready with professionally produced materials that those seeking official information about your business can access, reproduce and quote.

Most small businesses create media kits in two forms: in hard copy, usually contained in a folder called a *media kit,* and online as a page on their website.

Online, don't make people register to access your media kit contents, and do make it simple for them to leave their email addresses and requests for customised information. In hard copy or online, here's what to include:

- ✔ Business facts, including history and product and service profiles
- ✔ Head shots and bios of key people in your business in several forms – for example, 100-word, 50-word and 20-word descriptions
- ✔ Professionally produced photos and graphics, including high-resolution versions of your logo in several sizes
- ✔ A list of topics on which you're prepared to share expertise, each backed by a short statement that piques curiosity and sounds interesting and natural should a journalist choose to quote directly from your media kit
- ✔ Samples of or links to media appearances and coverage
- ✔ Background information such as white papers, fact sheets, speeches and links to demonstrations and presentations
- ✔ Social media links
- ✔ An invitation welcoming requests for guests' posts and original articles
- ✔ An invitation for media interview requests
- ✔ Contact information, including office phone and mobile phone numbers, email addresses and mailing address

Want to check out a few good examples? Here's one from an internationally known brand, one from a fellow *For Dummies* author and one from a small business branding powerhouse:

- ✔ www.crayola.com/mediacenter/index.cfm
- ✔ http://careerenlightenment.com/aboutcontact/press-kit
- ✔ http://duhmarketing.com/about_liz.html

Establishing and maintaining an all-important list of media contacts

The first step toward getting your news out there is to create a list of media contacts that serve the audience you want to reach. Target the following outlets:

- ✔ **Your local daily newspaper:** In making contacts, keep in mind that general and 'hot' news goes to the city or news desk. News that relates to feature sections of the paper – sports, home, business, entertainment and so on – goes straight to department editors. Go to your paper's website to find out the name of the person who covers your field, and make contact to find out whether you should deliver releases to the news desk, the section editor or directly to the beat reporter.

- ✔ **Regional weekly and business publications:** Study back issues and media kits to familiarise yourself with the regular columns and upcoming special focus topics. Think about angles for stories that you can discuss with the editor. Then call to introduce yourself and discuss ways that you can assist in providing information for news stories.

- ✔ **Radio and TV stations that broadcast in your local area:** Include those in nearby towns and cities where some of your customers may come from or you would be willing to travel for work.

- ✔ **Publications that serve your industry or business sector:** Go to the publication's *masthead,* which is the editorial staff listing that's normally listed on its website and on one of the early pages of each printed issue. Find out the names of the writers who cover the kind of news you generate and include them on your news release distribution list.

- ✔ **Blogs and electronic magazines that your target audience reads:** For blogs that reach your target audience, search the directory at http://technorati.com. Also do a general Google search for the name of your business arena or products, along with the word *blog* or *community.* When you find sites that address your audience and cover stories like the ones you plan to generate, add them to your media list. Even more important, start following them. Subscribe to their RSS feeds so you stay current on the nature and tone of the content they feature. Only then are you ready to make contact, following the advice in the sidebar later on in this chapter, 'A blueprint for blog PR'.

Establishing media contacts

Get familiar with the audience and content of each targeted media outlet and, if at all possible, introduce your business before the first news release arrives.

Contact editors or reporters to briefly introduce your business; to explain the kind of news it generates; to list the type of useful information, industry stats, market research or other helpful info you'd be glad to share; and to mention your availability to serve as a resource whenever you can be of assistance.

For online news sites, introduce yourself by participating through useful comments to blog or news posts.

Maintaining media relationships

You want to earn a reputation as a business that sends only newsworthy releases. Skip over any item that isn't timely, doesn't announce a major milestone or has no unique angle or hook.

Make yourself available to the media. Alert those who answer the phone at your company to direct media calls to you immediately. If you aren't the owner of your organisation, do all that you can to get the top person to be available as well. Nothing is more damaging to your efforts than the most powerful person in your company saying 'no comment' or refusing to be interviewed by news writers when they call.

Promptly return media calls and be sensitive to deadlines. Don't call near the deadline and don't take more time than you need. If your answers involve complex explanations, offer to email summaries of lengthy material. Also, don't assume that the media contact heard or understood everything you said. Follow each conversation with a short note summarising key points and providing links to additional relevant information.

Finally, always assume that you're on the record. See the section 'Managing media interviews' later in the chapter for more information.

Getting real with publicity expectations

The fable about the oil driller who threw in the towel just a few feet before reaching liquid gold is a good analogy for what most small businesses term their *failed publicity campaigns*. They send out five, maybe even ten, news releases, nothing happens, and they quit – disappointed and without a clue of how close they came to achieving the result they so badly desired.

To generate publicity, commit to a long-haul programme of activity and keep the following in mind:

✔ **Don't expect instant or even consistent results.** Here's the truth: Most news releases never make it into the media. In fact, personal contact and follow-up generates more coverage than just sending out pre-packaged news and crossing your fingers.

✔ **Don't carpet-bomb the media by sending the same release to all media outlets.** Instead, customise the story to specific audiences and news vehicles. Especially if you're aiming for coverage in well-read blogs, establish contact and inquire about interest in your story before sending a tailored release, and keep each release focused on a single topic of interest to each media outlet's audience.

✔ **Don't expect news coverage as a perk for your advertising investments.** Arm-twisting is the worst of all routes to good publicity. The only way your advertising investment helps your publicity effort is that your ads build awareness. As a result, when your release arrives, your editorial contacts may be familiar with your name and brand.

✔ **Don't peddle hype as news.** If your story's focus is why you think your product is better than that of a competitor, that's hype. But if your story describes a change of importance to the public, that's news. Newsworthy releases announce financial results, special events, awards given or received, staffing or management changes, reactions to legal or financial difficulties (see 'Crisis Communications: Dealing with Bad News' later in this chapter), and product, technology or industry announcements, all presented in terms that matter to the media outlet's audience.

✔ **Don't hound the media.** Never demand an explanation for why a release hasn't run. If you're concerned that your releases are being ignored, buy an hour or two of a publicist's time to get a professional assessment of your efforts, along with guidance for presenting your news in the future.

✔ **Aim for quality, not quantity.** Don't try to get publicity by blasting out endless releases, and don't write releases that are even one sentence longer than they need to be. Send releases only when you have news of interest to readers or viewers. Keep each release hype-free and to the point. Follow a standard news release format (see the following sections) and make sure that your grammar and spelling are flawless.

Spreading Your News

When you're ready to generate news coverage, start with this question: Is your story a local, industry or national/international story? The answer can focus your distribution strategy. Until recently, you had three essential avenues to circulate your news:

✔ **Distribute news releases on your own by hand, mail or email to a list your business has developed and maintained.** This approach is especially common for local or targeted industry news stories.

✔ **Hire a public relations firm.** Especially for stories with broad-reaching impact, professionals often have more open channels to news sources, and they distribute news through appropriate wire services and the Associated Press.

✔ **Use a news distribution wire service.** PR professionals and individual businesses use services such as Business Wire (www.businesswire. co.uk) for simultaneous release of material to news networks, newspapers, magazines, TV and radio stations, sites such as Google News and Yahoo and investment and research departments in the business and financial world. PR Newswire (www.prnewswire.com) provides the same service but isn't limited to business press.

Today, you've one more essential approach to news distribution: an evergrowing number of blogs.

Technorati, the world's first and largest blog search engine, indexes more than a million of what's estimated to be more than 100 million blogs. With numbers like that, anyone seeking publicity needs to know the route to blog coverage, which involves these key steps:

✔ **Follow the blogs that influence your target audience.** Don't even think about approaching a blogger until you're familiar with the blogger's content and tone, and preferably until the blogger has become familiar with you. How? Subscribe. Read. Comment. Repeat. See Chapter 12 for tips on how and when to comment on blogs.

✔ **Send customised news announcements to each blogger.** Follow the instructions each one posts regarding preferences for how to pitch stories. Anything less is considered the equivalent of PR spam. For a good example of how to customise your blogger approach, see the nearby sidebar, 'A blueprint for blog PR'.

Preparing news releases

News releases summarise stories appropriate for coverage in the editorial portion of news media. News releases are also called *press releases,* but the term *news release* provides a more appropriate label that encompasses the role of broadcast and Internet news.

Whether you distribute your release via traditional media or online, after you circulate it to media outlets, amplify your news in the following ways:

✔ Post your release on your own website *before* distributing it elsewhere. That way search engines point to your site as the origin of the content. Beyond that, when people, including reporters and bloggers, land on your site, your release can lead to unexpected and valuable coverage for your business.

✔ Post your release on social media.

A blueprint for blog PR

Joshua Waldman (www.careerenlighten ment.com) wrote *Job Searching with Social Media For Dummies* (Wiley), and, primarily by activating social media, he catapulted his book to the number two slot among all Amazon business books. He did it by reaching out to a carefully crafted list of 500 bloggers and media contacts with customised messages appropriate to their wants and needs. Here's a summary of the PR game plan he employed:

1. **Segment blogger contacts.** Top bloggers don't have time to read and review all the books they receive, so Waldman sent offers for free guest posts. Mid-tier bloggers are trying to draw traffic and build engagement, so with a review request Waldman offered a free review copy and five copies for competitions. He offered lower-tier blogs, which struggle with relevancy, a book for review.

2. **Always ask first.** Waldman didn't send any blogger a book or post out of the blue, which is considered intrusive new product spam. Instead, he sent introductory emails extending the offer and asking for their interest and response.

The result of Waldman's actions? Blogger coverage, Internet radio interviews and – thanks to traditional PR outreach and the reverberating effect of online visibility – features on CBS and ABC News and in the *Chicago Tribune* and *U.S. News & World Report*.

The lessons from Waldman's actions? Be persistent. Begin with an introductory email. To those who respond positively, send a reminder email before launch day. Remove those who respond negatively from the list. Send all others up to three email prompts ('Last week I sent you an email about my forthcoming book; I haven't heard from you. If you're interested. . . .'). Then, the day after launch, reconnect ('Wow, the book launched at number two on Amazon. Would love for you to review it. . . .').

The bottom line? Start making your blogger list – now.

✔ Distribute your release to those of influence to your business, including clients and those in a position to refer business your way.

✔ Post the release within your company. Employees should never have to find out their own company's news through the media.

Writing a news release

When developing news releases, whether for print or electronic distribution, first decide on an *angle* from which to present your news. This angle involves deciding what makes the facts you're sharing timely, interesting and worthy of media interest. Good publicists present the same news from a number of different angles – one for the local media, one for national media, one for industry media and so on.

In all cases, your release needs to cover the following points:

- **Contact information** so that recipients can find out more if they want to.

- **A date that the news can be released** – most often *For Immediate Release* but occasionally after a specified date or time.

- **A headline** that's active (in other words, it should include a verb), succinct (it should fit on no more than two lines), and benefit-oriented (it should tell what's in the news for the media audience).

- **A dateline** that states the city from which the release originated, followed by the date the release was issued.

- **A clear presentation of the facts,** including a summary of who, what, where, when, why and how in an *inverted pyramid style.* That means revealing the most important news details in the first sentence and unpacking your next most important facts sequentially into the following paragraphs, ending with the least important but necessary details.

- **A short closing paragraph**, called a *boilerplate,* that summarises information about your company.

Table 17-1 helps you put your release to a final test of newsworthiness before you put it into circulation.

Table 17-1	Spotting the Good and Bad in News Releases
Attributes of Releases That Get Results	*Attributes of Releases That Get Ignored*
Feature timely news about your products or services, your staff, recent legal or legislative actions, industry changes or other items of interest to the public	Contain promotional messages, convey recycled stories that have already been covered by competing news media, or present self-serving puff pieces
Are customised messages tailored to the audience of a specific news vehicle, often accompanied by a brief note written to an established editorial contact	Are blanket mailings that relay the same exact news to competing media with no unique angle, no offer for interviews or no other effort to customise the story
Contain crisp, clear, accurate and factual language	Are full of superlatives (biggest, brightest, strongest and so on), opinions and hype
Describe benefits to the target audience of the media outlet	Emphasise product features rather than benefits and use insider terminology
Make a clear point regarding why the news is important and how and when people can act upon the information conveyed	Fail to answer the fundamental question, 'Who cares?'

Attributes of Releases That Get Results	Attributes of Releases That Get Ignored
Use quotes from management, customers and industry leaders	Fail to make a clear point about how the news affects your industry, your business or, especially, your customers
Are intriguing and believable	Are boastful or stretch the bounds of credibility

Producing hard-copy news releases

If you deliver your release by mail, hand or fax (which is becoming rarer every day), prepare your story in the longstanding form of a printed release, illustrated in Figure 17-1.

The hard-copy printed release is becoming something of an antique in a world where news is increasingly submitted electronically, but the format is still the basis of official news announcements. Figure 17-1 shows what's involved.

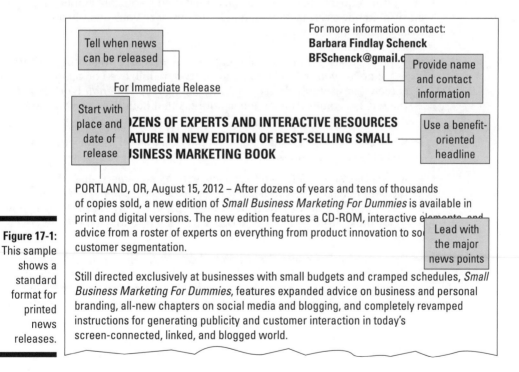

Figure 17-1: This sample shows a standard format for printed news releases.

Tell when news can be released

For more information contact:
Barbara Findlay Schenck
BFSchenck@gmail.c

Provide name and contact information

For Immediate Release

Start with place and date of release

)ZENS OF EXPERTS AND INTERACTIVE RESOURCES
ATURE IN NEW EDITION OF BEST-SELLING SMALL
JSINESS MARKETING BOOK

Use a benefit-oriented headline

PORTLAND, OR, August 15, 2012 – After dozens of years and tens of thousands of copies sold, a new edition of *Small Business Marketing For Dummies* is available in print and digital versions. The new edition features a CD-ROM, interactive elements and advice from a roster of experts on everything from product innovation to so customer segmentation.

Lead with the major news points

Still directed exclusively at businesses with small budgets and cramped schedules, *Small Business Marketing For Dummies*, features expanded advice on business and personal branding, all-new chapters on social media and blogging, and completely revamped instructions for generating publicity and customer interaction in today's screen-connected, linked, and blogged world.

Sending releases electronically

Emailing news releases is immediate, cost-efficient and effective – *if* you take a few steps first.

Start by checking media outlet websites to find out their news submission specifications and to obtain editorial email addresses. Or contact the assignments editor at your target media outlet (or better yet, the editor you hope will handle your news).

Explain that you've a news release you believe is of interest and ask if the editor prefers to receive submissions by email. The editor will probably ask the nature of your news, in part to provide accurate delivery directions, so be ready with a one-sentence answer.

If the editor prefers electronic delivery, confirm the email address. Also ask whether the editor prefers the release as an attachment or typed straight into the email message. Don't make assumptions. Most editors won't open attachments, so never send them unless requested.

If the editor requests your news as an attached file, you can simply email your printed news release document. If not, prepare your news in an email message following these guidelines:

- Type your subject line in uppercase and lowercase, presenting a short headline for your release that can be read, in full, even on a mobile screen. For example, *Lancaster Landscaping Free Waterfall Workshop.* If the release comes from an email address that includes your business name, you don't need to repeat it in your subject line.

- Write and send your email in plain text. Don't use HTML or other markup languages, as they can reduce the readability of your news.

- If possible, start each email message with a customised line. For example, you mayuse *News Release for [name of news contact] at [name of media outlet]*, followed by a short description of why the story is a good fit for the editor, reporter or blogger's audience and what type of coverage you're aiming for.

- Paste your release into the message box. Your release should begin with the words *For Immediate Release* and follow the content instructions for standard printed releases. Unlike printed releases, however, emailed releases are single-spaced except between paragraphs and are edited down to 500 words or fewer.

- Include hyperlinks that lead to supporting information or product landing pages on your website. The links provide helpful information to reporters or editors preparing stories based on your release, and they appear in any media outlets that post your release.

✔ End your release with an invitation to request additional information or interviews, followed by your contact information in this format:

- Contact person's name

- Company name

- Office and mobile phone numbers with area code

- Email, website and physical addresses

✔ Don't attach files, photos or artwork unless the recipient has specifically instructed you to do so. Instead, include a link to your website, where high-definition artwork is available. (See the sidebar below, 'Preparing and submitting artwork digitally'.)

✔ Print a copy of your email release so that you've a reference copy handy when editors respond to request additional information.

If you send an identical release to those on your media list instead of sending tailored releases to individual media contacts, take great care not to reveal the names and addresses on your list. Instead, use an email group or distribution list or send the release to yourself with all recipients listed in the blind carbon copy (Bcc) field.

Managing media interviews

When you hit the publicity jackpot and a reporter calls, be ready!

Before the interview

Get the details. Confirm the media outlet and deadline, along with the interview topic, the story's angle and the type of questions you'll be asked. Ask whether others the reporter is interviewing others for the same story. The answer gives you an indication of the nature of the story and allows you to prepare your remarks accordingly.

Then take time to prepare yourself. Unless the reporter is on a deadline or calling in response to a release that you put out (in which case you should have talking points prepared and by your phone), buy a couple of minutes' time by asking whether you can wind up a meeting or project before returning the call – and then do so, preferably within a half hour. But before hanging up, ask whether the reporter has specific questions in mind. That way you can be prepared when you call back.

Preparing and submitting artwork digitally

Increasingly, media outlets emphasise art in their page designs. They need good images to accompany stories, which presents a great opportunity for businesses that submit photos or graphics in easily usable formats.

Follow these steps as you make digital art submissions:

✓ Start with a clear, well-exposed image that has good composition, good focus and interesting subject matter.

✓ Submit an image that's at least the size you hope it's going to appear in the media outlet or, better yet, the size the editor has requested.

✓ Prepare your photo or art for adequate digital resolution before sending. Nearly any newspaper can use your image if you submit it at a resolution of 250 to 300 PPI, which means pixels per inch. (You'll also hear the term DPI, which means dots per inch.)

✓ Obtain permission to submit artwork before attaching your file to an email message. When writing the email that accompanies the file, type your caption into the subject line (for example, 'Photo: *Small Business*

Marketing For Dummies book cover'). In the message box, type your *cutline,* which is a more detailed caption of the photo or artwork. If your photo includes people, include the complete names of all who are recognisable. (Keep in mind that publications rarely use photos featuring groups of more than four.) Close your email with your name and contact information.

✓ Most media outlets can receive your image if you compress it and send it in JPEG format.

✓ Transmit your image in RGB (red, green, blue) colour format if possible. Most images originate in RGB, which is the most common colour mode for viewing digital images on-screen and the default setting in photo software.

✓ If you're submitting a digital photo, change the file name designated by the camera (which is probably something like DSCN0015.JPG) before submitting.

✓ One last step: Be patient. Your image may not be used this time, but if you're a good, reliable source, in time your efforts pay off.

After you find out the scope of the interview, jot down the two or three most important ideas that you want to convey about the topic. Grab any appropriate reference materials that help you make your points clearly. Consider negative issues that may arise and develop short responses. And think about what photos, charts, industry statistics or other materials you'd like to offer to the reporter to enhance the coverage.

During the interview

Proceed with confidence – and caution – during media interviews. Answer questions clearly and then stop talking. If you try to fill time with additional comments, you run the risk of overshadowing your message or saying something you don't want to see in print or hear on-air.

After the interview

Following the interview, thank the reporter and ask when the story will run or air. Don't demand prior review, but do offer to be available to assist in confirming any facts or quotes. Also, put your thanks into writing in a follow-up note that summarises key points and provides links to more information.

Be prepared for the fact that after interviews stories sometimes get cancelled or they don't run on the scheduled date. Also realise that you may notice discrepancies between the way the story is worded and what you thought you said. Request corrections only for actual and important errors, not for differences of opinion or approach. Instead, look for a positive aspect of the coverage and highlight that point in a thank-you note to the reporter. Good words get you further than nit-picking or criticising.

Staging news conferences – or not

Companies like the concept of news conferences a lot more than editors and reporters do. In fact, many media organisations, including many local newspapers and stations, simply won't attend ribbon-cutting and launch events, considering them promotional and easily described in simple news releases. Even the most newsworthy conference (in your view) can be eclipsed by late-breaking news.

Stage a news conference only for a huge and time-sensitive announcement and only in the following cases:

✔ When you need to announce important news simultaneously to all media

✔ When the news is best told in person, backed by displays and followed by the chance for reporters to ask questions

✔ When you're presenting important speakers or celebrities

Watch your words

People pay a big price for attacking someone's reputation in the media. To stay out of trouble in media interviews, steer clear of negative opinions about others.

For the record, here are two terms with which you don't ever want direct involvement:

✔ **Libel:** Printed statements that are untrue, defamatory and harmful.

✔ **Slander:** The verbal form of libel.

Schedule and announce the news conference well in advance. Send invitations in the form of brief letters or announcements that you format like news releases but with the words *Media Advisory* replacing the words *For Immediate Release.*

Crisis Communications: Dealing with Bad News

Chalk it up to bad decisions or just plain bad luck, but sometimes, bad news happens. When it does, work fast to find out what went wrong with your business, collect all pertinent facts and prepare to fix the problem, if possible.

Waste no time before circulating facts about what happened and, if possible, what actions you're taking to see that it won't happen again. As much as you'd like to run and hide, don't. The last thing you want is for those who care a lot less about your reputation than you do to be speculating or spinning the story for you. Almost certainly your business will fare better if you show a concerned face and release a truthful explanation through the same media channels in which the bad news is travelling.

Public relations strategists have complete scenarios to use in what are called *crisis communications.* If your event is likely to have negative ramifications that continue for more than a few days, and if the bad news seems likely to reach out further than your local market, call on pros to help you manage the story.

Part V
Winning and Keeping Customers

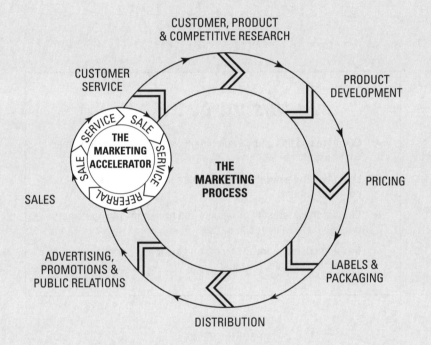

CUSTOMER, PRODUCT & COMPETITIVE RESEARCH

CUSTOMER SERVICE

PRODUCT DEVELOPMENT

THE MARKETING ACCELERATOR

SERVICE SALE SERVICE REFERRAL SALE

THE MARKETING PROCESS

PRICING

SALES

LABELS & PACKAGING

ADVERTISING, PROMOTIONS & PUBLIC RELATIONS

DISTRIBUTION

For Dummies can help you get started with a huge range of subjects. Visit www.dummies.com/extras/smallbusinessmarketing for free bonus content, including forms designed to help your marketing efforts.

In this part . . .

- ✔ Get priceless tips on how to contact, win and – crucially – keep your customers.

- ✔ Learn to network and introduce yourself and your business to potential punters.

- ✔ Capture the interest of prospects and turn them into customers through good sales techniques.

- ✔ Develop customer loyalty by making customer service a cornerstone of your business.

Chapter 18

Making Impressions through Networking and Presentations

*W*ith all the talk about advertising, publicity and social media, you can lose sight of the fact that the ultimate objective of marketing communications is to prompt person-to-person interactions. A phone call. An email. A meeting. A face-to-face presentation. A chance to personally make your pitch, launch a business relationship and begin the interaction that precedes a sale.

After you've developed awareness with business and customer contacts and spread your marketing message within your target audience, are you prepared for the person-to-person encounters that follow?

Whether you're seeking sales, publicity, favourable impressions that inspire industry or community recognition, or some other objective, success depends on what you do when the moment to make an in-person impression arrives.

Building a Far-Reaching Network

Networking isn't about meeting people, but about establishing connections with people who are likely to become customers, suppliers, associates or proponents of your business. Networking is about collecting contact information and following up to build meaningful business relationships. Make sure that you

✔ Introduce yourself and your business and make great first impressions on those with whom you aim to do business.

✔ Learn your prospective customers' interests and business concerns.

- ✔ Learn the problems they want solved or needs they want addressed.
- ✔ Establish common interests.
- ✔ Forge connections that lead to business relationships and referrals.

In person, networking is less about handing out business cards than handing your business cards to targeted prospects and getting their contact information in return. Online, networking is less about adding people to *your* circles or pages than getting others to add *you* to *theirs.* To succeed, you want to

- ✔ **Start with a well-prepared introduction,** described in the next section.

- ✔ **Network in person** in networking groups, conferences and at community, business, cultural, church, school and any other events where those who meet the profile of your target audience gather and interact. And don't rule out the old-fashioned network-building approach of making introductions by writing or phoning those you want to meet. See the sidebar, 'Pick up the phone', for advice from award-winning journalist and business coach Antonio Neves.

- ✔ **Network online,** using LinkedIn (see advice from LinkedIn expert Viveka von Rosen in Chapter 11) and other social networks.

- ✔ **Finish well** by entering all contacts into your database or contact-management system and following up on a regular basis to remind them of the value of your products, services and expertise.

Pick up the phone

Antonio Neves founded THINQACTION (http://thinqaction.com) to provide coaching and professional development workshops that help young professionals transform potential into exceptional performance. 'Look,' he says, 'I love emailing, texting, tweeting and Facebooking as much as the next person. But those actions are what you call *passive.* You have to wait for something to happen. Picking up the phone is *proactive.* It allows you to make things happen.'

When you pick up the phone, you show initiative, save time, build relationships, improve communication skills and get things done. And something else: Though people can easily delete an email or a text, they find it harder to 'delete' you on the phone or in person. Yet marketers avoid phone calls for predictable reasons. Neves has an answer for each:

'Some people don't like to be called.' Says who?

'If I call them, I'll inconvenience them.' You're probably inconveniencing yourself more.

'What if they pick up?' Introduce yourself and tell the person what you want.

'Unless told not to call, call,' Neves says. 'And sometimes, even then, I call.'

Making Introductions

To build a network and launch positive interactions, you need to be ready to make three kinds of introductions: your personal introduction, your business introduction and your introduction of two colleagues to each other. Each introduction gives you a moment in the limelight. Use it well.

Introducing yourself

People engage with people they find interesting, connected and able to make unique contributions. When they ask, 'What do you do?' they want to find out how your capabilities and interests align with their own wants and needs.

In person, you have about 20 seconds to answer, inspire and make others want to continue the conversation. Online, you have about 20 words. (See Chapter 11 for tips on compressing your introduction to fit the length limitations of most social media sites.) In presentations, you have about 50 words. After that, minds wander, which is the effect you want to avoid.

When introducing yourself, take these steps:

- ✔ **Begin with names.** 'Hi, Mike. I'm Jane. Jane Smith.' By stating the name of the person ('Hi, Mike') or people ('Good morning, everyone') you're addressing, you gain attention and establish a conversational tone. By stating and repeating your name (along with your business, if you're in a business setting), you help build name awareness and recall.

- ✔ **Provide a context for your relationship.** Establish a connection by saying something like, 'I'm one of today's panellists.' 'Our kids are on the same football team.' 'John Brown has told me good things about you.'

- ✔ **Deliver an interesting, informative and concise self-description.** Avoid openings that simply state your job description or dull introductions like, 'I sell life insurance', or, 'I'm a consultant'. Instead, give an engaging summary of what you do, the benefits you deliver and why you're a credible and interesting resource. Don't be dull and don't be stuffy. Aim for a description that rings true and that makes the person you're talking with nod – and smile.

For example, 'After years as a university admissions director, I now help 50 students a year get into their top-choice universities, coaching and calming them (and their parents!) through the high-tension process of making selections, completing applications and applying for financial aid.'

✔ **Launch a conversation.** Ask open-ended questions that prompt interaction and keep the conversation going. For example, 'What's your line of work?' 'How did you get started?' 'What's the most interesting project or customer you've worked with recently?' 'Who would you like to meet?' Really listen to the answers, because the whole point of networking is to establish contact with people who share your business interests and approaches.

✔ **Make your introduction memorable.** You want to make a lasting and positive impression. Beyond that, you want your introduction to be one that *you* remember and feel comfortable presenting. Keep it true. Keep it simple. And then keep it in your head.

Introducing your business

When people ask what your business does, if you reel off a summary of your business history or the bells and whistles of your product features, you'll lose their interest in a hurry. You want to tell them not what your business does but what it does for its customers. And you need to answer in a way that addresses the wants and needs of the person asking the question:

✔ Investors want to know whether your business can make them money.

✔ Journalists want to know whether your business can contribute to a good story.

✔ Business leaders want to know whether your business is likely to be a good industry or community partner.

✔ Consumers want to know whether your business addresses their wants or needs.

✔ Everyone wants to know what you do, whom you serve and what unique benefits you deliver.

That's why you need an *elevator pitch.* The term 'elevator pitch' comes out of the 1990s, when venture capitalists listened to full presentations only from entrepreneurs who first provided a great short answer (about the length of an elevator ride) to the question, 'What does your business do?'

The contents and order of a good elevator pitch – or business introduction – are as follows:

1. **A description of your business in a handful of non-technical words**

2. **A sentence telling what your business does and what unique benefits your products and services provide**

3. **A description of the target customer you reach and serve**

4. **A statement of the competitive edge that makes your business interesting, different and successful**

Introducing others to each other

Every time you can help a customer or business associate by making a referral or an introduction, the process is like putting money in the bank. Chances are more than good that the person will pay your kindness forward, not only by helping others but by helping you out sometime in the future too. Yet Ron J. Williams, the co-founder and CEO of Knodes (`http://knod.es`) and SnapGoods (`http://snapgoods.com`), says that most people aren't any good at introductions, and if you don't know how to make awesome introductions, Williams says, you're losing out on an opportunity to help two people connect and collaborate to do something amazing. And guess what? 'If they meet and make something awesome happen because *you* introduced them,' he says, 'then they always associate you with awesome. That makes you a rock star.' His advice for great introductions? Incorporate these three C's:

- ✔ **Context:** In business, there's little room for cold calls and cold introductions. An email out of nowhere that says, 'John, meet Ron. Ron, meet John' is inconsiderate. John doesn't know who Ron is. Ron doesn't know who John is. And neither knows who's supposed to do what next. Are you doing John a favour, in which case John should follow up? Is Ron looking for a job and wanting to grab coffee at John's company, in which case he better say 'Hi' first? Who knows? No one except you, so this intro isn't set up for success. Provide context by finding out and communicating what the person initiating the request wants out of an introduction.

- ✔ **Consideration:** Few relationships start or end on completely equal footing. Always consider how to make an introduction valuable for the person in the relative position of power. If you know a leading venture capitalist personally and want to offer intros to her every time you're out drinking, imagine how little time it would take for her to add you to her spam filter. What she'd value instead are relevant intros that are considerate of her schedule and interests.

- ✔ **Choice:** Remember, you have a choice about whether to make introductions. More importantly, you should give the choice to those you're introducing. For example, 'Hey, John wants to meet you, Paul. He's a smart tech dude working on some stuff I think you'll like. Worth a coffee. You game for an intro?' The request is simple, provides context, is immensely considerate of the relative schedules and standing of those you're introducing and sets up for a successful outcome. But if Ron says, 'No thanks,' John will appreciate your candour and won't be left wondering why he's heard nothing back.

Those who are serially poor introducers, who send context-free introductions or introductions via random tweets, are time-wasters. Those who take a few minutes to make sure that people want to be introduced and two more minutes to describe why the world would benefit from these two people meeting are real connectors – and a force for good.

For more information, follow Knodes and SnapGoods CEO Ron J Williams on Twitter at @ronjdub.

When you get your introduction down pat, practise it until you can convey it naturally and comfortably in well under a minute, with a relaxed smile on your face and enthusiasm in your tone. Then, when the time comes, relax. Introduce your business in a conversational tone – not as if you're reciting an anthem. You don't have to run through the whole introduction at once. If the person you're talking with interrupts you with questions or comments, accept the input gladly. Doing so is an indication of interest and exactly the kind of interaction great introductions aim to generate.

Polishing Your Presentation

When the time comes to move beyond introductions and shine in the limelight, be ready to take the microphone, make a great impression, make a difference and make those you're talking with want to take the next step toward a relationship with you and your business.

Stepping up to the microphone

You've probably heard of TED, a non-profit devoted to 'Ideas Worth Spreading' from the world's most remarkable thinkers and speakers. Presentations are posted free at www.ted.com. In addition to sharing amazing information, each TED talk runs not a second longer than 18 minutes, and all obey the following 'commandments', which provide great advice for any speaker to follow:

> Dream big. Show the real you. Make the complex plain. Connect with people's emotions. Don't flaunt your ego. No selling from the stage. Comment on other speakers' talks. Don't read your talk. End your talk on time. Rehearse your talk in front of a trusted friend – for timing, for clarity, for impact.

When preparing your next speech, consider the TED commandments and follow these steps:

✔ **Plan ahead:** For how-to instructions, pick up *Confessions of a Public Speaker* (O'Reilly Media), by Scott Berkun, who gives these tips:

- **Take a strong position in the title.** Avoid titles like 'Risk Management 101' (Berkun says that everyone remembers 101 courses as boring) in favour of titles like 'Mistakes I Made in *X* and What I Learned' or 'Why *X* Sucks and What We Can Do about It'.

- **Know your audience, including what they currently think and what they hope to learn.** Get audience information from meeting presenters. Further, search online to discover what people are saying about your topic on blogs and social media sites.

- **Be concise.** Build your talk around no more than five key points. Put them in order, commit them to memory and then turn them into powerful statements that your audience can grasp and remember.

- **Be ready for audience questions and counter-arguments.** Do some research to be clear about what people with the opposite point of view have to say so you're prepared with good responses if those comments arise.

✔ **Let your audience know what to expect.** Berkun gives this example: 'I have 30 minutes to talk to you and five points to make, so I will spend five minutes on each point and save the remaining time for questions.'

✔ **Finish on time and then follow up.** After the applause, leverage the success of your speech. Send thanks via email and social media to those who made your talk possible. Post your handout, slides, outline, audio or video for online reach and visibility. Search blogs and social media for mentions of your talk and respond or repost wherever appropriate. Then start making arrangements for your next speaking opportunity.

For advice as you prepare the slides that accompany your talk, pick up a copy of *PowerPoint For Dummies,* by Doug Lowe (Wiley) and the inspirational *Resonate: Present Visual Stories That Transform Audiences*, by Nancy Duarte (Wiley).

Presenting your proposal or product

When a business contact turns into a prospective purchase, how you present your offering can make or break your chance to close the deal. Successful sales presentations share three attributes:

✔ They describe the product or service by showing how it delivers benefits, solves problems or provides opportunities for the prospect.

✔ They focus on a few points that the prospect can relate to and remember.

✔ They're appropriately entertaining – grabbing and holding the prospect's interest while reinforcing the marketing message.

Preparing for sales presentations

Effective sales presentations match product benefits with customer needs or desires. Before you start, be ready with the following information:

✔ **Know your product.** Be clear about every customer want or need that your offering addresses. Then think about every question a prospect may ask and have the answers ready, linking each product fact to a customer benefit. Remember, people don't buy features. They buy benefits or, better yet, the personal outcomes or desirable solutions that the benefits deliver.

✔ **Know how to explain your offering in a sentence.** Condense everything you know into a brief explanation that grabs interest and causes the prospect to think, 'Hmm, this will benefit me.' Don't resort to jargon. Consider the difference between 'We offer aesthetic laser services' and 'We restore the look of youth and health using the most advanced laser, medical and therapeutic treatments.'

✔ **Know your prospect.**

- **For individual consumers,** consult your database to find out about previous interactions with or purchases from your business. Also, be observant. Notice the kind of car or clothes the customer arrives in and whether the person is accompanied by friends or family members. Know the typical buying pattern of all customers, including whether they make purchase decisions on the spot or after consultation with others. Plan your presentation accordingly.

- **For business customers,** visit websites, read company and competitor marketing material, talk to mutual associates and do any research necessary to understand wants and needs. Also, determine whether the prospect has the authority to say yes to your proposal. If not, be prepared to share information that can represent you well when your message is relayed to the decision maker.

✔ **Know what message your prospect is ready to receive.** (For more on the buying decision, turn to Chapter 19.)

- Especially if yours is a new or unusual offering, develop awareness and interest before asking for the order. Even the iPhone, now ubiquitous, didn't launch sales until Steve Jobs worked his magic, gaining worldwide awareness and interest for 'a revolutionary and magical product that is literally five years ahead of any other mobile phone'.

- When people are aware of the need that your product addresses, help them see it as the best and highest-value solution before asking for the buying decision.

- Even customers with awareness, interest and a desire to purchase may require more information or an incentive before they make the final decision. They may require information to share with others who influence the decision. Or maybe an incentive is necessary to spur action. Determine your prospect's mind-set and tailor your presentation accordingly.

✔ **Know your presentation goal.** Knowledge of your customer's position in the buying process determines the goal of your interaction. Sometimes, your goal is to make the sale and launch a celebration. More often, your aim is an incremental step – a request for a proposal, a meeting with a higher-level decision maker, a demonstration or some other step that moves the process toward a close. Be aware that if your product involves significant cost and deliberation, you may need a good number of interactions before you achieve the sale.

Making your presentation

After you're prepared, you're ready for show time. When presenting to your customer, take these steps:

✔ Establish rapport, taking care to notice the customer's body language and to match communication styles.

✔ Agree on goals so you're both clear about where the conversation is going.

✔ Identify the customer's wants and needs and explain how your offering provides the solution.

✔ Convey cost benefits by discussing the costs involved with the customer's current situation and the beneficial return the customer can expect from investing in your offering.

Translating your message into prospect benefits

The following is worth repeating: *People buy benefits, not features.* They don't buy all-natural, algae-based facial moisturiser; they buy the promise of firmer skin in four weeks. They don't care about lists of ingredients as much as the benefits those ingredients deliver. To keep your presentation focused on benefits, stay tuned at all times to your prospect's station WII-FM: What's In It – For *Me?*

Turning your presentation into a back-and-forth conversation

People *buy in* before they *buy.* The more your prospects are talking, the more involved they are, and the more likely a sale will occur. Great sales presenters follow these two steps:

✔ **Ask, then listen.** Make your introductory remarks and then ask questions that elicit more than yes or no answers. Nod to validate points, but don't interrupt. When the prospect pauses, say something like 'Tell me more' to find out as much as possible before you respond, share additional information or present another question.

✔ **Show, don't tell.** People start to *own* a product when they hold it in their hands, take it for a test drive, carry it into a fitting room or in some other way get involved in a tactile manner. This fact is why service businesses show samples of projects similar to the one the prospect is considering – and why they sometimes show speculative work conducted on the prospect's behalf.

Dealing with objections

In sales presentations, prospects raise objections as a means to gather information to pass along to decision influencers and also as a way to accumulate facts to justify the buying decision. Often, objections are questions in disguise. Encourage them, because when prospects ask questions, they're engaged in the presentation process.

When objections arise, validate input by saying things like, 'That's an important point. . . .' Then probe to find out more, paraphrase to show that you understand, and present a positive response, as described in Table 18-1.

Table 18-1	Responding to Prospect Objections
Objection	*Positive Response*
Lack of belief or trust in your business.	Share testimonials.
Preference for a competitor.	Never bad-mouth. Instead, present unique benefits included with your offering and show how the prospect can receive greater value and cost-effectiveness from your business. If you're familiar with the competitor, consider complimenting the competitor followed by 'and we do that and more'.
Concern over cost.	Present pricing options, volume discounts, payment terms or other incentives to address the concern. Then move quickly from emphasis on the cost expended to a discussion of the value received, including warranties, service, reliability, convenience and quality. If appropriate, discuss the cost of *not* making the purchase.

As long as your presentation is focused on price, you're emphasising what's in the purchase for you. Shift the focus to your offering's value to move the presentation to a discussion of what's in it for your prospect.

Chapter 19

Making the Sale

In This Chapter

▶ Using marketing communications to convert prospects into customers

▶ Leveraging each step of the sale process

*Y*ou have a great product or service (see Chapter 3). You project a clear, strong, positive business image (see Chapters 6 and 7). And you've run ads, sent direct mailers, optimised a website and driven traffic to your business (see the chapters in Parts III and IV). In other words, by now you have plenty of prospects. So what do you do next?

If you're like most businesses, you follow the *if it ain't broke, don't fix it* rule. You run more ads, send more mailers, pull more people to your website and, as a result, you keep building more and more interest in your offering.

But if you're like the most successful businesses, this point is the one at which you shift emphasis. After all, your ultimate goal isn't to gather prospects but to gain customers.

Prospect generation is a step on your marketing path, but this step is not your destination. After your prospect pipeline is full, you need to convert interest to action. That means making the sale, closing the deal and winning the customer. That's what this chapter is all about.

Turning Prospects into Customers

Most people become customers over time and after encountering multiple marketing messages from your business. Plan your marketing communications to move prospects through the steps illustrated in Figure 19-1 and described in this list:

1. **Gain positive attention and awareness.**

   Because people tend to do business with people and businesses they know and trust, prospect conversion begins with awareness development. Use advertising, one-to-one communications, publicity, networking and presentations to introduce your company and to develop positive perceptions in the minds of prospects and those who influence your prospects' purchase decisions.

2. **Generate interest in the advantages and benefits of your product or service.**

   Your objective at this stage is to convey how your offering provides a unique solution to customer wants and needs and to make people think, *this sounds worth looking into.*

3. **Heighten the prospect's purchase desire.**

   Use one-to-one communications, promotions and special offers to draw prospects to your business and to prompt them to schedule face-to-face meetings, watch product demonstrations, obtain samples or price proposals or take other steps that help deepen their belief that your product uniquely addresses their wants and needs.

4. **Close the sale.**

   Present your offer, address questions, overcome objections, help the customer reach a satisfying decision and then make the buying transaction an easy, efficient and enjoyable process.

Don't jump the gun. Plan each marketing communication to move prospects to the next step on the buying-decision path.

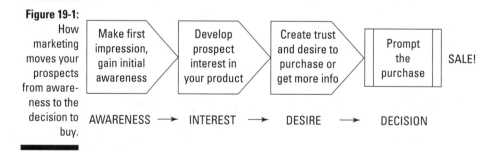

Figure 19-1: How marketing moves your prospects from awareness to the decision to buy.

| Make first impression, gain initial awareness | Develop prospect interest in your product | Create trust and desire to purchase or get more info | Prompt the purchase | SALE! |

AWARENESS → INTEREST → DESIRE → DECISION

In rare instances, the awareness-interest-desire-action scenario, called *AIDA* by marketers, happens with a single communication. Sometimes infomercials, retail websites or direct mailers lead prospects through all the steps in one fell swoop. But single-communication, on-the-spot selling usually occurs only with certain kinds of high-appeal, low-cost, low-involvement and low-risk products. More complex purchases require multiple marketing messages.

Suppose that a new pre-school wants to enrol 30 toddlers. With no existing awareness or reputation, the pre-school owners would be expecting parents to leapfrog over the decision process if they ran ads saying, 'Introducing our new pre-school. Call to register children between 2 and 4 years old.'

They'd be more apt to succeed if they precede the enrolment request with a programme that builds awareness, interest and trust. They may begin with a message saying: 'Our new pre-school and playground are ready to serve 30 lucky 2- to 5-year-olds. Please join us on Thursday afternoon for an open house and tour or call any time for a personal tour or appointment.'

The first approach calls for the order before the prospect is ready for the question. The second approach seeks to build a relationship and rapport. Which would you respond to more comfortably?

Another truth to remember as you seek to reach and convert customers is that unless a person is a true prospect for your offering – or someone who influences a prospect for your offering – any amount of communication amounts to wasted time and effort.

The number of *people* you reach with your marketing programme really doesn't matter. What's important is how many *qualified prospects* you reach and how you move them through the steps toward taking action – whether that means a purchase, a recommendation, a presentation invitation, inclusion in publicity coverage or any other marketing objective.

Think about the earlier pre-school example. Suppose that the owners run an ad in a newspaper delivered to 20,000 homes in the pre-school's market area. If 5 per cent of those homes have 2- to 4-year-olds, the ad reaches 1,000 prospects. But if only half of those prospects want and can afford pre-school, then the ad has the potential to reach only 500 *qualified* prospects.

Of those 500 qualified prospects, however, some miss the ad, some won't be interested, some already have a different solution and some (drum roll, please) convert into prospective customers, as shown in Table 19-1.

Table 19-1	Where Do All the Prospects Go?
Where Prospects Disappear	**Why Prospects Disappear**
The ad won't catch the majority of prospects.	If the ad has the potential to reach 500 qualified prospects, it may only gain the awareness of a few hundred. The others may not read the paper on the day the ad runs, the ad may not grab them or they may be too busy to notice the offer.
Many prospects who become aware won't have interest.	If 200 prospects notice the ad, only a portion will have interest. The others may be committed to a competitor, they may not be in the market for the offering or the message may not motivate them.
Of those with interest, only some will consider the offer.	If 50 prospects are interested, a portion may consider accepting the ad's offer. The others may decide, based on the specifics of the product, price, offer or presentation, not to part with their time or money at that moment.
Of those who take action, a few may ultimately decide to buy.	In other words, only a very few of the prospects that the ad reaches are likely to take the action or accept the offer presented in the ad. And of those, only a small percentage will convert to customers. That's why marketers need to communicate frequently using multiple forms of communication to keep the pump primed for success.

Navigating the Sale Process

The cost of your marketing programme is the price you pay to play in the business arena, and the sale is your first point of investment return and your chance at a big payoff:

- ✔ Seal the deal and you win a new customer and immediate revenue.

- ✔ Exceed the customer's expectations and you reap repeat purchases – each at a fraction of the cost of recruiting a new customer.

- ✔ Develop loyalty and you achieve positive word of mouth and reviews that lead to referrals, starting your chance at a new three-way payoff all over again.

Figure 19-2 illustrates a *marketing accelerator* – a circle within the marketing cycle where sales and service efforts intensify to convert prospects to customers, customers to repeat buyers and repeat buyers to loyalists who become ambassadors that recruit new prospects to your business (see Chapter 20 for information on building customer loyalty).

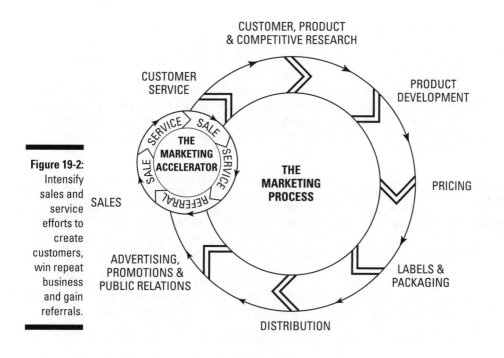

Figure 19-2: Intensify sales and service efforts to create customers, win repeat business and gain referrals.

Selling redefined

Forget terms like *high pressure, low pressure, hard sell* or *soft sell.* For that matter, forget about *selling* and concentrate on drawing people to your business and helping them *buy* your products and services.

As the seller in the buyer-seller relationship, your role involves knowing and believing in your offering, persuasively communicating your product's benefits and value, successfully leading the buyer through the decision process and facilitating an easy and satisfying purchase transaction.

Getting off to a good start

Closing a sale begins with opening a relationship, and the first step is to establish contact with your prospect, whether online, in person or by phone, mail or email.

Welcoming customers in person

Here's an amazing fact: Fewer than half of all people who enter a retail outlet make a purchase. What's more, as customers increasingly treat the bricks-and-mortar outlet as a showroom before buying at discounted prices online, the percentage of shoppers who become buyers continues to decline. The percentages are much higher in supermarkets and convenience stores and far lower in exclusive boutiques and galleries. But across the board, the *conversion rate* – the number of prospects who become buyers – is ripe for improvement.

No matter what kind of business yours is – business-to-consumer, business-to-business, bricks-and-mortar or online – you can calculate a conversion rate by counting the number of people who enter your business (or land on your website) and the number who make a purchase. Divide the number of purchasers by the number of shoppers or visitors to get your looker-to-buyer conversion rate, and then set a goal for improvement.

The rate you aim for depends on your business. Retailers that attract shoppers who arrive with a clear need that a purchase can fulfil experience higher conversion rates than those who attract people who are just shopping.

Publicly available web analytics from Fireclick (`http://index.fire click.com`) show average online retail conversion rates in the range of 2 to 3 per cent, and other reports show Amazon converting 8 per cent of visitors. In the bricks-and-mortar world, research shows conversion rates between 20 and 40 per cent, with fashion retailers on the low end and electronics retailers on the high end.

Interacting with shoppers

Especially in physical retail settings, the best way to grow retail conversions is to increase the number of prospects who have contact with your staff. It sounds too simple to be true, but retail scientists (they *do* exist) have validated the fact. They've also proven that staff contact increases the time a prospect spends in a retail setting, which directly affects spending levels.

Adopt these proven approaches:

- ✔ Use displays and personal contact to intercept shoppers upon arrival.

- ✔ Offer a shopping basket, explain a special offer or give a quick store orientation to increase interaction and shopper involvement.

- ✔ Enhance comfort by pointing out refreshment and sitting areas, play areas for children and fitting rooms for shoppers.

- ✔ When you see signs of shopper uncertainty, step in to reinforce decisions, suggest complementary items or alternative choices or make other recommendations to both facilitate and increase the sale.

- ✔ Don't prejudge prospects. Watch, listen and respond to prospect cues instead of letting first impressions limit your sales expectations.

For advice on retail success, see the nearby sidebar, 'Want more sales? Follow the retail rules'.

Want more sales? Follow the retail rules

Paco Underhill has researched and verified how people shop and buy in every kind of physical retail setting. His book, *Why We Buy: The Science of Shopping* (Simon & Schuster), sells tens of thousands of copies a year in more than two dozen languages. Among the findings he shares:

- ✔ Shoppers race through the entryway 'decompression zone' before slowing down and turning right. That means the space that's 5 to 15 paces beyond and to the right of your front door is your most valuable store real estate.

- ✔ They buy more if you free their hands by giving them a shopping basket or bag.

- ✔ They leave, abandoning intended purchases, if they see long queues at your cash register.

- ✔ Women make an immediate U-turn and leave an aisle if the aisle is so narrow that another shopper gives them a 'butt brush'.

- ✔ Store cleanliness matters, especially to female shoppers.

- ✔ Change drives sales. New windows and reorganisation on the floor give your retail space a sense of evolution and excitement.

- ✔ In small retail shops, owners need to be visible and to interact with customers.

- ✔ Shoppers are conscious of what they see, taste, smell, touch and hear, so engage them through all five senses. Use knowledge of your shopper profiles throughout the day to adjust music mixes and experiences accordingly.

Converting online visits to online sales

Going for the online sale means first designing and building a good website (see Chapter 10); then driving visits from qualified, interested customers (see Chapter 11); and finally, and most importantly, converting site visits to the action you're aiming to achieve.

When selling online, you've no opportunity for customised presentations or negotiations. Your site makes an immediate favourable impression, presents a good offer and provides an easy way to make the purchase or the customer clicks to another site within seconds.

To win the sale:

- ✔ You have only three to five seconds to convince a visitor to stay on your site. That means the page has to load immediately and present a balance of words and graphics that persuade a shopper to look further. Realise that most people direct their eyes first to the upper left-hand portion of your page, so use that space wisely. And don't pull attention away with irrelevant and annoying ads.

- ✔ Make viewing and selecting your product easy. Limit the number of products your customer has to consider and don't distract customers with irrelevant offerings.

- ✔ Don't make customers use pull-down menus, go through multiple clicks or register before purchasing. Simplify the process so that the shopper doesn't have to visit too many different pages to complete the transaction. Then be sure that making a purchase is a clear and easy process. Watch someone try to use your site from arrival through purchase. If you notice steps in the process that cause confusion or delay, work to alter and simplify them.

- ✔ Make the checkout easy, reassuring, trustworthy and well-supported by your business. See the nearby sidebar, 'Battling abandoned shopping carts' for advice. Chapter 10 includes information on building e-commerce sites with convenient and, most of all, secure online payment options.

Negotiating mutually agreeable solutions

If you're in sales, you're a negotiator.

Negotiation is the primary approach for dealing with the differences that precede nearly all major and even some minor purchase decisions, whether your customer is seeking a better price, faster delivery, added-value services, customised options or some other variation of the product or service under consideration.

Battling abandoned shopping carts

A company called 3dcart (www.3dcart.com) provides complete shopping cart solutions for online stores of all sizes, which all share one common goal – to get customers to complete the order and make the purchase. From the 3dcart eCommerce University (www.3dcart.com/ecommerce-university.html), follow these five steps to overcome the common enemy of online sales success: shopping cart abandonment.

1. Save shopping cart data even if the customer doesn't complete the form. The shopper's browser may have crashed or the person may have navigated away from the checkout page. Make sure that your site's cookies save form data so customers can easily pick up where they left off, upping your conversion rate as a result.

2. Give your customers a one-page checkout. When you go to the supermarket, you don't pick the longest queue. The same holds true online. A one-page checkout ensures that customers won't lose interest or get frustrated midway through the checkout. The 2010 Vancouver Olympics online store sent half of buyers to a two-page checkout and the other half to a one-pager. The single-page checkout form helped conversion rates jump by 21.8 per cent.

3. If a shopping cart is abandoned by a return customer, reach out with an email reminder to re-ignite interest. If the customer ditched his cart right when the shipping fee was added, include a voucher code or discount with the email. A few shopping carts even have built-in modules that save you time by sending automatic reminder emails.

4. Gain trust with security certificates. A little peace of mind goes a long way, so reassure customers that their personal data is safe. Post security certificates in visible areas of the checkout process, clearly identifying security programs like McAfee and SSL certificates to show customers that you care about their privacy. The result: higher trust, better conversion rates and fewer abandoned carts.

5. Offer support resources without making customers navigate from the checkout page. Assume that customers have questions and put the resources they need right at their fingertips. Place links and contact information for customer support right on the checkout page. Live chat is another great feature for addressing questions.

What's more, most negotiations involve people with whom you want to maintain relationships, which makes conducting a civilised negotiation that results in a mutually acceptable solution all the more important.

Negotiation experts offer this advice:

✔ Begin negotiations only after you've a firm purchase proposal from your customer.

✔ Know what you need out of the deal and what you're willing to offer to make the sale happen.

 ✔ Know the buyer's interests. Listen carefully – not just to words but to the issues the buyer is asking you to address – so you can craft solutions that address the real points of difference.

 ✔ Know your deal-breakers. Don't be unreasonable, but know your 'walk away' price or the kind of concessions that you simply aren't willing to make.

 ✔ Finally, whenever possible, negotiate calmly and in person. Email is a poor substitute because it allows little opportunity for discussion or compromise, and the whole point of negotiation is to arrive at a win-win solution that serves the interests of you and your buyer.

Watching for buying signals

Many salespeople miss the moment when the seller needs to give the prospect a chance to buy. Instead, they keep talking, unconsciously undoing the sale by raising issues that confuse rather than comfort the decision maker. As a result, they sell right past the point when the prospect was ready to become a customer.

The minute your prospect indicates a readiness to buy, *stop selling*.

As soon as a shopper starts agreeing with your responses to stated objections or you pick up non-verbal and verbal buying signals, such as the ones in Table 19-2, move from selling to affirming your prospect's good choice and get ready to close the deal.

Table 19-2	Buying Signals
Examples of Non-verbal Cues	*Examples of Verbal Cues*
Relaxed demeanour	Increased questions about product details
Increased eye contact	Requests to see features demonstrated a second or third time
Leaning forward, uncrossing arms or legs	Questions about customisation options
Showing enthusiasm beyond simple nods, which often indicate not purchase-readiness but agreement with points being made	Questions about delivery schedules
Making calculations, studying sales tags or a contract, reaching for a pen, wallet or handbag	Questions about payment plans or options

Asking for the order

WARNING!

More than half of all sales presentations drift to a finish without an order request. Don't let yours be among them.

Follow one of these closing approaches:

- ✔ **Ask for the order.** Don't rush it or you'll race the customer to the word *no,* which is a hard place from which to make a U-turn. Wait for buying cues and, after you receive them, present one more summary of benefits before moving toward closure with questions like, 'How many would you like?' and, 'When would you like it delivered?' Gain positive responses to those gateway questions and then close the deal.

- ✔ **Make a buying assumption.** For service or major-investment products, you may choose to replace the outright order request with a buying assumption. Using this approach, you paraphrase your prospect's needs, reiterate how your offering provides a cost-effective solution and explain when you can deliver or begin work, ending with a question such as, 'Will that schedule work for you?'

- ✔ **Gain agreement to a delivery plan.** This approach is similar to making a buying assumption, but it goes one step further in involving the prospect in the closing process. By presenting a detailed, written schedule, you convey your readiness to do the job, your ability to do it well and your willingness to adapt your plans to your prospect's wants and needs. By providing input to the plan, your prospect begins to take ownership, an important prerequisite to actually making the purchase.

Making buying easy

The sidebar 'Battling abandoned shopping carts' earlier in this chapter gives advice on easing the buying process online. In the bricks-and-mortar world, the transaction happens over a desk, or where a proposal or contract is signed, or at a cash register. Either way, this point is where relationships begin – and where loyalty or dissatisfaction starts to grow.

After your customer says yes, it's time to complete the transaction. You also need to begin delivering on all the promises you made as you presented the attributes, benefits and values of your offering and business.

Follow these steps:

- ✔ **Make the transaction flawlessly easy.** In professional service businesses, see that the contract is professionally produced, error-free, easy to understand and delivered in a manner that reinforces the calibre of your business and product. In retail settings, be sure that the cash/wrap area is clean, adequately sized, efficient and well-staffed with people trained to affirm the buyer's decision and begin the process of customer service. (Customers literally abandon the product in their hands and make a quick exit when they see long lines at a cash register.)

- ✔ **Add unexpected value.** Package your offering well and include an unexpected enclosure, be it a sincere thank-you note (*not* a one-size-fits-all pre-printed card), a thank-you gift, an invitation to a new-customer event, a next-purchase certificate or some other offer that inspires customer commitment to your business.

- ✔ **Make the purchase your first step in developing customer satisfaction and loyalty, which is the topic of Chapter 20.**

Chapter 20

Enhancing Customer Service and Developing Loyalty

In This Chapter

▶ Delivering the kind of service that customers want

▶ Using complaints as opportunities to improve your customer service

▶ Exceeding expectations to build customer loyalty

*G*reat companies know the profile of their most likely prospects, attract those people into their businesses, convert them to customers and lock them in with a level of service and appreciation they can't find elsewhere.

Especially during times of competitive or economic threat, developing unshakeable customer relationships is the smartest – and most economically efficient – way to proceed. Strong customer relationships protect your business from competitive assault. What's more, they lead to customer loyalty, which translates to repeat sales at a fraction of the marketing cost and effort required to find, inform, interest and sell new prospects. Plus, loyal customers spread goodwill for your business, bringing along a tide of new customers with their positive words.

Creating loyal customers through amazing customer service is essential to business success. This chapter shows why and how.

What Customers Want

Customers want product value that exceeds the product price, but that's not all. They also want interactions that exceed their expectations:

- ✔ They want to be greeted promptly, whether on the phone, in person or on a quick-loading website.
- ✔ They want their concerns addressed with expertise, efficiency and friendliness.
- ✔ They want clear communication from knowledgeable people.
- ✔ They want solutions that make them feel important and valued.

What they don't want: Long waits. In person, you test their tolerance at 90 seconds, and 2-minute waits are considered complete service failures. Online, they're willing to wait only a few seconds before they navigate away from your site. Waits are a signal of service indifference, and service indifference is the biggest reason for customer departure.

The Fundamentals of Customer Service

Services and *service* are not the same thing.

- ✔ *Services* are what you provide to customers as part of your product.
- ✔ *Service* is how well you do what you do – how well you deliver your product to your customer.

In many businesses, customer parking and free coffee are considered expected offerings. They become indicators of great service when they rise above standard levels. For example, a clean, well-signed car park with the most convenient spaces reserved not for staff but for customers, and refreshments provided in an inviting reception area, set service-oriented businesses apart.

To move your business into the circle of excellence, become familiar with each step in the service cycle. Then evaluate how your business currently performs at each point of service delivery, set improvement objectives, target your efforts toward those customers you're most likely to turn into loyalists, and build a company-wide environment in which excellent service becomes a required standard. The following sections take you through these steps.

Mastering the service cycle

Customer service starts before the sales presentation and continues well past the time of purchase. It includes these steps:

1. **Establish contact with a prompt, friendly greeting.**

2. **Build rapport.**

   A marketing truth goes like this: People don't buy because you make them understand. They buy because they feel understood.

3. **Present your product as a high-value solution to the customer's needs (see Chapter 18 for presentation tips).**

4. **Make the sale following the advice for reading buying signals and closing the deal in Chapter 19.**

5. **Make the sales transaction quick and efficient.**

   During the sales transaction isn't the time for lengthy customer research or promotional pitches for additional products. Don't complicate the moment of payment or you risk losing the sale.

6. **Deliver the product, reaffirm the buying decision, offer to be of ongoing service and invite future business.**

7. **Monitor customer satisfaction and troubleshoot any issues that cause customer concern.**

8. **Follow up to assess service satisfaction, confirm complete satisfaction and ask for future business.**

Evaluating and improving service levels

Products lead to sales, but service leads to loyalty, and only loyalty translates to relationships that deliver customer raves, referrals and repeat business.

Service – exemplary service – never goes out of style, nor does it ever reach a finish line. Customers expect every encounter with your business to exceed previously established expectations. As a result, your customer service programme needs to be ever-evolving through ongoing evaluation, discovery of weak spots and continuous improvement.

One evaluation step is to accompany every operational decision with the question, 'How does this help our customer?' Many business decisions unintentionally add management layers and cumbersome processes that detract from good customer service.

Another step is to test every aspect of service delivery on an ongoing basis, assessing not only customer perceptions of your service but also the commitment your business makes to a service culture.

As you work to improve your customer service levels, consider the following:

- ✔ **Make a guarantee that strips away buyer risk and demonstrates your belief in your product's quality.** Whether you offer a money-back guarantee or a price or performance guarantee, make the guarantee straightforward and liberal (no small print), relevant and substantial (worth the effort it takes to request it), available immediately (no management approvals required) and easy to collect.

- ✔ **Notice and immediately overcome dissatisfaction.** Compensate dissatisfied customers on the spot by offering upgrades, discounts or premiums when something goes wrong. Don't wait for a complaint. Most people never register dissatisfaction verbally. Instead, they quietly slip out the door once and for all, perhaps politely saying thanks as they exit your business for the final time. See the section 'Reading customer clues to dissatisfaction' later in this chapter.

Treat all customers with the utmost respect and the high level of service they deserve, and then double your efforts with customers who are most likely to be of high influence in their online and off-line worlds. More and more service establishments are checking out their customers on Twitter, Facebook and LinkedIn to see which ones actively communicate their impressions to strong online followings. Open a free account at www.klout.com, enter the names of customers and find out which ones score high in online influence.

Cultivating 'best customers'

Every person who buys from your business is an important asset who deserves your total courtesy and best service. But as you tailor unique solutions and extend special services, you want to direct the extra investment toward the kind of customer that's likely to become a profitable, loyal, repeat customer who speaks well on your company's behalf.

Some customers are never satisfied by anything other than the very lowest price. Others are never satisfied, even if you provide your products or services for free. Be aware of the following three customer categories and weight your efforts toward developing relationship customers in your business.

Relationship customers

Relationship customers value loyalty and commitment. They're the ones you invest in for the long haul. Recognise them, remember them, do them favours, offer them gifts, bend your rules, anticipate their needs and win their trust. They'll become loyal customers for life.

Defensive marketing

In sports, defenders protect their team from threats, withstand attacks and prevent opponents from gaining an advantage. Defenders protect the goal. They place more emphasis on stopping an opponent from gaining an advantage than on winning new territory or scoring points.

You can take's a customer service lesson from that analogy. When sales are down, many businesses go on the marketing offensive – reducing prices, launching promotions and increasing advertising to win new customers.

Defensive marketers place greatest value on keeping existing customers and protecting ongoing relationships by providing unrivalled service and communication. They fortify themselves against competitive attacks by training customers to expect service levels that other businesses can't meet. They build customer loyalty – and reap the resulting benefits – by delivering consistently enhanced value to customers, who grow ever more loyal as a result.

Transaction customers

Transaction customers are interested primarily in immediate convenience or price. They represent sales and generate word of mouth for your business, but they leave you for another company in a split second, so gauge your efforts to meet their high demands accordingly.

Toxic customers

Sooner or later, you'll encounter an excessively negative customer. When you do, you've two choices. One is to get defensive and try to prove why your business is right in spite of the bad opinion held by the person standing in front of you. This route almost certainly leads to an argument, which erodes your customer service standard, spurs negative word of mouth and leaves you in a losing position.

The better approach is to use the same friendly service style for which your business is known – listening, trying to solve the customer's complaint and working to arrive at a mutually agreeable outcome. Many times, this service approach calms the customer and leads to a positive outcome.

But some customers demand concessions you shouldn't make. Catering to unreasonable demands risks your company's financial stability and threatens your ability to retain good employees. When you encounter an overly negative or abusive customer, make a choice in favour of your company. Forgo the customer's business and dare to part ways if

- ✔ The customer acts abusively to you or your employees
- ✔ The customer abuses your systems
- ✔ The customer ignores your payment policies or refuses to pay what you know is the fair price for your offering

Creating a customer service environment

Make sky-high customer satisfaction a core value of your company. Treat employees and customers like VIPs by following these ten tips:

- ✔ Get to know your customers, recognise them as individuals and treat them like friends, insiders and valued partners.
- ✔ Create a team of great service people and reward their efforts with frequent and sincere gestures of recognition and appreciation.
- ✔ Communicate often – with customers and with employees.
- ✔ Anticipate customer needs.
- ✔ Thank customers for their business.
- ✔ Encourage customer requests and respond with tailor-made solutions.

Is your business beloved?

Jeanne Bliss has led the customer-experience strategies for Lands' End, Coldwell Banker, Allstate, Microsoft and Mazda. Below are ten questions she presents to help you determine whether your business is a 'beloved company'. See whether you can answer yes to eight or more.

- ❑ Do your customers talk about your belief in them?
- ❑ Do your customers give you referrals?
- ❑ Do your customers want you in their lives?
- ❑ Do your customers grow your business for you?
- ❑ Do your customers say that they love you?
- ❑ Do your employees feel treated like partners?

- ❑ Do your employees know that you believe in them?
- ❑ Do your employees have a seat at the table?
- ❑ Do your employees become part of the story of your business?
- ❑ Do your employees have permission to impact customers' lives?

© CustomerBliss 2010

Jeanne Bliss is the author of *I Love You More Than My Dog: Five Decisions That Drive Extreme Customer Loyalty in Good Times and Bad* (Portfolio Trade). For more information, visit www.customerbliss.com

✔ Empower employees to do the right thing for customers, including bending rules to keep loyal customers happy.

✔ Provide extra services and favours to high-volume, long-time customers.

✔ Make dealing with your business a highlight of your customer's day.

✔ Teach your customers to expect your company's level of service and keep your standard so high that no other business can rise to the level you set.

You know that you've succeeded when employees and customers share their praise. See the nearby sidebar, 'Is your business beloved?' for a quiz from internationally recognised customer-experience expert Jeanne Bliss.

Dealing with Concerns and Complaints

Dissatisfied customers complain to dozens of friends and post disparaging messages that go viral online, but remember that if you handle complaints well, you can circumvent potential damage and strengthen your customer relationships. Use customer complaints to lead your business to service improvements and higher satisfaction levels.

Understanding why customers don't complain

The Direct Selling Education Foundation reports that for every complaint that a customer makes, the average business has another 26 customers with unreported problems. Here's why disgruntled customers stay mum:

✔ They don't think that anyone in the company cares.

✔ They don't know where to register their dissatisfaction.

✔ They're embarrassed to say anything because they know the owner.

You can't fix it if you can't hear it. Talk with customers to hear their concerns, along with suggestions for how you can improve your service.

Encouraging complaints

You're better off hearing about dissatisfaction directly than indirectly – or not at all – so be open to concerns and comments, and study every word of feedback you receive. (See Chapter 11 for information on encouraging online reviews and keeping your cool when a bad review gets lobbed your way.)

✓ **Talk with current customers.** Find out their opinions and their ideas about how you can be of better service. Opt for ongoing conversation rather than one-time surveys, and give customers the chance to explain themselves fully and without interruption. In addition to what they say, watch for unstated clues to dissatisfaction (see the following section).

✓ **Talk with past customers to discover why they left, where they took their business and what differences they were seeking.**

✓ **Talk with employees.** Ask what kinds of concerns they're hearing. What needs do they sense? What do customers want that you aren't delivering?

✓ **Respond promptly and show appreciation for input.** When changes result, thank the person who shared the idea. If a change is in the pipe-line, explain your plan and listen for further input.

Encourage customer pickiness. Companies that win customers for life create discerning and demanding customers with expectations so high that no other business can rise to the occasion.

Reading customer clues to dissatisfaction

Many customers consider small business owners and employees their friends. For that reason, they hesitate to directly complain or criticise.

This fact means that small business owners need to watch for unstated clues to dissatisfaction, including the following:

✓ Customers compliment other suppliers.

✓ Customers reminisce about how things *used to be.*

✓ The compliments they used to offer stop coming.

✓ Customers return products, an act you should treat as a non-verbal form of customer dissatisfaction. If products are coming back, either they're faulty or your communication was unclear and the product was misrep-resented. Similarly, watch what's backlogged as an indicator of unmet consumer demand.

Hidden in your customers' comments may be concerns or complaints about your business, so listen carefully.

Turning complaints into loyalty springboards

When a customer is dissatisfied, stop whatever else you're doing and give your full attention. First deal with the customer and then deal with the problem. Follow these steps:

1. **Listen to the problem.**

   - Let the customer rant, preferably out of earshot of others.

   - Don't argue, make excuses or blame others. Don't make the problem seem routine by pulling out a form to complete.

   - Empathise. Paraphrase the problem and offer to help.

   - If your company is at fault, apologise. If you're not sure, give the customer the benefit of the doubt, within reason. Protect the relationship, the potential future business and the chance for good word of mouth.

2. **Take action.**

   - Offer options to allow the customer some control over the outcome.

   - Say what you can do, not what you can't. Opt for *I'll see that the refund is ready by 10 a.m. tomorrow* rather than *We can't refund you today*.

   - If your product or company is at fault, a refund or replacement isn't enough. Provide a no-strings-attached add-on that delivers value with no additional spending requirement.

   - Keep in mind that refunds or exchanges may address the complaint, but only personal service repairs the relationship.

3. **Follow up.**

   - Confirm that the problem was resolved to the customer's complete satisfaction and ask whether you can be of further help.

   - Thank the customer for voicing concern and letting your company make things right.

4. **Fix your business by revamping systems if necessary and asking:**

   - Is this the first complaint of its kind or one of many?

   - Can we eliminate this fault?

   - Did we address the customer concern promptly and well?

McKinsey & Company has conducted research showing that when a company resolves a complaint, more than half of initially dissatisfied customers buy again from that business. If the company resolves the complaint rapidly, the number rises to 80 per cent. If the company resolves the complaint on the spot, the chance of keeping the customer's business soars above 90 per cent, often higher than if the customer had never experienced the negative issue.

Making Loyal Customers for Life

Small businesses have an advantage over larger ones when it comes to making customers for life. In most small businesses, the person who facilitates the sale continues to have customer contact after the event. As a result, the style and service mode that attracted the customer continues unaltered, and the customer's buying decision is reaffirmed during every future contact.

As small businesses get larger, some adopt structures that resemble those of their big-business role models, and suddenly, their customer focus begins to change. Don't let this situation happen to you. Manage your business so that every person in your organisation realises the value of every customer – not only to your sales today but also to your sales tomorrow and well into the future, when the customer's positive comments will lead others to your business.

Research suggests that getting a new customer costs five times more than retaining a current one. Other studies show that customers who claim to be 'totally satisfied' are six times more likely to become repeat purchasers than customers who claim to be only 'satisfied' and that loyal customers are worth ten times the value of single-purchase buyers. Why else does loyalty matter? Consider this list:

- ✔ Loyal customers account for higher buying rates and lower marketing and service costs than other customers.

- ✔ Loyal customers involve fewer business risks because you know their credit status, buying preferences and purchasing patterns.

- ✔ Loyal customers respond to customer service that costs far less than the cost involved to recruit a new customer.

- ✔ Loyal customers are the best source of qualified referrals.

- ✔ Loyal customers lead to a loyal staff (and vice versa) because long-term relationships enhance the business environment.

Valuing your customers

Imagine that each of your customers arrived wearing a price tag that read *Replacement Cost: $1,000*. Imagine that even your inquiries and responses to ads came equipped with signs that said *I cost $75*. Don't you think that your employees would handle each contact with greater care if they realised what bringing that person into your business cost – and what recruiting a replacement would cost?

Estimating the cost of a new customer

To roughly estimate the cost of bringing a new customer into your business, apply the following formula:

Begin with the cost of last year's marketing programme. Even a wild guess at what your company spent in advertising, sales, public relations, promotions, signage, brochures and other communication vehicles provides a good starting point.

Subtract marketing costs that were directed toward repeat or loyal customer marketing communications – for example, customer newsletters, customer promotions and customer entertainment.

Divide by the number of new customers you attracted last year.

The result is a rough approximation of what it costs to develop a new customer for your business.

Share your findings so everyone in your business is aware of the valuable commodity they deal with each time they have customer contact.

After you know the cost of getting a customer, you have an indicator of how much expense you can justify to keep that customer on board.

If your calculations show that getting a new customer costs you £300, you know not to risk losing that person's business over a £50 dispute. Whether it means accepting a questionable return, writing off a contested charge or indulging a customer with extra service or an unexpected gift, the investment is likely to cost less than the expense and effort required to replace that customer with a new recruit.

Measuring customer economics

Whether a customer buys from you once or a hundred times, your initial marketing investment is the same. What changes is your customer's lifetime value (LTV) to your business.

LTV for a one-time customer = Profit from first and only sale

LTV for a long-term customer = Profit from first sale + profit from second sale + profit from third sale + profit from fourth sale + profits from all future sales over coming weeks and years

The most efficient way to put money on your bottom line is to develop relationships and satisfaction levels that lead to increases in purchases by established customers. Think of the initial sale as the first step toward winning the customer's business for life – or at least for as long as that person remains in the market for the kind of products or services you offer.

Benchmarking satisfaction levels and cultivating loyalty

Customers vote with their wallets, and your cash register is their ballot box. If your sales-per-customer and repeat business rates are increasing, you're doing something right. If they're declining, you need to go into repair mode.

Your business is on the right track if it has

✔ A growing number of new customers coming through the door

✔ A declining number of customers defecting after one or two purchases

✔ An increase in the expenditure per sales transaction

Good marketers consider the customer their boss. As you monitor customer satisfaction, ask yourself, 'Is my boss giving me a pay rise?'

The first step toward developing loyalty is to get real about the current satisfaction levels of those who buy from your business. Each of your customers falls into one of the following three categories:

✔ **Satisfied customers find their relationship with your business acceptable.** They have no complaints about the promptness with which they're served, the accuracy of their transactions, the responsiveness of your service or the effectiveness and friendliness of your staff. But neither are they amazed by their dealings with your business, and for that reason they're susceptible to better offers from competitors.

✔ **Dissatisfied customers believe that their value and service expectations were not met.** Perhaps they received outright poor service. More likely they received mediocre service based on how they were greeted, the time it took to help them, the way their complaints were handled or the quality of the service or product they received.

After customers reach dissatisfaction, they make an immediate or gradual departure from your business. Most pay their final bill politely and say thank you on the way out the door, and 94 out of 100 leave without a word of complaint to your business. But they won't remain silent. They personally share their dissatisfaction in conversations with anywhere from 5 to 20 other people, and they tell countless others if they choose to post word of their discontent on the Internet.

> ✔ **Loyal customers are the only customers safe from defection.** They reduce the cost side of your profit and loss statement while benefiting the revenue side by costing less, spending more and spreading the word better than others who buy from your business.

Refer to Table 20-1 as you work to move customers into the loyal customer category.

Table 20-1	Customer Loyalty Prescriptions	
Customer Type	**Customer Mind-set**	**Service Prescription**
Dissatisfied customers	Service expectations have not been met.	Establish rapport. Find out about and address concerns. The damage may be done, but try anyway.
Satisfied customers	Find your service acceptable but aren't overwhelmed. They leave for a better price, offer, convenience or recognition.	Treat them like VIPs. Demonstrate appreciation. Do them favours. Offer added value. Bend your rules. Anticipate their needs. Win their trust.
Loyal customers	Safe from defection as long as their sky-high service expectations are met.	Treat them like valuable assets. Follow the service prescriptions for satisfied customers but double the dosage. Don't take them for granted, burden them with your problems or test their patience while you court new customers.

Closing the quality gap

A *quality gap* occurs when a difference exists between a customer's service expectation and the perceived level of service received. The quality gap exists entirely in the customer's mind. Whether service is satisfactory depends completely on your customer's opinion. The litmus test is simply whether the customer's perception of your service exceeded or fell short of the customer's expectations.

Because you can't read your customers' minds, the best route to assessing how you're doing against customer service expectations is to understand the variables that affect customer satisfaction and to reach for optimal performance in each area.

To eliminate the possibility of a quality gap and to build customer loyalty, expect your customers to have high service expectations and then exceed them with each customer encounter.

Building loyalty through service

To walk into a business and be greeted by name is a customer luxury.

To check into a hotel and be welcomed as a frequent guest is a pleasure.

To be walked to your favourite table in a restaurant, to have your voice recognised in a phone call to a small business, to have a record of your purchases on file for easy reference – these things are the kinds of conveniences and service indicators that move satisfied customers into the loyal customer category.

Imagine this hotel check-in scenario:

> The receptionist enters your name in the computer, looks up and says, 'Welcome back! It's been nearly three months since your last stay, so you haven't seen our re-modelled restaurant. Let us know if we can make a reservation for you, and here's a card for a complimentary glass of wine with dinner. For now, let me get you registered. Last time you preferred a non-smoking room on the tenth floor. Do you have a different preference for this stay?'

> Now compare that with this approach: 'Good afternoon. Do you have a reservation? Under what name? Could you spell that again? Have you stayed with us before?'

To develop loyalty, never make a frequent guest feel like a first-time guest, and always aim to make even a first-time guest feel like a long-time friend.

Launching loyalty programmes

Loyalty programmes inspire increased business by rewarding repeat purchases with discounts or added-value offers. They also allow you to monitor what customers are buying – and with what frequency.

The concept of loyalty programmes took hold in the 1970s, when airlines launched the first frequent flyer reward programmes. Today, most consumers participate in at least one loyalty programme, and businesses everywhere are working to figure out how to add a loyalty programme to their marketing efforts.

Playing the 80/20 customer odds

The 80/20 rule maintains that 20 per cent of your consumers account for 80 per cent of your sales. Conversely, 80 per cent of your problems come from 20 per cent of your customers. The concept actually has a title, *Pareto's Law,* named after the economist who developed the theory formally known as the *law of misdistribution.*

Your goal: To acquire customers in the trouble-free, highly profitable 20 per cent group without being derailed by the problematic 20 per cent who gladly consume your time instead.

The approach: Listen to discontented customers and do what you can to right the wrongs they cite. But don't allow your energy to be consumed by those who may never be entirely happy with you or your business – or any other business, for that matter. Tip the marketing odds in favour of your business by focusing on your most content and profitable customers. Plan your marketing programme to cater to their wants and needs, telegraph their satisfactions to your market and let them serve as a magnet to attract more people just like them to your business.

Before launching a programme, establish your loyalty programme goals:

✔ To maintain customer spending habits in an effort to reverse the natural decline in buying activity that otherwise tends to occur over time.

✔ To increase sales by enhancing a feeling of customer inclusion.

✔ To show customer appreciation by providing rewards for past purchases, which tends to inspire additional buying activity.

✔ To collect information on customer buying patterns and preferences. Be cautious, though: Customers can feel duped if your programme looks more like an effort to conduct research than to extend rewards.

Consider the following loyalty programme formats:

✔ **Buy-ahead discounts:** Lock in loyalty at the time of a first purchase by providing an immediate bonus along with discounts on future purchases.

Benefit: Upfront revenue and customer commitment.

Downside: Because buy-ahead discounts require a purchase, customers view them more as product promotions than customer rewards.

✔ **Purchase-level rewards or discounts:** Offer customers a free gift or discount when they pass a certain spending level.

Benefit: Increased same-visit purchases in order to obtain the bonus.

Downside: The programme often requires small print clarification regarding which kinds of purchases apply, what spending level needs to be reached and what time period is involved. Its appeal relies on the reward's significance and simplicity.

✓ **Rebates against spending levels:** Offer a reward upon achievement of a spending level, usually in the form of a year-end rebate.

Benefit: Increased long-term purchases to obtain end-of-year payoff.

Downside: Success relies on the rebate's size and often inspires only the most cost-sensitive consumers.

✓ **Upgrades and special treatments:** Rely on the value of surprise rewards. Imagine driving into a car wash and having the attendant say, 'Our license plate reader tells us this is your tenth trip through our car wash, so let's make this one on us.'

Benefit: Spontaneous recognition and individualised customer service is a sure-fire loyalty-development formula.

Downside: Customers begin to anticipate and expect this kind of acknowledgement, so be prepared for ongoing rewards to keep your best customers inspired by your demonstration of appreciation.

Avoid programmes that look more like promotions than rewards or that provide incentives with too many strings attached. For example, a £10 certificate 'valid until the end of this month on any in-stock, regularly priced item of £24.99 or more' looks more like a come-on than a gift.

In customer service and in customer loyalty programmes, give customers what they want, deliver consistently, show true appreciation and exceed expectations that only your business can meet.

Part VI
The Part of Tens

For Dummies can help you get started with a huge range of subjects. Visit www.dummies.com/extras/smallbusinessmarketing for free bonus content, including forms designed to help your marketing efforts.

In this part . . .

✔ Grasp the ten most important questions to ask and answer before naming or renaming your business or one of its products.

✔ Understand the ten steps to getting active online.

✔ Follow ten steps to build your own easy-to-assemble marketing plan.

Chapter 21

Ten Questions to Answer before Choosing a Business Name

In This Chapter

▶ Selecting a business name that's available, original and memorable

▶ Taking steps to claim your new business name

*I*n your customer's mind, your name is the key to your brand image. Chosen well, your name can advance an image for your business that's unique, memorable, appropriate and likeable. This chapter provides ten questions to ask before committing to a new business name.

What Kind of Name Do You Want?

Most business names fit into one of the following categories:

✔ **The owner's name:** If Jim Smith opens an accounting firm, he can name it Jim Smith Accounting. The name is easy to choose, easy to register and sure to put forth the promise that Jim Smith is proud of this business, though it also screams 'solopreneur' and is hard to pass on if Jim decides he wants to sell his practice.

✔ **A geographic name:** A financial institution that calls itself Central Coast Bank has a name with local market appeal, but the name also restricts the institution from expanding outside the central coast area.

✔ **An alphabet name:** A name like ABC Paving used to have value because it topped the Yellow Page listings. With fewer people searching printed alphabetical listings, though, alphabet soup names offer few benefits, and their lack of personality or brand promise puts the businesses they label at a marketing disadvantage.

✔ **A descriptive name:** This type of name tells people what you do and how you do it. A consulting firm specialising in business turnarounds may call itself U-Turn Strategies to convey its offerings and its promise to clients.

✔ **A borrowed-interest name:** This type of name incorporates a word around which a business can build a story that becomes an accurate reflection of its brand promise. Borrowed-interest names require heavy marketing to link the name to the business image, but done right, they can work marketing magic. Just look at Apple, Nike or Starbucks.

✔ **A fabricated name:** You can create a name from an acronym, from words or syllables linked to form a new word or by stringing together letters that result in a pleasant sound with no dictionary meaning. Famous examples include Microsoft, Comcast, Groupon and Zappos. A fabricated name is likely to be available and protectable.

Is the Name You Want Available?

The law stops you from using a name that's too similar to an existing business name or trademark. To find out whether the name you want is available, take these steps:

✔ **Search business and trademark name databases.** Start by visiting the Companies House website (www.companieshouse.gov.uk) where the free WebCheck service allows you to search for company information and if a business name is available to register for yourself.

✔ **Search online.** Enter the name plus '.com' in at least three search engines to see whether the name is already claimed as a URL. Also search the URL at sites such as www.123-reg.co.uk or www.godaddy.com.

If searches turn up no prior claims to the name, protect it. For widespread and stronger protection of your name, consider filing for a trademark, which helps you prevent others from promoting a similar name. You can file for a trademark via the Intellectual Property Office (IPO) website at www.ipo.gov.uk where you can search for and register a Patent, Trademark or Copyright for your business.

Is It Easy to Spell?

The best names have four to eight letters and are spelled just like they sound. Unless you've the budget to educate your target audience, avoid unusual spaces, hyphens or symbols. Aim instead for a straightforward presentation that consumers are almost certain to spell correctly based on guesswork alone.

Names with odd spelling (*compleat* instead of *complete*) and names that begin with *The* or *A* are confusing to find in online and off-line searches.

Is It Easy to Say?

Ask others to read the name out loud. Do they pronounce it correctly? Is it phonetically pleasing? Does it work well in normal business conversation? As a test, imagine answering the phone using the name: 'Good morning, this is Greatname Consulting. How can I help you?'

Is It Original in Your Market Area?

Look up the name in directories for your local area and for the biggest city in your region to see whether other companies have sound-alike names.

To stand apart from the pack, avoid names tied to dominant local geographic features, as they tend to get lost in a lineup of similarly named businesses. For example, in a mountainous area, you can find names like Mountain View, Mountain Comfort, Mountain Shadow and a mountain of other similar and easy-to-confuse names.

Is It Unconventional?

Finding good, available business names isn't easy, which makes choosing an unusual name (think *Lady Gaga* or *Twitter*) not just popular but smart. On the plus side, unusual names are most likely available as domain names and probably won't be buried in an avalanche of search results, because few others have the same or a similar name. Foreign words fall into this category and are a good choice, especially when they share common roots with English and therefore sound somewhat familiar to English speakers.

On the flip side, unusual names require you to define and commit to how the name reflects your business or product, and they require explanation, education and consistent use to achieve market awareness. In the end, they pay off by establishing a good foundation for marketplace dominance.

Does It Work in Markets Far and Wide?

The Internet gives every company access to a worldwide market, so think globally. Look for a name that has a positive connotation in a range of major languages – especially in the languages of those you feel may represent future markets for your business.

Is It Memorable?

Choose a name that reflects a distinct, memorable aspect of your business or one around which you can develop a strong connection to your product or service. Companies named after their founders are easy to remember because they link to the owner's face, which triggers recollection of the name. Similarly, companies named after a physical characteristic (Pebble Beach, for example) are memorable because the unique attribute can create a strong impression – unless the feature is overused in other business names (refer to the earlier section 'Is It Original in Your Market Area?'). You can also make a name memorable with a logo that reinforces the name and by developing a strong brand story (see Chapter 7).

Can You Live and Grow with This Name?

You'll probably have this name for a long time, so the most important question of all may be, *Do you like it?* Ponder this question alone. It's your business. Be sure that you like the name, that you're comfortable saying it and that you can be proud repeating it countless times over years to come. And that leads to the next question: *Will the name adapt to your future?* Be careful about names that tie you to a geographic area or product offering, and be especially careful about names with faddish buzzwords that can get stuck in time. Examples of names that became outdated include BankAmericard, which became VISA to appeal to an international market, and MasterCharge, which became MasterCard to reflect a broader range of payment options.

Are You Ready to Commit to the Name?

After you settle on a name and determine that people can spell it, say it, remember it and relate well to it (even in other cultures), take these steps:

1. **Register the name with Companies House, file for a trademark if you choose to and secure the domain name if you can.**

2. **Create a professional logo to serve as the face of your name.**

3. **Introduce your new name and logo at each point where your business makes an impression on consumers.**

If you change your name, launch a name-introduction programme to inform your customers, prospects, suppliers, colleagues and friends about the reasons behind the new name. Move quickly to replace all items that carry your old identity with the new name you want your market to remember and embrace.

Chapter 22

Ten Ways to Attract People to Your Business Online

In This Chapter
▶ Increasing the odds that your business is found online
▶ Using social media to make your business an online magnet

*A*ny business – no matter its sector, market area or customer base – needs to be findable online. Worldwide, more than 2 billion people are online, including 21 million households (80 per cent) in Great Britain. They're researching products and services, learning about people they're about to meet or have just met, seeking directions to business locations, checking out reviews and ratings, and – perhaps most importantly – forming opinions that affect how they think and what they buy. This chapter covers the least you need to know – and do – to draw some of those potential online customers to your business.

Commit to Becoming Findable Online

Your business reputation isn't what *you* think it is. It's what your customers and those who advise your customers think and believe. More often than not, people form first impressions by what they discover about you online, which is why you need to commit to becoming findable online and to developing search results that consistently lead to accurate, trustworthy information about you and your business. Chapter 10 tells you how to optimise your website for search engines.

Set a Goal for Your Online Activity

Start by evaluating the current state of your online presence, and then decide what changes you want to achieve (see Chapter 3 for tips):

- ✔ If web searches don't deliver results for your business – whether people are searching for your business in particular or for businesses of your type in your market area in general – set a goal to develop an online presence so that you appear prominently in future search results.

- ✔ If your business has a strong online presence but search results lead to outdated, irrelevant or inaccurate information, set a goal to boost credibility by creating a website and online profiles that you control.

- ✔ If you've a good online presence with credible results, set a goal to deepen relationships with those in your target audience by increasing online participation and interaction.

No matter what goal you're reaching for, don't make sales your primary aim online. Selling repels people rather than attracting them to your business, especially on social media sites.

Decide on Your Online Identity

Just as you present your business using a single name in the physical world, you want to present it using the same name online.

But if others have already claimed your business name as a domain name or on social networks, or if your name is too long to work as a social network name (for example, Twitter limits names to 15 characters), you need a strategy for claiming an online alias that's tightly linked to your business name. That way, a search for either name leads to results for both names – and maximum exposure for your business. (Chapter 10 includes advice for claiming your online identity.)

If you can't use the same name everywhere, take these steps:

1. **Decide on no more than two names under which you'll present your business.**

   These names are likely to include the name under which your business was established and has long been marketed and a second name that you can use when your longstanding name isn't available or appropriate, because the name is too long or too difficult to spell.

2. **Claim one name or the other as your domain name and across all social media channels you may ever want to use.**

3. **Develop a strategy that links your names together.**

   Use your longstanding name as a prominent keyword in all descriptions for your online name, and use your online name as a prominent keyword in all descriptions for your longstanding name.

Establish Your Online Introduction

Online, you've about 20 words (160 characters on Twitter) to introduce your business and make others want to find out more. Follow this advice for getting the most from your brief introduction:

✔ Pack your introduction with keywords that people searching for businesses or products like yours are likely to use.

✔ Describe what your business does and for whom, along with what makes it trustworthy, distinct and likeable. Especially on social media, people want to connect with people and businesses with which they sense a personal connection.

✔ Deliver a sense of the kind of information people can count on you to deliver, as well as the tone – whether humorous, serious, controversial, authoritative, whatever – your messages convey.

✔ If you're the primary player in your business, help people locate you by your personal or business name by incorporating both into your description.

✔ Introduce yourself consistently across online channels so people on any site get a similar sense of your business and its brand image even though the length, tone and wording of your introduction needs to vary to fit the requirements of each online channel. It should be highly professional on LinkedIn, relaxed and informal on Facebook and short and punchy on Twitter.

Stake an Online Home Base

To be credible online, you need a site you control and can update that's findable by a search for your business name. Your own website, with a domain name that includes your business name, is the gold standard for online home bases. Your own blog (see Chapter 12) is a good alternative or a great complement, as both provide an updatable online location where you can share expertise, present offerings and invite customer interaction.

As an alternative – or as a placeholder until you establish your website or blog – set up business pages on Facebook and Google+. Both are free, easy to establish, great for customer interaction and highly findable in web searches.

See Chapter 10 for information on creating websites, including how to make your website mobile-friendly for the escalating numbers of people looking for you from mobile devices.

Build an Online Media Centre

Creating an online media centre can help you increase your media coverage, establish your business as a leader in its market area or industry and become a valuable resource for opinions, presentations and advice. Include easily accessible, high-quality, reproducible information, photos and videos that present your business, your owners and business principles, recent media appearances and coverage, contact information including social media links and an invitation welcoming requests for interviews, presentations and guest articles or blog posts. Chapter 17 provides advice for creating this one-stop media shop.

Get Active Across Social Media

Right now, if you haven't already done so, claim your name on every social network you may ever want to use, even if you don't plan to use the network quite yet. Sites like http://checkusernames.com, http://knowem.com and http://namechk.com provide free, almost instantaneous services for checking to see whether user names are available across social media networks. If the one you want isn't taken, grab it.

Then start participating. Figure out which networks your customers use and make those sites your starting points. Also consider which networks those with whom you want to achieve awareness or credibility use, and get involved there, too. For networking, target-audience interaction and search engine optimisation, the dominant players are Facebook, LinkedIn, Twitter and Google+. For retailers, restaurants and others with strong visuals to share, Pinterest became an essential site in 2012.

If your business has a street location and customers who use mobile phone apps to look for businesses, move sites like foursquare (http://foursquare.com) to the top of your list. And if customer reviews affect your business, claim pages on sites like Yelp (www.yelp.com) and

TripAdvisor (www.tripadvisor.com), along with any industry-specific sites that affect your business.

Use Chapter 11 to help you plan your social media programme, and be sure to add sites such as www.socialmediaexaminer.com and http://mashable.com to your reading list to stay on top of social network news and advice.

Develop a Content-Sharing Programme

Businesses that pull people to their online pages do so with useful, relevant, consistently presented information that takes time and discipline to create. If you have a blog (see Chapter 12 if you don't), your blog is the hub of your content-sharing programme. You write posts and then share links back to your blog on all your social media pages.

Beyond that, share links to useful news articles, white papers, podcasts and speeches you or others have given or attended. About the only rule is to share only information you believe is helpful, entertaining, interesting, humorous or otherwise useful to your target audience. Don't share just to prompt a sale; social media isn't the place for sales pitches. Chapter 11 gives you more advice on using social media to interact with customers.

Commit to a content-sharing or posting schedule that ensures that you're consistently visible online, with perhaps a couple of blog posts a week, a couple of Twitter posts a day and a Facebook entry every couple of days. Involve your staff to help you share the burden – and the enthusiasm. Beyond that, participate. Engage in online conversations and share interesting things posted by others. Social media is about interacting, not talking to yourself or shouting out your own message.

Monitor Your Online Reputation

You can't interact online if you're not tuned in to what's being said. Nor can you repost, share, thank people for good words or respond to concerns, criticisms or inaccurate comments, should they arise.

Social networks make monitoring easy by offering you the option of requesting alerts whenever your user name is mentioned. Opt in.

Also set up requests for free online-mention alerts through sites like Google Alerts, Bing Alerts (going through your Windows Live ID account) and Social Mention, directing responses to a single RSS aggregator like Feedly so you can open that one resource and see alerts for all your mentions in one place.

And from time to time, Google your business name to see whether your alerts have missed any mentions. You may find information worth sharing or commenting on.

Get and Stay Active Online

Remember that social media involvement, like marketing in general, has no finish line.

Post content that others want to see. Repost and share content you see and want to pass on to your social media audience. Post polls and questionnaires to generate involvement and to get opinions that you can – you guessed it – add to your content-sharing programme.

Above all else, interact. Follow people you find interesting and whose content you find useful. Follow people who follow you. Subscribe to blogs in your business and interest areas. Comment on page and blog posts. Comment on comments people post on your pages. Join groups. Ask and answer questions. Add your expertise to online conversations.

Become a resource. Become a thought leader. Become known and well-regarded in your business community and within your target audience. Watch your online presence, your search results and your business success expand as a result.

Turn to the chapters in Part III for more information and advice on connecting with your customers online.

Chapter 23

Ten Steps to a Great Marketing Plan

In This Chapter

▶ Tailoring a marketing plan for your small business

▶ Using the plan to reach your goals

*T*hough every other page of *Small Business Marketing For Dummies* is new and adapted to the changing marketing world we live in, this chapter remains relatively untouched because the steps you follow to write a marketing plan are the same, regardless of new communication channels and ever-changing customer mind-sets. You still have to know what you want to achieve. You still have to know about your target audience, your market environment and your competitive situation. You still need to be clear about the image and message that you want to convey. You still have to be certain about the strategies you're going to follow to achieve success. And you still have to choose the tactics to employ to reach your customers and move them to action.

Yes, marketing tactics have changed over the past few years – dramatically. And yes, customers have changed. They've been empowered by social media, review and rating sites, and interactive communication tools that give them not just any seat at the table but the best seat in the house.

The rest of this book provides information and advice for shifting your marketing tactics from traditional one-way, outbound, intrusive communications to two-way, inbound, engaging tactics that pull customers to your business, your products, and your cash register.

This chapter is about putting your marketing plan into words so that, even as you adjust your route through the ever-changing world around you, you know your destination and the navigational beacons that steer your way. Here are the ten planning steps to follow.

Step 1: State Your Business Purpose

Write your business purpose (see Chapter 5). For example, the purpose statement for *Small Business Marketing For Dummies* could be this:

> *To fuel the success of small business leaders and entrepreneurs by providing big-time marketing advice and tools scaled to fit the clocks, calendars, budgets, and pressing realities of small businesses in today's customer-empowered, screen-connected world.*

Step 2: Analyse Your Market Situation

Describe the changes, problems and opportunities that your business currently faces. In analysing your situation, consider the following factors:

- **Your customers:** Are they undergoing economic or lifestyle changes that affect their buying decisions? Are they using new communication or purchasing channels that require adjustments in how you reach and serve them? Are their numbers growing or declining in your current market area? (See Chapter 2 for help defining your customers and their needs.)

- **Your competition:** How much direct and indirect competition do you face? Are businesses entering your market arena to compete for your customers' money? Are competitors making moves that threaten your business? Have competitors closed, leaving a hole that you can fill? (See Chapter 4 for help assessing your competitive situation.)

- **Your market environment:** Do you foresee economic changes that will affect your business? What about building or road changes that may alter buying patterns or access to your business? Will your company be affected by regional or industry events that can boost business if you promote around them? If your business is weather-reliant, are forecasts in your favour? Factor such conditions into your situation analysis.

Step 3: Set Goals and Objectives

Arriving at your destination starts with naming where you want to go. Before planning your marketing strategies, establish what you aim to achieve. For example, *win three new major clients* or *increase revenue by 10 per cent*.

Your *goal* defines *what* you want your marketing plan to achieve. Your *objectives* define *how* you're going tol achieve your goal.

Put your goal and objectives in writing and then stick with them for the duration of the marketing-plan period. Each time a marketing opportunity arises, ask, 'Will this opportunity help us meet our goal? Does this opportunity support one or more of our objectives?' If the answer to either question is no, quickly pass on the opportunity. Chapter 5 provides step-by-step advice for setting goals and objectives, which are the foundation of a marketing programme.

Step 4: Define Your Market

Define your market in terms of *geographics* (where target customers live), *demographics* (who your customers are in factual terms such as age, gender, religion, ethnicity, marital status, income level, education and household size) and *psychographics* (how your customers live, including their attitudes, behavioural patterns, beliefs and values). See Chapter 2 for assistance.

By defining your market and knowing your customer profile, you can

- ✔ Develop marketing tactics that reach and appeal to your target market

- ✔ Create advertising messages that align with the unique interests and emotions of existing and prospective customers

- ✔ Select effective communication vehicles

- ✔ Weigh marketing opportunities based on their ability to reach those who match your customer profile – accepting opportunities with confidence or rejecting them quickly if they don't provide a cost-effective way to reach and interact with your defined target audience

Step 5: Advance Your Position, Brand and Creative Strategy

Begin with your company's position and brand statements, along with the creative strategy you'll follow to ensure that all marketing efforts you implement over the marketing-plan period advance a single, unified image for your company. Here are a few definitions to help you with this step:

- ✔ Your *position* is the available and meaningful niche that only your business can fill in your target consumer's mind.

- ✔ Your *brand* is the set of characteristics, attributes and implied promises that people remember and trust to be true about your business.

- ✔ Your *creative strategy* is the formula you follow to uphold your position and brand in all your marketing communications.

See Chapter 7 for information, examples and advice for creating position, brand and creative strategy statements.

Step 6: Set Your Marketing Strategies

In your marketing plan, detail the strategies you'll follow, including

- ✔ **Product strategies:** How will you add, alter or promote products to develop customers and sales? Will you introduce products, revise products or shift emphasis to a certain product or range of products? See Chapter 3 for information on analysing your product line, enhancing the appeal of existing products and developing new products.

- ✔ **Distribution strategies:** Will you alter the means by which you get your product to customers? Will you partner with other businesses or open outlets for off-site sales? Will your website play an expanded role in getting your message or product to customers? Chapter 2 includes a section on how and why to analyse and adjust distribution channels.

- ✔ **Pricing strategies:** Over the marketing-plan period, will you adjust the pricing strategy of your business – by, for instance, moving up from low-cost pricing or adding more affordable alternatives to your current premium-price position? Will you announce new prices or payment options, a frequent buyer pricing schedule, quantity discounts, rebates or other pricing offers? Chapter 3 includes pricing facts to consider, along with advice for establishing a profitable pricing strategy.

- ✔ **Promotion strategies:** How will you use advertising, online communications, public relations and promotions to support your marketing strategies? For example, if your product strategy calls for a new product introduction, your promotion strategy needs to reflect that effort through a new product promotion campaign.

After you set your strategies, you can spend time implementing an orchestrated and well-planned marketing programme rather than frantically reacting to a non-stop string of advertising pitches and ideas all year long.

Step 7: Outline Your Tactics

The next section of your marketing plan details the tactics you're going to employ to implement your strategies. For example, if one of your strategies is to introduce a new product, the sequence of tactics may look like this:

1. **Select an ad agency and develop product identity and ads.**

2. **Establish a direct-mail programme and direct-mail list.**

3. Create sales literature and product landing pages.

4. Develop a publicity plan.

5. Place ads.

6. Implement social media and blogger outreach programs.

7. Send direct mailshots.

8. Generate industry and regional-market publicity.

9. Train your staff.

10. Unveil the product at a special event.

11. Track results.

12. Adjust communications prior to a second wave of communications.

Parts III and IV of this book describe the marketing tools that you can use in your tactical plan.

Step 8: Establish Your Budget

No one ever built a successful business by marketing with leftover time or money. Your plan needs to define how much your business is going to devote to its marketing programme. Avoid pulling out last year's budget and adding *x* per cent for inflation. Opt instead for a *zero-based* budget, which means starting with nothing and adding in costs to cover the development of each element in your plan. Include costs for ad creation, media placements, direct mail, website and new page designs, trade show fees, displays, packaging and other tactics.

If you're planning to employ the professional assistance of freelancers or an agency or if you require additional staffing to implement your plan, incorporate those costs into your budget. Then add a contingency of up to 10 per cent to cover unanticipated costs. Include your marketing budget as an integral part of your marketing plan, get it approved and invest the money wisely.

Most businesses invest a combination of marketing budget and marketing hours to achieve success. The more time you invest – in networking, social media and one-to-one outreach – the less money you need to budget. In general, mature businesses aiming to maintain market share and growth levels usually budget 2–5 per cent of annual sales for marketing. Start-ups, those aiming for high growth levels and those trying to overcome strong competition or marketplace changes budget as much as 7–10 per cent.

Step 9: Blueprint Your Action Plan

This part of your plan brings all your strategies and tactics together into an action plan. One easy way to prepare this blueprint is to create an action agenda in calendar form. Begin by entering all key events that affect your marketing plan, such as trade shows, community events and major buying season launch dates. Then use the calendar to detail the marketing actions your plan requires, along with the budget for each action, the deadline and the responsible party. If the marketing action is on the calendar and someone is responsible for meeting a deadline, chances are better than good that it will actually happen.

Step 10: Think Long Term

In the final section of your marketing plan, list growth opportunities to research over the coming year for possible action in future marketing-plan periods. Some ideas can't be (or shouldn't be) rushed into. Spend time as you produce *this* year's marketing plan to think of ideas to research for possible implementation over the course of *next* year's plan, focusing on one or several of the following areas:

- ✔ New or expanded business locations to serve more consumers
- ✔ New geographic market areas outside your current market area
- ✔ New customers different from those in your current customer base
- ✔ New products or product ranges that inspire additional purchases
- ✔ New pricing strategies
- ✔ New distribution channels
- ✔ New customer-service programmes
- ✔ Mergers, business acquisitions, recruitment of key executives and formation of new business alliances

Choose one to three opportunities to explore and commit to producing an analysis before development of next year's marketing plan begins.

One Final Step: Use Your Plan

This step is the easiest to state and the most important: *Use your plan.* Share it with key associates. Provide it when you give background information to those helping to create and implement your marketing efforts. And use it to stay on track as you steer your business toward its goals and to higher levels of success.

Index

• _N_ •

Notes

Notes

About the Authors

Paul Lancaster is a digital marketing and social media expert based in Newcastle upon Tyne.

As a passionate supporter of start-ups and small businesses everywhere, Paul spent 7yrs at PNE Group, a Newcastle-based local enterprise agency and 4yrs at Shell LiveWIRE, one of the UK's longest running youth enterprise schemes, before joining the Sage One team at Sage (UK) Ltd.

With a wide range of IT, web and marketing roles for small businesses, not-for-profits and large corporates (including Sage and British Airways), plus a brief spell in the music industry, Paul now spends much of his time blogging and Tweeting about business start-ups and marketing.

Paul also worked on Seth Godin's Domino Project, introduced the first annual 'No Email Day' on 11/11/11 and runs his own marketing, PR and social media consultancy, Plan Digital UK.

To find out more, visit www.plandigitaluk.com and follow him on Twitter @lordlancaster.

If you'd like to comment on or share tips from this book on Twitter, please send Paul an @mention including the #DummiesSBM hashtag in your Tweets.

Barbara Findlay Schenck helps business leaders start, grow, market, brand, and, when they're ready, sell their companies.

She's worked internationally as a community development Peace Corps volunteer in Malaysia. She's served as a college administrator and writing instructor in Hawaii. And she started and sold an advertising agency in Oregon, which she co-founded with her husband, business partner, and the collaborator on this book, marketing strategist Peter V. Schenck.

She has worked with hundreds of businesses and shares what she's learned in a shelf-full of business books that include the book you're holding (including its first and second editions), *Selling Your Business For Dummies,* and *Business Plans Kit For Dummies* (now in its 3rd edition), all published by Wiley.

Barbara is a marketing strategist and small business advocate who contributes to a number of news sites and is called upon for presentations and advice by a long list of businesses and business groups.

For more information on Barbara's background, books, and business advice, visit her website at www.bizstrong.com. You can also follow her on facebook.com/bizstrong and at twitter.com/bizstrong.

Dedication

From Paul: For Lisa, Jake and Amber.

Authors' Acknowledgments

From Paul: First, thank you to my friends and family and to my beautiful wife Lisa for supporting me with everything, for being a fantastic proof reader and for our two wonderful children Jake and Amber.

Thank you Zeinab Lenton, Nick Goode, Sarah Woods, Richard Hughes, Michael Maddison, Deborah Nolan and everyone in the Sage One team for pushing me to greater heights and for being such incredibly smart and talented people to work with. I've learned a lot from you all.

Thanks to Stuart Anderson for giving me the opportunity to work alongside him at Shell LiveWIRE which ignited my passion for start-ups and small business support. Thanks also to Dawn Cranswick, Gary Nagel, Richard Clark, Melissa Middleton and everyone else at PNE Group for their dedication to helping small businesses, voluntary organisations and individuals reach their potential (including me).

Thanks to Claire Ruston, Raichelle Weller, Katie Moffat, Sarah Upstone and Simon Bell in the *For Dummies* team at Wiley for giving me the opportunity to publish this, my very first book!

Finally, thanks to everyone who Follows and Retweets me on Twitter @lordlancaster, including Michael Raven @micrv, Charlie Nettle @ NECCCharlie and Coraline Despeyroux @beingcoraline.

From Barbara: *Thank you to every business owner, marketer, and strategist I've ever had the honor of working with.* We are living in an age of collaboration, and only because you shared your issues and insights was I able to discover the solutions and advice shared in this book.

Thank you to Microsoft, MSN, and BusinessonMain.com. For years I've had the pleasure of writing marketing lessons and articles for your incredible small business resource programs. Because of you I've collected a good many of the examples shared in this book, and I've connected with many of the experts who shared their talent in the book's sidebars and how-to sections.

Thank you to the experts featured throughout this book. In the order their advice appears: Jim Bonfield of CustomerLink; Sohrab Vossoughi of Ziba Design; Janine Warner of DigitalFamily; Liz Goodgold of Red Fire Branding; Eric Swartz of Tagline Guru; the marketing software geniuses at HubSpot; Annette Tonti and Rich Kolman of MoFuse; the site-creation pros at Weebly and WordPress; Viveka von Rosen of Linked Into Business; Michael Katz of Blue Penguin Development; Joshua Waldman of Career Enlightenment; Antonio Neves of THINQACTION; Ron J. Williams of SnapGoods and Knodes; the e-commerce solution providers at 3dcart; and Jeanne Bliss of CustomerBliss. Also thanks to the long list of authors whose books I love to cite and recommend, headed by Paco Underhill's (Simon & Schuster) and Scott Berkun's (O'Reilly Media).

You have opened doors, enabled conversations, and kindled business relationships that simply would not have been possible a decade ago.

You manage to make each publishing experience yet more enjoyable. This time, heartfelt kudos go to executive editor Lindsay Lefevere, project editor Elizabeth Rea, copy editor Todd Lothery, tech reviewer Lorraine Ball, digital team leader Laura Moss-Hollister, and publicist Adrienne Fontaine. Calling this an amazing team is an understatement.

Your research, reporting, editing, and inspiration merits a byline on the cover. This book wouldn't exist without your talent.

Starting with Peter, my husband, business partner, and the person who improves every writing and business project we undertake; and Matthew, our son, who opens doors to new media, new business opportunities, and new ways of looking at strategy – and success. And finally, thanks to those who have been with me longest: My late dad, Walt; my dear mom, Julie; and my sisters, Carole, Mary Lynn, and Pam.

Publisher's Acknowledgments

Project Editor: Simon Bell

(Previous Edition: Elizabeth Rea)

Commissioning Editor: Claire Ruston

(Previous Edition: Lindsay Lefevre)

Assistant Editor: Ben Kemble

Development Editor: Simon Bell

Copy Editor: Todd Lothery

Technical Editor: Lorraine Ball

Proofreader: Kim Vernon

Production Manager: Daniel Mersey

Publisher: Miles Kendall

Vertical Websites: Rich Graves

Cover Photos: ©iStockphoto.com/Peter Booth

Project Coordinator: Kristie Rees